SCHAUM'S OUTLINE OF

THEORY AND PROBLEMS

of

ACCOUNTING I

Second Edition

•

by

JAMES A. CASHIN, M.B.A., CPA

Emeritus Professor of Accounting
Hofstra University

and

JOEL J. LERNER, M.S., P.D.

Chairman, Faculty of Business
Sullivan County Community College

SCHAUM'S OUTLINE SERIES

McGRAW-HILL BOOK COMPANY

New York   St. Louis   San Francisco   Auckland   Bogotá   Düsseldorf   Johannesburg
London   Madrid   Mexico   Montreal   New Delhi   Panama   Paris
São Paulo   Singapore   Sydney   Tokyo   Toronto

JAMES A. CASHIN is Emeritus Professor of Accounting at Hofstra University, where he was formerly Chairman of the Accounting Department. His publishing credits include some fifteen titles: he is a coauthor of several accounting textbooks, of the Schaum's Outlines of *Accounting II*, *Cost Accounting*, *Intermediate Accounting I*, and *Tax Accounting*, and he is Editor-in-Chief of the *Handbook for Auditors*. Professor Cashin is a Certified Public Accountant and a Certified Internal Auditor. He holds a B.S. degree in Accounting from the University of Georgia and an M.B.A. from New York University. He has wide experience in business with large industrial companies and has taught in the Graduate School of City University of New York and New York University.

JOEL LERNER is Professor and Chairman of the Business Division at Sullivan County Community College, Loch Sheldrake, New York. He received his B.S. from New York University and his M.S. and P.D. from Columbia University. Professor Lerner has published a booklet for *The New York Times* on teaching college business courses and has acted as editor for both *Readings in Business Organization and Management* and *Introduction to Business: A Contemporary Reader*. He has coauthored the Schaum's Outlines of *Accounting II* and *Introduction to Business* and authored *Bookkeeping and Accounting*.

Schaum's Outline of Theory and Problems of
ACCOUNTING I

7 8 9 10 11 12 13 14 15 16 17 18 19 20   SH   SH   8 5

Sponsoring Editor, John A. Aliano
Editing Supervisor, Denise Schanck
Production Manager, Nick Monti

Library of Congress Cataloging in Publication Data

Cashin, James A.
  Schaum's outline of theory and problems of
accounting I.

  (Schaum's outline series)
  Includes index.
  1. Accounting—Problems, exercises, etc.
I. Lerner, Joel J., joint author. II. Title.
III. Title: Outline of theory and problems of
accounting I.
HF5661.C37   1980   657'.076   79-26048
ISBN 0-07-010251-1

Preface

The second edition of *Accounting I* brings to the study of Accounting the same *solved-problems approach* which has proved so successful in the disciplines of Engineering and Mathematics. In contrast to previous supplementary materials, which have been little more than summary textbooks, the Accounting Series is organized around the *practical application* of basic accounting concepts. By providing the student with:

1. concise definitions and explanations, in easily understood terms

2. fully worked-out solutions to a large range of problems (against which the student can check his or her own solutions)

3. review questions

4. sample examinations typical of those used by two-year and four-year colleges

these books help the student to develop the all-important know-how for solving problems—on the CPA examination and in professional practice.

Accounting I and its sequel, *Accounting II*, parallel the full-year introductory course offered in most colleges and universities. Subject matter in this newly revised edition has been carefully coordinated with the leading textbooks, so that any topic can easily be found from the Table of Contents or the Index. In addition, this book should prove a valuable supplement to other accounting courses and to individual study. Today, there are an increasing number of programs offering college credit by examination, such as the College Level Examination Program (CLEP) and the New York College Proficiency Examination. Advanced placement, too, is now possible. Veterans and others who may have taken Introductory Accounting some years ago will find much-needed aid in brushing up for the next course.

Among the many individuals the authors have to thank for contributions to *Accounting I*, they would like to single out the members of a student panel who offered suggestions and helped in designing the problems. They are: Richard S. Clarke, Pat Herrmann, Louis Lucido, Vi Messerli, Herman J. Ortmann, and Gary Weller. The authors would also like to thank their wives, Nancy Lou Cashin and Anita Lerner, and families for their support and encouragement in writing this book.

JAMES A. CASHIN
JOEL J. LERNER

CONTENTS

CONTENTS

CONTENTS

Chapter 1

Accounting Concepts

1.1 NATURE OF ACCOUNTING

Every element of society — from the individual to an entire industry or government branch — has to make decisions on how to allocate its resources. *Accounting is the process which aids these decisions by (1) recording, (2) classifying, (3) summarizing, and (4) reporting business transactions and interpreting their effects on the affairs of the business entity.* This definition makes it clear that the recording of data, or *bookkeeping*, is only the first and simplest step in the accounting process.

The financial information provided by accounting is used both directly and indirectly, as summarized in the following table.

DIRECT USERS	INDIRECT USERS
Owners	Labor unions
Managers	Financial analysts
Creditors	Stock exchanges
Suppliers	Lawyers
Taxing authorities	Regulatory authorities
Employees	Financial press
Customers	Trade associations

1.2 BRANCHES AND SPECIALIZATIONS

Like many professions, the field of accounting has expanded into separate branches and further into many different specializations.

BRANCHES

(1) *Private accounting.* Accountants employed by a company to work on its own affairs are engaged in *private accounting.* Some private accountants become controllers (the chief accounting officer), vice presidents of finance, or even presidents of companies.

(2) *Public accounting.* Accountants who offer their professional services to the public for a fee, as does a doctor or lawyer, are engaged in *public accounting.* These are Certified Public Accountants, or CPAs, who have passed a very rigorous examination.

(3) *Governmental accounting.* Accountants working in the large number of federal, state, and local government units are engaged in *governmental accounting.* Sometimes this group is broadened to include accountants employed by hospitals, colleges, etc.

(4) *Teaching.* Accountants teach accounting courses in colleges and universities, junior colleges, and some high schools. Most high school courses are really oriented to bookkeeping rather than accounting.

SPECIALIZATIONS

The six principal specializations of private accounting are indicated in Fig. 1-1. These same specializations may be performed in other branches of accounting. For example, auditing is performed by public accountants, by private accountants who are called internal auditors, and by governmental auditors.

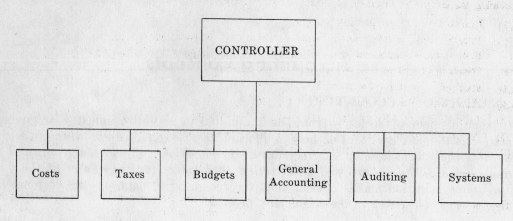

Fig. 1-1

1.3   BASIC ELEMENTS OF FINANCIAL POSITION: THE ACCOUNTING EQUATION

The financial condition or position of a business enterprise is represented by the relationship of assets to liabilities and capital.

Assets.   Properties that are owned and have monetary value; for instance, cash, inventory, buildings, equipment.

Liabilities.   Amounts owed to outsiders, such as notes payable, accounts payable, bonds payable. Liabilities may also include certain deferred items, such as income taxes to be allocated.

Capital.   The interest of the owners in an enterprise.

These three basic elements are connected by a fundamental relationship called the *accounting equation.* This equation expresses the equality of the assets on one side with the claims of the creditors and owners on the other side:

$$\text{ASSETS} \quad = \quad \text{LIABILITIES} \quad + \quad \text{CAPITAL}$$

According to the accounting equation, a firm is assumed to possess its assets subject to the rights of the creditors and owners.

EXAMPLE 1.

Assume that a business *owned* assets of $100,000, *owed* creditors $70,000, and *owed* the owner $30,000. The accounting equation would be:

$$\text{ASSETS} \quad = \quad \text{LIABILITIES} \quad + \quad \text{CAPITAL}$$
$$\$100,000 \qquad\qquad \$70,000 \qquad\qquad \$30,000$$

If over a certain period the firm had a net income of $10,000, representing an increase of net assets, the change may be reflected as increased cash, increased inventory or other assets, or as a decrease in liabilities. Suppose that $6,000 was used to reduce liabilities and the balance remained in assets. The equation would then be:

$$\text{ASSETS} \quad = \quad \text{LIABILITIES} \quad + \quad \text{CAPITAL}$$
$$\$104,000 \qquad\qquad \$64,000 \qquad\qquad \$40,000$$

We shall call any business event which alters the amount of assets, liabilities, or capital a *transaction*. In Example 1, the net changes in asset groups were discussed; in Example 2, we show how the accountant makes a meaningful record of a series of transactions, reconciling them step by step with the accounting equation.

EXAMPLE 2.

During the month of January, Mr. Alan Bagon, Lawyer,

(1) Invested $5,000 to open his law practice.

(2) Bought supplies (stationery, forms, pencils, etc.) for cash, $300.

(3) Bought office equipment from Altway Furniture Company on account, $2,500.

(4) Received $2,000 in fees earned during the month.

(5) Paid office rent for January, $500.

(6) Paid salary for part-time help, $200.

(7) Paid $1,000 to Altway Furniture Company on account.

(8) After taking an inventory at the end of the month, found he had used $200 worth of supplies.

(9) Withdrew $300 for personal use.

These transactions might be analyzed and recorded as follows.

Transaction (1).　Mr. Bagon invested $5,000 to open his law practice. There are two accounts that are affected: the asset Cash is increased, and the capital of the firm is increased by the same amount.

	ASSETS	=	LIABILITIES	+	CAPITAL
	Cash				A. Bagon, Capital
(1)	+ $5,000	=			+ $5,000

Transaction (2).　Bought supplies for cash, $300. In this case, Mr. Bagon is substituting one asset for another: he is receiving (+) the asset Supplies and paying out (−) the asset Cash. Note that the capital of $5,000 remains unchanged.

	ASSETS		=	LIABILITIES	+	CAPITAL
	Cash + Supplies					A. Bagon, Capital
	$5,000					$5,000
(2)	− 300	+ $300				
	$4,700 +	$300	=			$5,000

Transaction (3).　Bought office equipment from Altway Furniture Company on account, $2,500. He is receiving the asset Equipment but is not paying for it with the asset Cash. Instead, he will *owe* the money to the Altway Furniture Company. Therefore, he is *liable* for this amount in the future, thus creating the liability Accounts Payable.

	ASSETS			=	LIABILITIES	+	CAPITAL
	Cash + Supplies + Equipment				Accounts Payable		A. Bagon, Capital
	$4,700	$300					$5,000
(3)			+ $2,500		+ $2,500		
	$4,700 +	$300 +	$2,500	=	$2,500	+	$5,000

Transaction (4).　Received $2,000 in fees earned during the month. Because he received $2,000, the asset Cash increased and also his capital increased. It is important to note that he labels the $2,000 *Fees Income* to show its origin.

	ASSETS			=	LIABILITIES	+	CAPITAL
	Cash + Supplies + Equipment				Accounts Payable		A. Bagon, Capital
	$4,700	$300	$2,500		$2,500		$5,000
(4)	+ 2,000						+ 2,000 Fees Income
	$6,700 +	$300 +	$2,500	=	$2,500	+	$7,000

Transaction (5). Paid office rent for January, $500. When the word "paid" is stated, you know it means a deduction from Cash, since he is paying *out* his asset Cash. Payment of expense is a reduction of capital. It is termed *Rent Expense*.

	ASSETS			=	LIABILITIES	+	CAPITAL
	Cash	+ Supplies	+ Equipment		Accounts Payable		A. Bagon, Capital
	$6,700	$300	$2,500		$2,500		$7,000
(5)	− 500						− 500 Rent Expense
	$6,200 +	$300 +	$2,500	=	$2,500	+	$6,500

Transaction (6). Paid salary for part-time help, $200. Again the word "paid" means a deduction of cash and a reduction in capital. This time it refers to *Salaries Expense*.

	ASSETS			=	LIABILITIES	+	CAPITAL
	Cash	+ Supplies	+ Equipment		Accounts Payable		A. Bagon, Capital
	$6,200	$300	$2,500		$2,500		$6,500
(6)	− 200						− 200 Salaries Expense
	$6,000 +	$300 +	$2,500	=	$2,500	+	$6,300

Transaction (7). Paid $1,000 to Altway Furniture Company on account. Here he is reducing the asset Cash because he is paying $1,000, and reducing the liability Accounts Payable. He will now owe $1,000 less.

	ASSETS			=	LIABILITIES	+	CAPITAL
	Cash	+ Supplies	+ Equipment		Accounts Payable		A. Bagon, Capital
	$6,000	$300	$2,500		$2,500		$6,300
(7)	− 1,000				− 1,000		
	$5,000 +	$300 +	$2,500	=	$1,500	+	$6,300

Transaction (8). After taking an inventory at the end of the month, Mr. Bagon found he had used $200 worth of supplies. The original amount of supplies purchased has been reduced to the amount that was found to be left at the end of the month. Therefore, the difference was the amount used ($300 − $100 = $200). This reduces the asset Supplies by $200, and reduces capital by the same amount. It is termed *Supplies Expense*.

	ASSETS			=	LIABILITIES	+	CAPITAL
	Cash	+ Supplies	+ Equipment		Accounts Payable		A. Bagon, Capital
	$5,000	$300	$2,500		$1,500		$6,300
(8)		− 200					− 200 Supplies Expense
	$5,000 +	$100 +	$2,500	=	$1,500	+	$6,100

Transaction (9). Withdrew $300 for personal use. The withdrawal of cash is a reduction not only in Mr. Bagon's cash position but also in his capital. This is not an expense but a personal withdrawal, a reduction of the amount invested.

	ASSETS			=	LIABILITIES	+	CAPITAL
	Cash	+ Supplies	+ Equipment		Accounts Payable		A. Bagon, Capital
	$5,000	$100	$2,500		$1,500		$6,100
(9)	− 300						− 300 Drawing
	$4,700 +	$100 +	$2,500	=	$1,500	+	$5,800

Summary of Transactions
Month of January, 19X2

	ASSETS			=	LIABILITIES	+	CAPITAL	
	Cash +	Supplies +	Equipment		Accounts Payable		A. Bagon, Capital	
(1)	+$5,000						+$5,000	
(2)	− 300 +	$300						
	$4,700 +	$300		=			$5,000	
(3)			+ $2,500		+ $2,500			
	$4,700 +	$300 +	$2,500	=	$2,500	+	$5,000	
(4)	+ 2,000						+ 2,000	Fees Income
	$6,700 +	$300 +	$2,500	=	$2,500	+	$7,000	
(5)	− 500						− 500	Rent Expense
	$6,200 +	$300 +	$2,500	=	$2,500	+	$6,500	
(6)	− 200						− 200	Salaries Expense
	$6,000 +	$300 +	$2,500	=	$2,500	+	$6,300	
(7)	− 1,000				− 1,000			
	$5,000 +	$300 +	$2,500	=	$1,500	+	$6,300	
(8)		− 200					− 200	Supplies Expense
	$5,000 +	$100 +	$2,500	=	$1,500	+	$6,100	
(9)	− 300						− 300	Drawing
	$4,700 +	$100 +	$2,500	=	$1,500	+	$5,800	

Summary

(1) The four phases of accounting are _recording_, _classifying_, _summarizing_ and _reporting_ .

(2) The accounting equation is _assets_ = _Liabilities_ + _Capital_ .

(3) Items owned by a business that have money value are known as _assets_ .

(4) _Capital_ is the interest of the owners in a business.

(5) Money owed to an outsider is a _liability_ .

(6) The difference between assets and liabilities is _capital or equity_

(7) Financial events that occur in a business are termed _transactions_

(8) An investment in the business increases _assets_ and _capital_ .

(9) To purchase "on account" is to create a _liability_ .

(10) When the word "paid" occurs, it means a deduction of _cash_ .

(11) Income increases net assets and also _capital_ .

(12) A withdrawal of cash reduces cash and _capital_ .

Answers: (1) recording,   classifying,   summarizing,   reporting;   (2) assets,   liabilities,   capital;   (3) assets; (4) capital; (5) liability; (6) capital; (7) transactions; (8) assets, capital; (9) liability; (10) cash; (11) capital; (12) capital

Solved Problems

1.1. What effect do the transactions below have on the owner's equity (capital)?

(a) The owner invested $5,000 in the business. *increase*

(b) He bought equipment on account, $2,400. *no effect*

(c) He paid 1/2 of the bill owed to the creditor. *no effect*

(d) He received $2,000 in fees. *increase*

(e) He paid salaries for the week, $800. *decrease*

(f) He withdrew $400 from the business. *decrease*

(g) He paid rent for the month, $320. *decrease*

(h) Inventory of supplies decreased $350 during the month. *decrease*

SOLUTION

(a) increase		(c) no effect		(e) decrease		(g) decrease	
(b) no effect		(d) increase		(f) decrease		(h) decrease	

1.2. Compute the amount of the missing element:

	ASSETS	LIABILITIES	CAPITAL
(a)	$24,000	$19,000	5,000 ?
(b)	16,500	? 4,200	12,300
(c)	? 16,700	2,700	14,000
(d)	15,665	9,406	? 6,259

SOLUTION

(a)	$ 5,000	($24,000 − $19,000)
(b)	$ 4,200	(16,500 − 12,300)
(c)	$16,700	(2,700 + 14,000)
(d)	$ 6,259	(15,665 − 9,406)

1.3. Transactions completed by J. Epstein, M.D., appear below. Indicate the increase (+), decrease (−), or no change (0) in the accompanying table.

		ASSETS	=	LIABILITIES	+	CAPITAL
(a)	Paid rent expense for month.	−		0		−
(b)	Paid bi-weekly salary for lab assistant.	−		0		−
(c)	Cash fees collected for the week.	+		0		+
(d)	Bought medical equipment, paying cash.	+ −		0		0
(e)	Bought equipment on account.	+		+		0
(f)	Paid a creditor (liability) money owed.	−		−		0

SOLUTION

		ASSETS	=	LIABILITIES	+	CAPITAL
(a)	(reduction of cash and capital)	−		0		−
(b)	(reduction of cash and capital)	−		0		−
(c)	(increase in cash and capital)	+		0		+
(d)	(increase in equipment, reduction in cash)	+ −		0		0
(e)	(increase in equipment and in accounts payable)	+		+		0
(f)	(decrease in cash and in accounts payable)	−		−		0

1.4. Mr. Allen begins business, investing $4,000 in cash, equipment valued at $12,000, and $1,000 worth of supplies. What is the capital of the firm? *17,000*

SOLUTION

ASSETS	=	LIABILITIES	+	CAPITAL
$ 4,000				
12,000				
1,000				
$17,000	=	0	+	$17,000

Mr. Allen's capital is $17,000, as it is the total of all his assets, less his liabilities (0).

1.5. If in Problem 1.4, Mr. Allen had included a $6,000 note payable (written liability), what would his capital then have been?

SOLUTION

ASSETS	=	LIABILITIES	+	CAPITAL
$17,000	=	$6,000	+	$11,000

The total assets of $17,000, reduced by liabilities of $6,000, results in $11,000 capital. Stated a different way:

$$\text{ASSETS } (\$17,000) = \text{LIABILITIES } (\$6,000) + \text{CAPITAL } (?)$$
$$17,000 = 6,000 + ?$$
$$17,000 = 6,000 + 11,000$$

1.6. Supplies had a balance of $2,400 at the beginning of the year. At the end of the period, its inventory showed $1,400. How is this decrease recorded?

SOLUTION

ASSETS	=	LIABILITIES	+	CAPITAL
Supplies				
Balance $2,400				$2,400
Decrease − 1,000				− 1,000 *Supplies Expense*
Balance $1,400				$1,400

1.7. Illustrate the difference between *supplies* and *supplies expense*.

SOLUTION

Supplies is an asset and represents the value of supplies owned (supplies on hand). *Supplies Expense* is the value of supplies *used* during the period and is a reduction of capital.

Supplies (Asset)	$2,400	(beginning)
Supplies Expense	−1,000	(used during year)
Supplies (Asset)	$1,400	(end)

The value of supplies at the end of the period is the difference between the beginning balance and the amount that has been used.

1.8. The Supplies account had a balance of $3,850 at the beginning of January. At the end of the month it was discovered that $1,425 remained.

(*a*) What was the Supplies *Expense* for the month? 2425.

(*b*) What was the *balance* of the asset, Supplies? 1425

SOLUTION

(*a*) $3,850   Supplies, January 1 (asset)
       −1,425   Supplies, January 31 (asset)
        $2,425   Supplies Expense (used during month)

(*b*) $1,425.   This is the amount that remains at the end of the month and is considered an asset.

1.9. The Supplies account had a balance of $3,850 at the beginning of January. At the end of the month it was discovered that $1,425 had been used.

(*a*) What was the Supplies *Expense* for the month? 1425

(*b*) What was the *balance* of the asset, Supplies? 2425

SOLUTION

(*a*) $1,425.   This is the amount that has been used.

(*b*) $3,850   Supplies, January 1 (asset)
       −1,425   Supplies Expense (used)
        $2,425   Supplies, January 31 (asset)

1.10. Record the following transaction in the space provided: Bought equipment for $22,000, paying $6,000 in cash and owing the balance.

	ASSETS	=	LIABILITIES	+	CAPITAL
	Cash + Equipment		Accounts Payable		
Balance	$30,000				$30,000
Entry (?)	−6000 22,000	=	16,000		30,000
Balance (?)	24 000				

SOLUTION

Step 1.   Reduce the cash account by the amount paid, $6,000.

Step 2.   Record the purchase of the equipment at its cost, $22,000.

Step 3.   Increase Accounts Payable for the amount owed, $16,000.

	ASSETS	=	LIABILITIES	+	CAPITAL
	Cash + Equipment		Accounts Payable		
Balance	$30,000				$30,000
Entry	− 6,000 + $22,000		+ $16,000*		
Balance	$24,000 + $22,000	=	$16,000	+	$30,000

       *$22,000   (equipment)
        −6,000   (paid in cash)
        $16,000   (balance owed)

1.11. Based on the information in Problem 1.10, what effect does the purchase of the equipment on account have on capital?

SOLUTION

No effect.

	ASSETS		**=**	**LIABILITIES**	**+**	**CAPITAL**
	Cash	+ Equipment		Accounts Payable		
Balance	$30,000					$30,000
Entry	−$6,000	+$22,000		+$16,000		
Balance	$24,000 +	$22,000	=	$16,000	+	$30,000

Note that the capital before and after the transaction remains the same. The only areas that are affected are assets and liabilities.

1.12. In Problem 1.10 what effect does the payment of the liability in full have on the capital account?

SOLUTION

No effect.

	ASSETS		**=**	**LIABILITIES**	**+**	**CAPITAL**
	Cash +	Equipment		Accounts Payable		
Balance	$24,000	$22,000		$16,000		$30,000
Entry	− 16,000			− 16,000		
Balance	$ 8,000 +	$22,000	=			$30,000

The reduction of cash is accompanied by an equal reduction of the accounts payable.

1.13. The summary data of the Boyd Taxi Company for May are presented below in equation form. Describe each of the transactions that occurred during the month.

	Cash	+ Supplies	+ Equipment	=	Liabilities	+ Capital	
(1)	+ $6,600					+ $6,600	Investment
(2)	− 3,200		+ $3,200				
(3)	− 500	+ $500					
(4)			+ 2,000		+ $2,000		
(5)	+ 2,500					+ 2,500	Fares Income
(6)	− 1,100					− 1,100	Salaries Expense
(7)	− 500				− 500		
(8)	− 300					− 300	Drawing
	$3,500 +	$500 +	$5,200	=	$1,500 +	$7,700	

SOLUTION

(1) An investment was made by the owner.
(2) Equipment was bought and *paid* for.
(3) Supplies were bought and paid for.
(4) Additional equipment was bought *on account*, thus creating the liability.
(5) Income from taxi fares is recorded.
(6) Salaries were paid to the company's drivers.
(7) Cash was paid, reducing the liability.
(8) Owner *withdrew* funds for his personal use.

1.14. The following transactions occurred during the year for the Ken Stanton Musical Band. **(1)** Invested $2,000 in the formation of a band. **(2)** Bought instruments costing $1,200, on account. **(3)** Bought musical supplies for cash, $300. **(4)** Received $600 for services rendered. **(5)** Paid salaries of $250. **(6)** Paid in full the amount owed on instruments. **(7)** Travel expenses of $150 were paid. **(8)** Withdrew $200 for personal use.

Record the effect of each transaction in the table below. (*Note*: The term *element* refers to assets, liabilities, or capital; *account* refers to the individual item within an element.)

	Increase			Decrease		
	Element	Account	Amount	Element	Account	Amount
(1)	Assets	Cash	$2,000			
	Capital	K. Stanton, Capital	2,000			
(2)	*Assets*	*Instruments*	*1,200*			
	Liabilities	*Accts. Payable*	*1,200*			
(3)	*Assets*	*Supplies*	*300*	*Assets*	*Cash*	*300*
(4)	*Asset*	*Cash*	*600*			
	Capital	*K.Stanton Cap.*	*600*			
(5)				*Assets*	*Cash*	*250*
				Liabilities	*Wages*	*250*
(6)				*Assets*	*Cash*	*1200*
				Liabilities	*Acct. Payable*	*1200*
(7)				*Assets*	*Cash*	*150*
				Liabilities	*Travel Exp.*	*150*
(8)						

SOLUTION

	Increase			Decrease		
	Element	Account	Amount	Element	Account	Amount
(1)	Assets	Cash	$2,000			
	Capital	K. Stanton, Capital	2,000			
(2)	Assets	Equipment	1,200			
	Liabilities	Accounts Payable	1,200			
(3)	Assets	Supplies	300	Assets	Cash	$ 300
(4)	Assets	Cash	600			
	Capital	Music Income	600			
(5)				Capital	Salaries Expense	250
				Assets	Cash	250
(6)				Liabilities	Accounts Payable	1,200
				Assets	Cash	1,200
(7)				Capital	Travel Expense	150
				Assets	Cash	150
(8)				Capital	K. Stanton, Drawing	200
				Assets	Cash	200

1.15. The following transactions were engaged in during the month of March by Dr. M. Spring, Physician.

    (1)   Opened his practice by investing $10,000 in the business.

    (2)   Bought office equipment for $7,000 on account from Medical Products, Inc.

    (3)   Paid $2,000 for various medical supplies for the office.

    (4)   Received $1,600 in fees earned during the first month of operations.

    (5)   Paid office rent for the month, $200.

    (6)   Paid medical assistant salary for the month, $400.

    (7)   Paid Medical Products, Inc., $3,000 on account.

    (8)   Withdrew $500 for personal use.

    Enter each transaction in the following form.

	Cash	+ Supplies	+ Equipment	=	Liabilities	+ Capital
(1)						
(2)	____	____	____		____	____
Balance						
(3)	____	____	____		____	____
Balance						
(4)	____	____	____		____	____
Balance						
(5)	____	____	____		____	____
Balance						
(6)	____	____	____		____	____
Balance						
(7)	____	____	____		____	____
Balance						
(8)	____	____	____		____	____
Balance						

SOLUTION

	Cash	+ Supplies	+ Equipment	=	Liabilities	+ Capital	
(1)	+$10,000					+$10,000	Investment
(2)			+ $7,000		+ $7,000		
Balance	$10,000		$7,000		$7,000	$10,000	
(3)	− 2,000	+ $2,000					
Balance	$ 8,000 +	$2,000 +	$7,000	=	$7,000 +	$10,000	
(4)	+ 1,600					+ 1,600	Fees Income
Balance	$ 9,600 +	$2,000 +	$7,000	=	$7,000 +	$11,600	
(5)	− 200					− 200	Rent Expense
Balance	$ 9,400 +	$2,000 +	$7,000	=	$7,000 +	$11,400	
(6)	− 400					− 400	Salaries Expense
Balance	$ 9,000 +	$2,000 +	$7,000	=	$7,000 +	$11,000	
(7)	− 3,000				− 3,000		
Balance	$ 6,000 +	$2,000 +	$7,000	=	$4,000 +	$11,000	
(8)	− 500					− 500	Drawing
Balance	$ 5,500 +	$2,000 +	$7,000	=	$4,000 +	$10,500	

1.16. Summary financial data of the Nu-Look Dry Cleaning Co. for November are presented below in transaction form.

- **(1)** Opened a business bank account, depositing $12,000.
- **(2)** Purchased supplies for cash, $220.
- **(3)** Purchased dry cleaning equipment from Hill Cleaning Equipment Inc. for $3,500, paying $1,500 in cash with the balance on account.
- **(4)** Paid rent for the month, $425.
- **(5)** Cash sales for the month totaled $1,850.
- **(6)** Paid salaries of $375.
- **(7)** Paid $500 on account to Hill Cleaning Equipment Inc.
- **(8)** The cost of supplies used was determined to be $60.

Record the transactions and running balances in the form below.

	ASSETS			=	LIABILITIES	+	CAPITAL
	Cash +	Supplies +	Equipment		Accounts Payable		Nu-Look Dry Cleaning Co.
(1)							
(2)	____	____	____		____		____
Balance							
(3)	____	____	____		____		____
Balance							
(4)	____	____	____		____		____
Balance							
(5)	____	____	____		____		____
Balance							
(6)	____	____	____		____		____
Balance							
(7)	____	____	____		____		____
Balance							
(8)	____	____	____		____		____
Balance							

SOLUTION

	ASSETS			=	LIABILITIES	+	CAPITAL
	Cash +	Supplies +	Equipment		Accounts Payable		Nu-Look Dry Cleaning Company
(1)	$12,000						$12,000 Investment
(2)	− 220 +	+ $220					
Balance	$11,780 +	$220					$12,000
(3)	− 1,500		+ $3,500		+ $2,000		
Balance	$10,280 +	$220 +	$3,500	=	$2,000	+	$12,000
(4)	− 425						− 425 Rent Expense
Balance	$ 9,855 +	$220 +	$3,500	=	$2,000	+	$11,575
(5)	+ 1,850						+ 1,850 Cleaning Income
Balance	$11,705 +	$220 +	$3,500	=	$2,000	+	$13,425
(6)	− 375						− 375 Salaries Expense
Balance	$11,330 +	$220 +	$3,500	=	$2,000	+	$13,050
(7)	− 500				− 500		
Balance	$10,830 +	$220 +	$3,500	=	$1,500	+	$13,050
(8)		− 60					− 60 Supplies Expense
Balance	$10,830 +	$160 +	$3,500	=	$1,500	+	$12,990

1.17. Mike Jameson operates a shoe repair shop known as the Repair Center. The balances of his accounts on June 1 of the current year are as follows: Cash, $5,400; Supplies, $600; Equipment, $3,200; Accounts Payable, $3,000; Capital, $6,200. The transactions during the month of June appear below.

(1) Paid salaries of $350.

(2) Paid creditors on account $2,000.

(3) Bought additional equipment on account for $3,100.

(4) Received cash from customers for repair service, $3,600.

(5) Paid delivery expense, $140.

(6) Inventory of supplies at the end of the month was $275.

(7) Mr. Jameson withdrew for his personal use $250.

Record the transactions below in the form provided.

	ASSETS			=	LIABILITIES	+	CAPITAL
	Cash +	Supplies +	Equipment		Accounts Payable		M. Jameson, Capital
Balance, June 1	$5,400	$600	$3,200		$3,000		$6,200
(1)	___	___	___		___		___
Balance							
(2)	___	___	___		___		___
Balance							
(3)	___	___	___		___		___
Balance							
(4)	___	___	___		___		___
Balance							
(5)	___	___	___		___		___
Balance							
(6)	___	___	___		___		___
Balance							
(7)	___	___	___		___		___
Balance, June 30							

SOLUTION

	ASSETS			=	LIABILITIES	+	CAPITAL	
	Cash +	Supplies +	Equipment		Accounts Payable	+	M. Jameson, Capital	
Balance, June 1	$5,400 +	$600 +	$3,200	=	$3,000	+	$6,200	Investment
(1)	− 350						− 350	Salaries Expense
Balance	$5,050 +	$600 +	$3,200	=	$3,000	+	$5,850	
(2)	− 2,000				− 2,000			
Balance	$3,050 +	$600 +	$3,200	=	$1,000	+	$5,850	
(3)			+ 3,100		+ 3,100			
Balance	$3,050 +	$600 +	$6,300	=	$4,100	+	$5,850	
(4)	+ 3,600						+ 3,600	Repair Income
Balance	$6,650 +	$600 +	$6,300	=	$4,100	+	$9,450	
(5)	− 140						− 140	Delivery Expense
Balance	$6,510 +	$600 +	$6,300	=	$4,100	+	$9,310	
(6)		− 325*					− 325	Supplies Expense
Balance	$6,510 +	$275 +	$6,300	=	$4,100	+	$8,985	
(7)	− 250						− 250	Drawing
Balance, June 30	$6,260 +	$275 +	$6,300	=	$4,100	+	$8,735	

* $600 (beginning inventory) − $275 (ending inventory) = $325 (amount used, or supplies expense)

Chapter 2

Financial Statements

2.1 INTRODUCTION

The two principal questions that the owner of a business asks periodically are:

    (1)   What is my net income (profit)?

    (2)   What is my capital?

The simple balance of assets against liabilities and capital, provided by the accounting equation, is insufficient to give complete answers. For (1) we must know the type and amount of income and the type and amount of each expense for the period in question. For (2) it is necessary to obtain the type and amount of each asset, liability, and capital account at the end of the period. This information is provided by (1) the *income statement* and (2) the *balance sheet*.

EXAMPLE 1.

    After the transactions for the month of January have been recorded in the books of Mr. Alan Bagon, the accounts show the following balances (see page 5).

ACCOUNTS	ASSETS	LIABILITIES AND CAPITAL
Cash	$4,700	
Supplies	100	
Equipment	2,500	
Accounts Payable		$1,500
A. Bagon, Capital		5,800
Total	$7,300	$7,300

    It is seen that the assets of the business changed from the original $5,000 invested by Mr. Bagon at the beginning of January to $7,300 at the end of January. Does that represent the amount of profit earned? It does not, because (1) liabilities have changed and (2) some of the transactions affecting capital were those relating to his investment; that is, he withdrew some of his original investment. It is apparent that his liabilities increased: they are now $1,500 more than the beginning liabilities (the balance due on the equipment).

    His net assets or his capital is now $5,800, an increase of $800 over the beginning amount. That would represent his profit if he had not withdrawn some of his investment.

2.2 INCOME STATEMENT

    The income statement may be defined as *a summary of the revenue, expenses, and net income or net loss of a business entity for a specific period of time*. This may also be called a Profit & Loss Statement, Operating Statement, or Statement of Operations. Let us review the meanings of the elements entering into the income statement.

Revenue. The increase in capital resulting from the delivery of goods or rendering of services by the business. In amount, the revenue is equal to the cash and receivables gained in compensation for the goods delivered or services rendered.

Expenses. The decrease in capital caused by the business's revenue-producing operations. In amount, the expense is equal to the value of goods and services used up or consumed in obtaining revenue.

Net Income. The increase in capital resulting from profitable operation of a business; it is the excess of revenues over expenses for the accounting period.

Net Loss. The decrease in capital resulting from the operations of a business. It is the excess of expenses over revenues for the accounting period.

It is important to note that a cash receipt qualifies as revenue only if it serves to increase capital. Similarly, a cash payment is an expense only if it decreases capital. Thus, for instance, borrowing cash from a bank does not contribute to revenue.

EXAMPLE 2.

Mr. A. Bagon's total January income and the totals for his various expenses can be obtained by analyzing the transactions shown under the heading "Capital" on page 5. The income from fees amounted to $2,000 and the expenses incurred to produce this income were: rent, $500; salaries, $200; and supplies, $200. The formal Income Statement can now be prepared.

Alan Bagon
Income Statement
month of January, 19X2

Fees Income		$2,000
Operating Expenses		
Rent Expense	$500	
Salaries Expense	200	
Supplies Expense	200	
Total Operating Expenses		900
Net Income		$1,100

In many companies there are hundreds and perhaps thousands of income and expense transactions in one month. To lump all these transactions under one account would be very cumbersome and would, in addition, make it impossible to show relationships among the various items. For example, we might wish to know the relationship of selling expenses to sales and whether the ratio is higher or lower than in previous periods. To solve this problem we leave the investment or permanent entries in the capital account and then set up a *temporary* set of income and expense accounts. The net difference of these accounts, the net profit or net loss, is then transferred in one figure to the capital account.

2.3   ACCRUAL BASIS AND CASH BASIS OF ACCOUNTING

Because an income statement pertains to a definite period of time, it becomes necessary to determine just *when* an item of revenue or expense is to be accounted for. Under the *accrual basis of accounting,* revenue is recognized only when earned and expense recognized only when incurred. This differs significantly from the *cash basis of accounting,* which recognizes revenue and expense generally with the receipt and payment of cash. Essential to the accrual basis is the *matching* of expenses with the revenue that they helped produce. Under the accrual system the accounts are adjusted at the end of the accounting period to properly reflect the revenue earned and the cost and expenses applicable to the period.

Most business firms use the accrual basis, while individuals and professional people generally use the cash basis. Ordinarily the cash basis is not suitable when there are significant amounts of inventories, receivables, and payables.

2.4 BALANCE SHEET

The information needed for the balance sheet items are the net balances at the end of the period, rather than the total for the period as in the income statement. Thus, management wants to know the balance of cash in the bank, the balance of inventory, equipment, etc., on hand at the end of the period.

The balance sheet may then be defined as *a statement showing the assets, liabilities, and capital of a business entity at a specific date*. This statement is also called a Statement of Financial Position or Statement of Financial Condition.

In preparing the balance sheet, it is not necessary to make any further analysis of the data. The needed data — that is, the balances of the asset, liability, and capital accounts — are already available.

EXAMPLE 3. Report Form

Alan Bagon
Balance Sheet
January 31, 19X2

ASSETS

Cash	$4,700
Supplies	100
Equipment	2,500
Total Assets	$7,300

LIABILITIES AND CAPITAL

Liabilities			
Accounts Payable			$1,500
Capital			
Balance, January 1, 19X2		$5,000	
Net Income for January	$1,100		
Less: Withdrawals	300		
Increase in Capital		800	
Total Capital			5,800
Total Liabilities and Capital			$7,300

The close relationship of the income statement and the balance sheet is apparent. The net income of $1,100 for January, shown as the final figure on the income statement of Example 2, is also shown as a separate figure on the balance sheet of Example 3. The income statement is thus the connecting link between two balance sheets. As discussed earlier, the income and expense items are actually a further analysis of the capital account.

The balance sheet of Example 3 is arranged in *report form*, with the liabilities and capital sections shown below the asset section. It may also be arranged in *account form*, with the liabilities and capital sections to the right of, rather than below, the asset section, as shown in Example 4.

EXAMPLE 4. Account Form

Alan Bagon
Balance Sheet
January 31, 19X2

ASSETS   **LIABILITIES AND CAPITAL**

Cash	$4,700	Liabilities			
Supplies	100	Accounts Payable			$1,500
Equipment	2,500	Capital			
		Balance, January 31, 19X2		$5,000	
		Net Income for January	$1,100		
		Less: Withdrawals	300		
		Increase in Capital		800	
		Total Capital			$5,800
Total Assets	$7,300	Total Liabilities and Capital			$7,300

Instead of showing the details of the capital account in the balance sheet, we may show the changes in a separate form called the Capital Statement. This is the more common treatment. In that case, we have three interrelated statements, as shown in Example 5.

EXAMPLE 5.

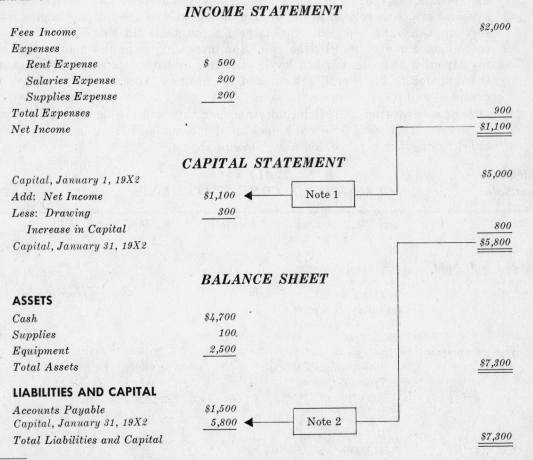

INCOME STATEMENT

Fees Income		$2,000
Expenses		
Rent Expense	$ 500	
Salaries Expense	200	
Supplies Expense	200	
Total Expenses		900
Net Income		$1,100

CAPITAL STATEMENT

Capital, January 1, 19X2		$5,000
Add: Net Income	$1,100	Note 1
Less: Drawing	300	
Increase in Capital		800
Capital, January 31, 19X2		$5,800

BALANCE SHEET

ASSETS

Cash	$4,700	
Supplies	100	
Equipment	2,500	
Total Assets		$7,300

LIABILITIES AND CAPITAL

Accounts Payable	$1,500	
Capital, January 31, 19X2	5,800	Note 2
Total Liabilities and Capital		$7,300

Note 1. The net income of the income statement, $1,100, is transferred to the capital statement.
Note 2. The capital is summarized in the capital statement and the final balance included in the balance sheet.

2.5   CLASSIFIED FINANCIAL STATEMENTS

Financial statements become more useful when the individual items are classified into significant groups for comparison and financial analysis. The classifications relating to the primary statements, the income statement and the balance sheet, will be discussed in this section.

THE INCOME STATEMENT

The classified income statement sets out the amount of each function and enables management, stockholders, analysts, and others to study the changes in function costs over successive accounting periods. There are four functional classifications of the income statement.

(1) *Revenue.* This includes gross income from the sale of products or services. It may be designated as Sales, Income from Fees, etc., to indicate gross income. The gross amount is reduced by Sales Returns and Allowances and by Sales Discounts to arrive at Net Sales.

(2) *Cost of goods sold.* This includes the costs related to the products or services sold. It would be relatively simple to compute for a firm that retails furniture; it would be more complex for a manufacturing firm that changes raw materials into finished products.

(3) *Operating expenses.* This includes all expenses or resources consumed in obtaining revenue. Operating expenses are further divided into two groups. *Selling expenses* are those related to the promotion and sale of the company's product or service. Generally, one individual is held accountable for this function and his performance is measured by the results in increasing sales and maintaining selling expenses at an established level. *General and administrative expenses* are those related to the overall activities of the business, such as the salaries of the president and other officers.

(4) *Other expenses (net).* This includes nonoperating and incidental expenses such as interest expense. Often any incidental income, such as interest income, is offset against the expense and a net amount shown.

EXAMPLE 6.

Gross Sales

J. ALES
CLASSIFIED INCOME STATEMENT

Sales of Goods or Services		$25,000	
Less: Sales Returns and Allowances	$1,250		
Sales Discounts	750	2,000	
Net Sales			$23,000
Cost of Goods Sold			
Inventory, January 1		$ 2,500	
Purchases		16,500	
Available for Sale		19,000	
Inventory, December 31		3,000	
Cost of Goods Sold			16,000
Gross Profit			$ 7,000
Operating Expenses			
Selling Expenses			
Sales Salaries Expense	$1,200		
Travel Expense	200		
Advertising Expense	600	$ 2,000	
General Expenses			
Officers' Salaries Expense	1,000		
Insurance Expense	600	1,600	
Total Operating Expenses			3,600
Net Income from Operations			$ 3,400
Other Expenses (net) Interest Expense		$ 500	
Less: Interest Income		100	
Other Expenses (net)			400
Net Income			$ 3,000

THE BALANCE SHEET

The balance sheet becomes a more useful statement for comparison and financial analysis if the asset and liability groups are classified. For example, an important index of the financial state of business, derivable from the classified balance sheet, is the ratio of current assets to current liabilities. This *current ratio* ought generally to be at least 2 to 1; that is, current assets should be twice current liabilities. For our purposes we will designate the following classifications.

ASSETS	LIABILITIES
Current	Current
Fixed	Long-term
Other	

Current assets. Assets reasonably expected to be converted into cash or used in the current operation of the business. (The current period is generally taken as one year.) Examples are cash, notes receivable, accounts receivable, inventory, and prepaid expenses (prepaid insurance, prepaid rent, etc.).

Fixed assets. Long-lived assets used in the production of goods or services. These assets, sometimes called *fixed assets* or *plant assets*, are used in the operation of the business rather than being held for sale, as are inventory items.

Other assets. Various assets other than current assets, fixed assets, or assets to which specific captions are given. For instance, the caption Investments would be used if significant sums were invested. Often companies show a caption for intangible assets such as patents or goodwill. In other cases, there may be a separate caption for deferred charges. If, however, the amounts are not large in relation to total assets, the various items may be grouped under one caption, Other Assets.

Current liabilities. Debts which must be satisfied from current assets within the next operating period, usually one year. Examples are accounts payable, notes payable, the current portion of long-term debt, and various accrued items such as salaries payable and taxes payable.

Long-term liabilities. Liabilities which are payable beyond the next year. The most common examples are bonds payable and mortgages payable.

Example 8, on the following page, shows a classified balance sheet of typical form.

EXAMPLE 7.

J. ALES
CAPITAL STATEMENT

Capital		$4,750
J. Ales, Capital January 1		
Net Income for the year	$3,000	
Less: Withdrawals	2,000	
Increase in Capital		1,000
J. Ales, Capital December 31		$5,750

EXAMPLE 8.

J. ALES
BALANCE SHEET

ASSETS

Current Assets		
Cash	$5,400	
Accounts Receivable	1,600	
Supplies	500	
Total Current Assets		$7,500
Fixed Assets		
Land	$4,000	
Building	8,000	
Equipment	2,000	
Total Fixed Assets		14,000
Total Assets		$21,500

LIABILITIES AND CAPITAL

Current Liabilities		
Notes Payable	$1,750	
Accounts Payable	2,000	
Total Current Liabilities		$ 3,750
Long-Term Liabilities		
Mortgage Payable		12,000
Total Liabilities		$15,750
Capital, December 31		5,750
Total Liabilities and Capital		$21,500

Summary

(1)   Another term for an accounting report is an _____.

(2)   The statement that shows net income for the period is known as the _____ statement.

(3)   The statement that shows net loss for the period is known as the _____ statement.

(4)   Two groups of items comprising the income statement are _____ and _____.

(5)   The difference between income and expense is known as _____.

(6) Withdrawal of money by the owner is not an expense but a reduction of _____ .

(7) To show the change in capital of a business, the _____ statement is used.

(8) The balance sheet contains _____ , _____ , and _____ .

(9) Assets must equal _____ .

(10) Expense and income must be matched in the same _____ .

Answers: (1) accounting statement   (6) capital

               (2) income   (7) capital

               (3) income   (8) assets, liabilities, capital

               (4) income, expense   (9) liabilities and capital

               (5) net income   (10) year or period

Solved Problems

2.1. Discuss the underlying rules which govern the preparation of the income statement and the balance sheet.

SOLUTION

Clearly, there must exist such rules; for otherwise it would be necessary to state for each financial statement the specific assumptions used in preparing it. Over the years, certain principles have been developed on the basis of experience, reason, custom, and practical necessity. We may call these "generally accepted accounting principles."

Business entity. Accounts are kept for business entities rather than for the persons who own or are associated with the business.

Continuity. Unless there is strong evidence to the contrary, it is assumed that the business will continue to operate as a going concern. If it were not to continue, then liquidation values, generally much lower, would apply.

Unit of measure. It is assumed that the most practical unit of measure is money and that changes in investment and income will be measured in money. So far, no better unit of measure has been found.

Time period. An essential function of accounting is to provide information for decision making. To accomplish this it is necessary to establish accounting periods, or systematic time intervals, so that timely accounting data can be developed.

Cost. The properties and services acquired by an enterprise are generally recorded at cost (the cash or its equivalent given to acquire the property or service). The cost is spread over the accounting periods which benefit from the expenditure.

Revenue. Revenue relates to the output of goods and services. In most cases revenue is recognized when goods are delivered or services rendered. In some cases revenue is recognized (1) during production, (2) when production is completed, or (3) when cash is collected.

Matching. In determining the proper periodic income, it is necessary to match related costs and expenses to revenue for the period.   The cost of the product sold and all expenses incurred in producing the sale should be matched against the revenue.

Objectivity. Accounting entries should be based on objective evidence to the fullest possible extent.   Business documents originating outside the firm provide the best evidence.   Estimates should be supported by verifiable objective data.

Consistency.   A standard method of treatment is necessary if periodic financial statements are to be compared with one another.   Where a different method will state results and financial position more fairly, the change may be made if the effect upon the statements is clearly disclosed.

Disclosure.   Financial statements and notes to financial statements should contain all relevant data of a material nature.   They should disclose such things as a change in accounting methods, contingent liabilities, etc.

Materiality. The accountant must be practical and must consider the relative importance of data.   The decision as to what is material and what is unimportant requires judgment rather than inflexible rules.

Conservatism.   Accountants necessarily make many value judgments which affect financial statements.   In these judgments it is desirable that they provide for all possible losses and not anticipate profits as yet unrealized.

2.2. Based on the following information, prepare an income statement: Fees Income, $38,000; Supplies Expense, $16,000; Salaries Expense, $12,000; Miscellaneous Expense, $7,000.

SOLUTION

INCOME STATEMENT		
Fees Income		*$38,000*
Expenses		
Supplies Expense	*$16,000*	
Salaries Expense	*12,000*	
Miscellaneous Expense	*7,000*	
Total Expenses		*35,000*
Net Income		*$ 3,000*

2.3. Based on Problem 2.2, what would the net income or net loss be if in addition to the listed expenses, there was an additional expense of $5,000 charged to Rent?

SOLUTION

INCOME STATEMENT		
Fees Income		$38,000
Expenses		
Supplies Expense	$16,000	
Salaries Expense	12,000	
Rent Expense	5,000	
Miscellaneous Expense	7,000	
Total Expenses		40,000
Net Loss		$ 2,000

Note: When expenses exceed income, a net loss results. This will have the effect of reducing capital.

2.4. The following information was taken from an income statement: Fees Income, $14,000; Rent Expense, $2,000; Salaries Expense, $5,000; Miscellaneous Expense, $1,000. If the owner withdrew $2,000 from the firm, what is the increase or decrease in capital?

SOLUTION

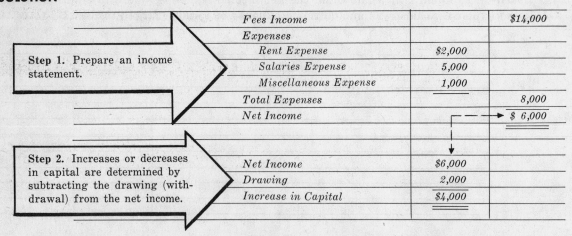

Fees Income		$14,000
Expenses		
Rent Expense	$2,000	
Salaries Expense	5,000	
Miscellaneous Expense	1,000	
Total Expenses		8,000
Net Income		$ 6,000
Net Income	$6,000	
Drawing	2,000	
Increase in Capital	$4,000	

2.5. Based on the information in Problem 2.4, if the withdrawal were $9,000 instead of $2,000, what would his increase (decrease) become?

SOLUTION

If the withdrawal is larger than the net income, a decrease in capital will result.

Net Income	$6,000
Drawing	9,000
Decrease in Capital	$3,000

2.6. If the capital account has a balance, January 1, of $32,000, what will be the balance, December 31, (a) based on Problem 2.4? (b) based on Problem 2.5?

SOLUTION

(a)
Capital, January 1		$32,000
Net Income	$6,000	
Drawing	2,000	
Increase in Capital		4,000
Capital, December 31		$36,000

(b)
Capital, January 1		$32,000
Net Income	$6,000	
Drawing	9,000	
Decrease in Capital		3,000
Capital, December 31		$29,000

2.7. Based on the following information, determine the capital as of December 31, 19X2: Net Income for period, $18,000; Drawing, $6,000; Capital (January 1, 19X2), $20,000.

SOLUTION

Capital, January 1, 19X2		$20,000
Net Income	$18,000	
Less: Drawing	6,000	
Increase in Capital		12,000
Capital, December 31, 19X2		$32,000

2.8. Based on the following information, determine the capital as of December 31: Capital (January 1), $26,000; Net Income, $18,000; Drawing, $20,000.

SOLUTION

Capital, January 1		$26,000
Net Income	$18,000	
Drawing	20,000	
Decrease in Capital		2,000
Capital, December 31		$24,000

Note: It is possible to withdraw more than net income provided that your beginning capital has an adequate balance. This will result in a decrease in capital and will be subtracted from the beginning capital.

2.9. Determine the Capital as of December 31, given the following information: Capital (January 1), $30,000; Net Loss for period, $18,000; Drawing, $4,000.

SOLUTION

Capital, January 1		$30,000
Net Loss	$18,000	
Drawing	4,000	
Decrease in Capital		22,000
Capital, December 31		$ 8,000

2.10. Based on the following information, determine the capital on December 31.

Cash	$6,000
Supplies	400
Equipment	8,000
Accounts Payable	4,500
Notes Payable	2,500

SOLUTION

ASSETS		LIABILITIES AND CAPITAL	
Cash	$ 6,000	Accounts Payable	$ 4,500
Supplies	400	Notes Payable	2,500
Equipment	8,000	Total Liabilities	7,000
Total Assets	$14,400	Capital	7,400*
		Total Liabilities and Capital	$14,400

*$14,400	Assets
−7,000	Liabilities
$ 7,400	Capital

2.11. Selected accounts of the Ruez Company produced the following balances:

	JANUARY 1	DECEMBER 31
Assets	$16,000	$19,000
Liabilities	4,000	3,000

What was the net income of the firm assuming that there were no withdrawals?

SOLUTION

Capital, January 1	$12,000*
Capital, December 31	16,000**
Increase in Capital	$ 4,000

Because there was no drawing, $4,000 must also be the net income as net income minus drawing equals Increase in Capital.
 * ($16,000 − $4,000) Based on the concept, Assets − Liabilities = Capital
** ($19,000 − $3,000) Based on the concept, Assets − Liabilities = Capital

2.12. Based on the information in Problem 2.11, determine the net income if $1,500 was withdrawn from the company.

SOLUTION

Capital, January 1	$12,000
Capital, January 31	16,000
Increase in Capital	$ 4,000

We know that:
         Net Income − Drawing = Increase in Capital

Therefore: Net Income − $1,500 = $4,000.   Net Income must be $5,500.

2.13. Prepare a balance sheet and a capital statement as of December 31, 19X2 from the data below.

Accounts Payable	$ 3,000
Cash	4,000
Equipment	16,000
Notes Payable	12,000
Supplies	200
Net Income	11,400
Drawing	10,200
Capital, January 1, 19X2	4,000

CAPITAL STATEMENT		
Capital, January 1, 19X2		
Net Income		
Drawing		
Increase in Capital		
Capital, December 31, 19X2		
BALANCE SHEET		
ASSETS		
Cash		
Supplies		
Equipment		
Total Assets		
LIABILITIES AND CAPITAL		
Notes Payable		
Accounts Payable		
Total Liabilities		
Capital, December 31, 19X2		
Total Liabilities and Capital		

SOLUTION

CAPITAL STATEMENT		
Capital, January 1, 19X2		$ 4,000
Net Income	$11,400	
Drawing	10,200	
Increase in Capital		1,200
Capital, December 31, 19X2		$ 5,200
BALANCE SHEET		
ASSETS		
Cash		$ 4,000
Supplies		200
Equipment		16,000
Total Assets		$20,200
LIABILITIES AND CAPITAL		
Notes Payable		$12,000
Accounts Payable		3,000
Total Liabilities		$15,000
Capital, December 31, 19X2		5,200
Total Liabilities and Capital		$20,200

2.14. Classify the following accounts by placing a check in the appropriate column.

		Current Asset	Fixed Asset	Current Liability	Long-Term Liability
(1)	Accounts Receivable				
(2)	Accounts Payable				
(3)	Notes Payable				
(4)	Mortgage Payable				
(5)	Cash				
(6)	Supplies				
(7)	Salaries Payable				
(8)	Bonds Payable				
(9)	Equipment				
(10)	Land				

SOLUTION

		Current Asset	Fixed Asset	Current Liability	Long-Term Liability
(1)	Accounts Receivable	✓			
(2)	Accounts Payable			✓	
(3)	Notes Payable			✓	
(4)	Mortgage Payable				✓
(5)	Cash	✓			
(6)	Supplies	✓			
(7)	Salaries Payable			✓	
(8)	Bonds Payable				✓
(9)	Equipment		✓		
(10)	Land		✓		

2.15. From the information that follows, prepare a classified balance sheet as of December 31: Cash, $6,000; Accounts Receivable, $3,000; Supplies, $1,000; Equipment, $14,000; Accounts Payable, $2,500; Notes Payable, $1,500; Mortgage Payable, $12,000; Capital, December 31, $8,000.

ASSETS		
Current Assets		
Total Current Assets		
Fixed Assets		
Total Assets		
LIABILITIES AND CAPITAL		
Current Liabilities		
Total Current Liabilities		
Long-Term Liabilities		
Total Liabilities		
Capital		
Total Liabilities and Capital		

SOLUTION

ASSETS		
Current Assets		
Cash	$6,000	
Accounts Receivable	3,000	
Supplies	1,000	
Total Current Assets		$10,000
Fixed Assets		
Equipment		14,000
Total Assets		$24,000
LIABILITIES AND CAPITAL		
Current Liabilities		
Notes Payable	$1,500	
Accounts Payable	2,500	
Total Current Liabilities		$ 4,000
Long-Term Liabilities		
Mortgage Payable		12,000
Total Liabilities		$16,000
Capital		8,000
Total Liabilities and Capital		$24,000

2.16. What is the current ratio in Problem 2.15?

SOLUTION

$$\text{Total Current Assets} \quad \$10,000$$
$$\text{Total Current Liabilities} \quad 4,000$$

$$\frac{10,000}{4,000} = 2.5 : 1$$

The firm has $2.50 in current assets for every $1 in current liabilities.

2.17. Complete the chart by writing in the appropriate column the name of the account group in which the particular account belongs and check the appropriate column in the balance sheet for its classification.

	Income Statement	Balance Sheet	Current Asset	Fixed Asset	Current Liability	Long-Term Liability
Accounts Payable						
Accounts Receivable						
Advertising Expense						
Cash						
Capital						
Equipment						
Fees Income						
Machinery						
Mortgage Payable						
Notes Receivable						
Other Income						
Salaries Expense						
Supplies						
Supplies Expense						

SOLUTION

	Income Statement	Balance Sheet	Current Asset	Fixed Asset	Current Liability	Long-Term Liability
Accounts Payable		Liability			✓	
Accounts Receivable		Asset	✓			
Advertising Expense	Expense					
Cash		Asset	✓			
Capital		Capital				
Equipment		Asset		✓		
Fees Income	Income					
Machinery		Asset		✓		
Mortgage Payable		Liability				✓
Notes Receivable		Asset	✓			
Other Income	Income					
Salaries Expense	Expense					
Supplies		Asset	✓			
Supplies Expense	Expense					

2.18. Prepare (*a*) an income statement and (*b*) a balance sheet, using the data of Problem 1.15.

(a)

Dr. M. Spring		
Income Statement		
Month of March		

(b)

Dr. M. Spring		
Balance Sheet		
March 31		

ASSETS

LIABILITIES AND CAPITAL

SOLUTION

(a)

Dr. M. Spring		
Income Statement		
Month of March		
Fees Income		$1,600
Expenses		
Rent Expense	$200	
Salaries Expense	400	
Total Expenses		600
Net Income		$1,000

(b)

Dr. M. Spring		
Balance Sheet		
March 31		
ASSETS		
Cash	$ 5,500	
Supplies	2,000	
Equipment	7,000	
Total Assets		$14,500
LIABILITIES AND CAPITAL		
Accounts Payable	$ 4,000	
Capital	10,500*	
Total Liabilities and Capital		$14,500

*If capital statement is not required, capital is computed as follows:

Capital (beginning)		$10,000
Add: Net Income	$1,000	
Less: Drawing	500	
Increase in Capital		500
Capital (end)		$10,500

2.19. Below are the account balances as of December 31, 19X2, of Mr. R. Gregg, owner of a movie theater.

Accounts Payable	$11,400
Admissions Income	34,200
Capital, January 1, 19X2	16,000
Cash	7,500
Drawing	5,400
Equipment	18,500
Film Rental Expense	6,000
Miscellaneous Expense	4,000
Notes Payable	1,000
Rent Expense	10,000
Salaries Expense	7,000
Supplies	4,200

Prepare (a) an income statement, (b) a capital statement, (c) a balance sheet.

(a)

	R. Gregg		
	Income Statement		
	Year ended December 31, 19X2		

(b)

	R. Gregg		
	Capital Statement		
	Year ended December 31, 19X2		

(c)

	R. Gregg		
	Balance Sheet		
	December 31, 19X2		

SOLUTION

(a)

	R. Gregg		
	Income Statement		
	Year ended December 31, 19X2		
Income			$34,200
Expenses			
Rent Expense		$10,000	
Salaries Expense		7,000	
Film Rental Expense		6,000	
Miscellaneous Expense		4,000	
Total Expenses			27,000
Net Income			$ 7,200

(b)   The capital statement is needed to show the capital balance at the *end* of the year.   Mr. Gregg's capital balance above is at the beginning.   Net income increases capital and drawing reduces capital.

R. Gregg		
Capital Statement		
Year ended December 31, 19X2		
Capital, January 1, 19X2		$16,000
Add: Net Income	$ 7,200	
Less: Drawing	5,400	
Increase in Capital		1,800
Capital, December 31, 19X2		$17,800

(c)

R. Gregg		
Balance Sheet		
December 31, 19X2		
ASSETS		
Cash	$ 7,500	
Supplies	4,200	
Equipment	18,500	
Total Assets		$30,200
LIABILITIES AND CAPITAL		
Accounts Payable	$11,400	
Notes Payable	1,000	
Total Liabilities		$12,400
Capital		17,800
Total Liabilities and Capital		$30,200

2.20.   The balances of the accounts of Dr. J. Hoflich, Dentist, appear as follows:

Accounts Payable	$ 2,800
Accounts Receivable	3,600
Building	12,000
Capital, January 1, 19X2	19,000
Cash	12,200
Dental Income	38,000
Drawing	6,000
Equipment	15,000
Furniture	3,000
Mortgage Payable	10,000
Miscellaneous Expense	2,000
Notes Payable	2,000
Supplies	6,000
Salaries Expense	8,000
Supplies Expense	4,000

Using the forms provided below, prepare   (*a*) an income statement,   (*b*) a capital statement, and   (*c*) a classified balance sheet.

(a)

Dr. J. Hoflich		
Income Statement		
Year ended December 31, 19X2		
Income from Fees		
Expenses		
Total Expenses		
Net Income		

(b)

Dr. J. Hoflich		
Capital Statement		
Year ended December 31, 19X2		
Capital, January 1, 19X2		
Add: Net Income		
Less: Drawing		
Increase in Capital		
Capital, December 31, 19X2		

(c)

Dr. J. Hoflich		
Balance Sheet		
December 31, 19X2		
ASSETS		
Current Assets		
Total Current Assets		
Fixed Assets		
Total Fixed Assets		
Total Assets		
LIABILITIES AND CAPITAL		
Current Liabilities		
Total Current Liabilities		
Long-Term Liabilities		
Total Liabilities		
Capital		
Total Liabilities and Capital		

SOLUTION

(a)

Dr. J. Hoflich		
Income Statement		
Year ended December 31, 19X2		
Income from Fees		$38,000
Expenses		
Salaries Expense	$ 8,000	
Supplies Expense	4,000	
Miscellaneous Expense	2,000	
Total Expenses		14,000
Net Income		$24,000

(b)

Dr. J. Hoflich		
Capital Statement		
Year ended December 31, 19X2		
Capital, January 1, 19X2		$19,000
Add: Net Income	$24,000	
Less: Drawing	6,000	
Increase in Capital		18,000
Capital, December 31, 19X2		$37,000

(c)

Dr. J. Hoflich		
Balance Sheet		
December 31, 19X2		
ASSETS		
Current Assets		
Cash	$12,200	
Accounts Receivable	3,600	
Supplies	6,000	
Total Current Assets		$21,800
Fixed Assets		
Building	$12,000	
Equipment	15,000	
Furniture	3,000	
Total Fixed Assets		30,000
Total Assets		$51,800
LIABILITIES AND CAPITAL		
Current Liabilities		
Accounts Payable	$ 2,800	
Notes Payable	2,000	
Total Current Liabilities		$ 4,800
Long-Term Liabilities		
Mortgage Payable		10,000
Total Liabilities		$14,800
Capital (see Capital Statement)		37,000
Total Liabilities and Capital		$51,800

Chapter 3

Analyzing and Classifying Transactions

3.1 INTRODUCTION

Preparing a new equation $A = L + C$ after each transaction would be cumbersome and costly, especially when there are a great many transactions in an accounting period. Also, information for a specific item such as cash would be lost as successive transactions were recorded. This information could be obtained by going back and summarizing the transactions but that would be very time-consuming.

A much more efficient way is to classify the transactions according to items on the balance sheet and income statement. The increases and decreases are then recorded according to type of item by means of a summary called an *account*.

3.2 THE ACCOUNT

A separate account is maintained for each item that appears on the balance sheet (assets, liabilities, and capital) and on the income statement (revenue and expense). Thus an account may be defined as *a record of the increases, decreases, and balances in an individual item of asset, liability, capital, revenue, or expense.*

The simplest form of the account is known as the "T" account because it resembles the letter "T". The account has three parts: (1) the name of the account and the account number, (2) the debit side (left side), and (3) the credit side (right side). The increases are entered on one side, the decreases on the other. Which change goes on which side will be discussed in Section 3.3. The balance (the excess of the total of one side over the total of the other) is inserted near the last figure on the side with the larger amount.

3.3 DEBITS AND CREDITS. THE DOUBLE-ENTRY SYSTEM

When an amount is entered on the left side of an account, it is a *debit* and the account is said to be *debited*. When an amount is entered on the right side, it is a *credit* and the account is said to be *credited*. The abbreviations for debit and credit are Dr. and Cr., respectively.

Whether an increase in a given item is credited or debited depends on the category of the item. By convention, asset and expense increases are recorded as debits, while liability, capital, and income increases are recorded as credits. Asset and expense decreases are recorded as credits, while liability, capital, and income decreases are recorded as debits. The following tables summarize the rule.

ASSETS AND EXPENSES		LIABILITIES, CAPITAL, AND INCOME	
Dr.	Cr.	Dr.	Cr.
+	−	−	+
(Increases)	(Decreases)	(Decreases)	(Increases)

EXAMPLE 1.

Let us re-examine the transactions that occurred in Mr. A. Bagon's law firm during the first month of operation. These are the same as in Chapter 1, except that accounts are now used to record the transactions.

Transaction (1). Mr. Bagon opened his law practice, investing $5,000 in cash. The two accounts affected are Cash and Capital. Remember that an increase in an asset (cash) is debited, whereas an increase in capital is credited.

Cash		Capital	
Dr.	Cr.	Dr.	Cr.
+	−	−	+
(1) 5,000			5,000 (1)

Transaction (2). Bought supplies for cash, $300. Here we are substituting one asset (cash) for another asset (supplies). We debit Supplies, because we are receiving more supplies. We credit Cash, because we are paying out cash.

Cash		Supplies	
Dr.	Cr.	Dr.	Cr.
+	−	+	−
5,000	300 (2)	(2) 300	

Transaction (3). Bought equipment from Altway Furniture Company on account, $2,500. We are receiving an asset (equipment), and therefore debit Equipment to show the increase. We are not paying cash, but creating a new liability, thereby increasing the liability account (Accounts Payable).

Equipment		Accounts Payable	
Dr.	Cr.	Dr.	Cr.
+	−	−	+
(3) 2,500			2,500 (3)

Transaction (4). Received $2,000 in fees earned during the month. In this case, we are increasing the asset account Cash, as we have received $2,000. Therefore, we debit it. We are increasing the capital, yet we do not credit Capital. It is better temporarily to separate the income from the owner's equity (capital) and create a new account, Fees Income.

Cash		Fees Income	
Dr.	Cr.	Dr.	Cr.
+	−	−	+
5,000	300		2,000 (4)
(4) 2,000			

Transaction (5). Paid office rent for January, $500. We must decrease the asset account Cash, because we are paying out money. Therefore, we credit it. It is preferable to keep expenses separated from the owners' equity. Therefore, we open a new account for the expense involved, Rent Expense. The $500 is entered on the left side, as expenses decrease owner's equity.

Cash		Rent Expense	
Dr.	Cr.	Dr.	Cr.
+	−	+	−
5,000	300	(5) 500	
2,000	500 (5)		

Transaction (6).   Paid salary for part-time help, $200.   Again, we must reduce our asset account (Cash), because we are paying out money.   Therefore, we credit the account.   Bagon's capital was reduced by an expense and we open another account, Salary Expense. A debit to this account shows the decrease in capital.

Cash				Salary Expense	
Dr. +	Cr. −			Dr. +	Cr. −
5,000	300		(6) 200		
2,000	500				
	200 (6)				

Transaction (7).   Paid $1,000 to Altway Furniture Company, on account.   This transaction reduced our asset account (Cash), since we are paying out money.   We therefore credit Cash. We also reduce our liability account (Accounts Payable) by $1,000; we now owe that much less.   Thus, we debit Accounts Payable.

Cash				Accounts Payable	
Dr. +	Cr. −			Dr. −	Cr. +
5,000	300		(7) 1,000		2,500
2,000	500				
	200				
	1,000 (7)				

Transaction (8).   After taking inventory at the end of the month, Mr. Bagon found he had used $200 worth of supplies.   We must reduce the asset account Supplies by crediting it for $200.   Supplies Expense is debited for the decrease in capital.   This is computed as follows: beginning inventory of $300, less supplies on hand at the end of the month ($100), indicates $200 must have been used during the month.

Supplies				Supplies Expense	
Dr. +	Cr. −			Dr. +	Cr. −
300	200 (8)		(8) 200		

Transaction (9).   Withdrew $300 for personal use.   The withdrawal of cash means there is a reduction in the asset account Cash.   Therefore, it is credited.   The amount invested by the owner is also $300 less.   We must open the account Drawing, which is debited to show the decrease in capital.

Cash				Drawing	
Dr. +	Cr. −			Dr. +	Cr. −
5,000	300		(9) 300		
2,000	500				
	200				
	1,000				
	300 (9)				

An account has a debit balance when the sum of its debits exceeds the sum of its credits; it has a credit balance when the sum of the credits is the greater.   In *double-entry accounting*, which is in almost universal use, there are equal debit and credit entries for every transaction.   Where there are only two accounts affected, the debit and credit amounts are equal.   If more than two accounts are affected, the total of the debit entries must equal the total of the credit entries.

3.4 THE LEDGER

The complete set of accounts for a business entity is called a ledger. It is the "reference book" of the accounting system and is used to classify and summarize transactions and to prepare data for financial statements. It is also a valuable source of information for managerial purposes, giving, for example, the amount of sales for the period or the cash balance at the end of the period. Depending on what method of data processing is used, the ledger may take the form of a bound book with a page for each account, punched cards, or magnetic tapes or disks. In any case, the accounting principles are the same. Further information on data processing methods is given in the Appendix.

3.5 THE CHART OF ACCOUNTS

It is desirable to establish a systematic method of identifying and locating each account in the ledger. The *chart of accounts*, sometimes called the *code of accounts*, is a listing of the accounts by title and numerical designation. In some companies the chart of accounts may run to hundreds of items.

In designing a numbering structure for the accounts it is important to provide adequate flexibility to permit expansion without having to revise the basic system. Generally, blocks of numbers are assigned to various groups of accounts, such as assets, liabilities, etc. There are various systems of coding, depending on the needs and desires of the company.

EXAMPLE 2.

A simple chart structure is to have the first digit represent the major group in which the account is located. Thus accounts which have numbers beginning with 1 are assets; 2, liabilities; 3, capital; 4, income; and 5, expenses. The second or third digit designates the position of the account in the group.

In the more common two-digital system, assets are assigned the block of numbers 11–19, and liabilities 21–29. In larger firms a three-digital (or higher) system may be used, with assets assigned 101–199 and liabilities 201–299. Following are the numerical designations for the account groups under both methods.

ACCOUNT GROUP	TWO-DIGITAL	THREE-DIGITAL
1. Assets	11–19	101–199
2. Liabilities	21–29	201–299
3. Capital	31–39	301–399
4. Income	41–49	401–499
5. Expense	51–59	501–599

Thus Cash may be account 11 under the first system and 101 under the second system. The cash account may be further broken down as: 101, Cash – First National Bank; 102, Cash – Second National Bank; etc.

3.6 THE TRIAL BALANCE

As every transaction results in an equal amount of debits and credits in the ledger, the total of all debit entries in the ledger ought to equal the total of all credit entries. At the end of the accounting period we check this equality by preparing a two-column schedule called a *trial balance*, which compares the total of all debit *balances* with the total of all credit *balances*. The procedure is as follows:

1. List account titles in numerical order in two columns of a work sheet.
2. Record balances of each account, entering debit balances in the left column and credit balances in the right column. (*Note*: Asset and expense accounts are debited for increases and would normally have debit balances. Liabilities, capital, and income accounts are credited for increases and would normally have credit balances.)
3. Add the columns and record the totals.
4. Compare the totals.

    If the totals agree, the trial balance is in balance, indicating the equality of the debits and credits for the hundreds or thousands of transactions entered in the ledger. While the trial balance provides *arithmetic* proof of the accuracy of the records, it does not provide *theoretical* proof. For example, if the purchase of a machine was incorrectly charged to Expense, the trial balance columns may agree, but theoretically the accounts would be wrong, as Expense would be overstated and Machinery understated. In addition to providing proof of arithmetic accuracy in accounts, the trial balance facilitates the preparation of the periodic financial statements. Generally the trial balance comprises the first two columns of a work sheet, from which financial statements are prepared.

EXAMPLE 3.

    The summary of the transactions for Mr. Bagon (see Example 1), and their effect on the accounts, is shown below. The trial balance is then taken. Note that each account now has a numerical designation. In this case, a two-digit base.

ASSETS	LIABILITIES	CAPITAL

Cash 11

(1)	5,000	300	(2)
(4)	2,000	500	(5)
		200	(6)
		1,000	(7)
		300	(9)

Accounts Payable 21

(7)	1,000	2,500	(3)

A. Bagon, Capital 31

	5,000 (1)

Drawing 32

(9) 300	

Supplies 12

(2)	300	200	(8)

Fees Income 41

	2,000 (4)

Equipment 13

(3) 2,500	

Rent Expense 51

(5) 500	

Salaries Expense 52

(6) 200	

Supplies Expense 53

(8) 200	

A. Bagon, Lawyer
Trial Balance
January 31, 19X2

	Dr.	Cr.
Cash	$4,700	
Supplies	100	
Equipment	2,500	
Accounts Payable		$1,500
A. Bagon, Capital		5,000
Drawing	300	
Fees Income		2,000
Rent Expense	500	
Salaries Expense	200	
Supplies Expense	200	
	$8,500	$8,500

Summary

(1) To classify and summarize a single item of an account group, we use a form called an _____.

(2) The accounts comprise a record called a _____.

(3) The left side of the account is known as the _____, while the right side is the _____.

(4) Increases in all asset accounts are _____.

(5) Increases in all liability accounts are _____.

(6) Increases in all capital accounts are _____.

(7) Increases in all income accounts are _____.

(8) Increases in all expense accounts are _____.

(9) Expenses are debited because they decrease _____.

(10) The schedule showing the balance of each account at the end of the period is known as the _____.

Answers: (1) account; (2) ledger; (3) debit side, credit side; (4) debited; (5) credited; (6) credited; (7) credited; (8) debited; (9) capital; (10) trial balance

Solved Problems

3.1. Revenue and expense accounts are designated as *temporary* or *nominal* accounts (accounts in name only). Explain.

SOLUTION

The increase in capital resulting from revenue is temporary, since capital will be reduced by expenses in the same period. These accounts are closed out at the end of the accounting period and the net balance (for example, the excess of revenue over expenses for the period) is then transferred to the capital account.

The *permanent* or *real account* balances—assets, liabilities, and capital—are not closed out at the end of the accounting period. For example, the cash or inventory balance at the end of one period becomes the beginning balance in the following period.

3.2. Interpret the balance in the supplies account at the end of the period.

SOLUTION

The book figure before adjustment is the amount on hand at the beginning of the period plus the amount purchased during the period. The sum is the total amount that was available during the period and was either used up or is still on hand. When an inventory count is made at the end of the period, the amount still on hand is determined, and the difference between that amount and the available amount above represents what was used during the period, which is an expense (supplies expense). The balance on hand is an asset (supplies on hand).

3.3. In each of the following types of "T" accounts, enter an increase (by writing +) and a decrease (by writing −).

ASSETS		LIABILITIES		CAPITAL	
Dr.	Cr.	Dr.	Cr.	Dr.	Cr.

INCOME		EXPENSES	
Dr.	Cr.	Dr.	Cr.

SOLUTION

ASSETS		LIABILITIES		CAPITAL	
Dr.	Cr.	Dr.	Cr.	Dr.	Cr.
+	−	−	+	−	+

INCOME		EXPENSES	
Dr.	Cr.	Dr.	Cr.
−	+	+	−

3.4. Indicate in the columns below the increases and decreases in each account by placing a check in the appropriate column.

	Debit	Credit
(a) Capital is increased		
(b) Cash is decreased		
(c) Accounts Payable is increased		
(d) Rent Expense is increased		
(e) Equipment is increased		
(f) Fees Income is increased		
(g) Capital is decreased (through drawing)		

SOLUTION

(a) Cr.   (b) Cr.   (c) Cr.   (d) Dr.   (e) Dr.   (f) Cr.   (g) Dr.

3.5. For each transaction in the table below, indicate the account to be debited and the account to be credited by placing the letter representing the account in the appropriate column.

Name of Account	Transaction	Dr.	Cr.
(a) Accounts Payable	1. Invested cash in the firm		
(b) Capital	2. Paid rent for month		
(c) Cash	3. Received cash fees for services		
(d) Drawing	4. Paid salaries		
(e) Equipment	5. Bought equipment on account		
(f) Fees Income	6. Paid 1/2 balance on equipment		
(g) Notes Payable	7. Bought supplies on account		
(h) Rent Expense	8. Borrowed money from bank, giving a note in exchange		
(i) Salaries Expense	9. Supplies inventory showed 1/3 used during the month		
(j) Supplies	10. Withdrew cash for personal use		
(k) Supplies Expense			

SOLUTION

	Dr.	Cr.
1.	(c)	(b)
2.	(h)	(c)
3.	(c)	(f)
4.	(i)	(c)
5.	(e)	(a)
6.	(a)	(c)
7.	(j)	(a)
8.	(c)	(g)
9.	(k)	(j)
10.	(d)	(c)

3.6. Record each transaction in the accompanying accounts.

(a) Bought equipment for cash, $600.

Equipment			Cash	
			Bal. 2,000	

(b) Bought additional equipment for $2,700, paying 1/3 down and owing the balance.

Equipment		Cash		Accounts Payable	
Bal. 600		Bal. 1,400			

(c) Gave a note in settlement of transaction (b).

Accounts Payable		Notes Payable	
	Bal. 1,800		

(d) Received $700 in plumbing fees.

Cash		Fees Income	
Bal. 500			

SOLUTION

(a)

Equipment		Cash	
600		Bal. 2,000	600

(b)

Equipment		Cash		Accounts Payable	
Bal. 600		Bal. 1,400	900		1,800
2,700					

(c)

Accounts Payable		Notes Payable	
1,800	Bal. 1,800		1,800

(d)

Cash		Fees Income	
Bal. 500			700
700			

3.7. The ten accounts which follow summarize the first week's transactions of the Willis Taxi Company.

Cash 11		Equipment 13		Fees Income 41	
(a) 14,000	10,000 (b)	(b) 10,000			1,000 (e)
(e) 1,000	200 (d)	(c) 6,000			
	300 (f)			**Salaries Expense 51**	
	500 (g)	**Accounts Payable 21**		(f) 300	
	100 (h)	(i) 2,000	6,000 (c)		
	2,000 (i)			**Rent Expense 52**	
	300 (j)	**Capital 31**		(g) 500	
			14,000 (a)		
				Gasoline Expense 53	
Supplies 12		**Drawing 32**		(j) 300	
(d) 200		(h) 100			

Complete the form below. (The analysis of the first transaction is given as a sample.)

Transaction	Account Debited	Effect of Debit	Account Credited	Effect of Credit
(a) Invested $14,000 in firm	Cash	Increased asset	Capital	Increased capital
(b)				
(c)				
(d)				
(e)				
(f)				
(g)				
(h)				
(i)				
(j)				

SOLUTION

Transaction	Account Debited	Effect of Debit	Account Credited	Effect of Credit
(a) Invested $14,000 in firm	Cash	Increased asset	Capital	Increased capital
(b) Bought equipment for cash	Equipment	Increased asset	Cash	Decreased asset
(c) Bought additional equipment on account	Equipment	Increased asset	Accts. Payable	Increased liability
(d) Paid $200 for supplies	Supplies	Increased asset	Cash	Decreased asset
(e) Received $1,000 in fees	Cash	Increased asset	Fees Income	Increased income
(f) Paid $300 for salaries	Salaries Expense	Increased expense	Cash	Decreased asset
(g) Paid $500 for rent	Rent Expense	Increased expense	Cash	Decreased asset
(h) Withdrew $100 for personal use	Drawing	Decreased capital	Cash	Decreased asset
(i) Paid $2,000 on account	Accounts Payable	Decreased liability	Cash	Decreased asset
(j) Paid $300 for gasoline	Gasoline Expense	Increased expense	Cash	Decreased asset

3.8. Rearrange the following list of accounts as they would appear in the ledger and assign a numerical designation for each one based on a two-digit system.

Fees Income
Salaries Expense
Supplies Expense
Supplies
Cash
Accounts Receivable
Accounts Payable
Notes Payable
Capital
Equipment
Drawing

SOLUTION

ACCOUNT	DESIGNATED NUMBER
Cash	11
Supplies	12
Accounts Receivable	13
Equipment	14
Accounts Payable	21
Notes Payable	22
Capital	31
Drawing	32
Fees Income	41
Salaries Expense	51
Supplies Expense	52

3.9. Rearrange the alphabetical list of the accounts and produce a trial balance.

Accounts Payable	$ 6,000
Accounts Receivable	14,000
Sarah Hudson, Capital	32,000
Cash	20,000
Sarah Hudson, Drawing	4,000
Equipment	15,000
Fees Income	26,000
General Expense	1,000
Notes Payable	11,000
Rent Expense	5,000
Salaries Expense	8,000
Supplies	6,000
Supplies Expense	2,000

SOLUTION

	Dr.	Cr.
Cash	$20,000	
Accounts Receivable	14,000	
Supplies	6,000	
Equipment	15,000	
Accounts Payable		$ 6,000
Notes Payable		11,000
Sarah Hudson, Capital		32,000
Sarah Hudson, Drawing	4,000	
Fees Income		26,000
Salaries Expense	8,000	
Rent Expense	5,000	
Supplies Expense	2,000	
General Expense	1,000	
	$75,000	$75,000

3.10. In the following trial balance for R. Romez Company, certain accounts have been recorded improperly, therefore, it does not balance. Prepare a corrected Trial Balance.

R. Romez		
Trial Balance		
December 31, 19X2		
	Debit	*Credit*
Cash	$26,000	
Accounts Receivable	14,000	
Supplies		$ 6,000
Equipment	12,000	
Accounts Payable	14,000	
R. Romez, Capital	30,000	
R. Romez, Drawing		4,000
Fees Income		38,000
Rent Expense	6,000	
Supplies Expense	2,000	
Salaries Expense		12,000
	$104,000	$60,000

	Debit	Credit

SOLUTION

	Debit	Credit
Cash	$26,000	
Accounts Receivable	14,000	
Supplies	6,000	
Equipment	12,000	
Accounts Payable		$14,000
R. Romez, Capital		30,000
R. Romez, Drawing	4,000	
Fees Income		38,000
Rent Expense	6,000	
Supplies Expense	2,000	
Salaries Expense	12,000	
	$82,000	$82,000

3.11. The trial balance of Joan Howard Co. does not balance. In reviewing the ledger, the following information was discovered: (1) The debits and credits in the cash account total $24,100 and $21,400 respectively. (2) A $400 check received in settlement of an accounts receivable account was not posted to the accounts receivable account. (3) The balance of the rent expense should be $200 less. (4) As of December 31, there are no notes payable outstanding. (5) Each account should have a normal balance. Prepare a corrected trial balance.

Joan Howard Co.		
Trial Balance		
December 31, 19X2		
	Debit	Credit
Cash	$ 3,000	
Accounts Receivable	11,800	
Supplies		$ 800
Equipment	18,500	
Accounts Payable		1,500
Notes Payable		300
Joan Howard, Capital		15,400
Joan Howard, Drawing		500
Fees Income		29,000
Salary Expense	8,200	
Rent Expense	3,000	
Supplies Expense		200
General Expense		800
	$44,500	$48,500

	Debit	Credit

SOLUTION

	Debit	Credit
Cash	$ 2,700	
Accounts Receivable	11,400	
Supplies	800	
Equipment	18,500	
Accounts Payable		$ 1,500
Notes Payable		
Joan Howard, Capital		15,400
Joan Howard, Drawing	500	
Fees Income		29,000
Salary Expense	8,200	
Rent Expense	2,800	
Supplies Expense	200	
General Expense	800	
	$45,900	$45,900

3.12. Using the information of Problem 1.15, record the entries in the accounts below for Dr. M. Spring, labeling each item by number as in Problem 1.15. Then prepare a trial balance.

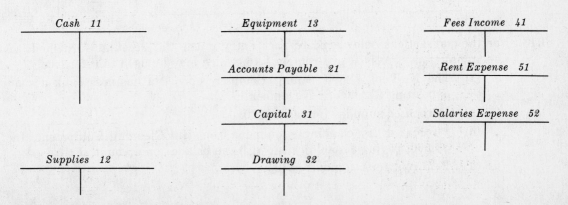

Dr. M. Spring		
Trial Balance		
December 31, 19X2		
Cash		
Supplies		
Equipment		
Accounts Payable		
Dr. M. Spring, Capital		
Dr. M. Spring, Drawing		
Fees Income		
Rent Expense		
Salaries Expense		

SOLUTION

Cash 11			Equipment 13			Fees Income 41	
(1) 10,000	2,000 (3)		(2) 7,000				1,600 (4)
(4) 1,600	200 (5)						
	400 (6)		**Accounts Payable 21**			**Rent Expense 51**	
	3,000 (7)		(7) 3,000	7,000 (2)		(5) 200	
	500 (8)						
			Capital 31			**Salaries Expense 52**	
Supplies 12				10,000 (1)		(6) 400	
(3) 2,000							
			Drawing 52				
			(8) 500				

Dr. M. Spring		
Trial Balance		
December 31, 19X2		
Cash	$ 5,500	
Supplies	2,000	
Equipment	7,000	
Accounts Payable		$ 4,000
Dr. M. Spring, Capital		10,000
Dr. M. Spring, Drawing	500	
Fees Income		1,600
Rent Expense	200	
Salaries Expense	400	
	$15,600	$15,600

3.13. For the transactions below, record each entry in the "T" accounts furnished. (*Note:* The transactions are those of Problem 1.16, which may be used in reference.)

(1) The Nu-Look Dry Cleaning Company opened a business bank account by depositing $12,000 on November 1.

(2) Purchased supplies for cash, $220.

(3) Purchased dry cleaning equipment from Hill Cleaning Equipment, Inc. for $3,500, paying $1,500 in cash with the balance on account.

(4) Paid rent for the month, $425.

(5) Cash sales for the month totaled $1,850.

(6) Paid salaries of $375.

(7) Paid $500 on account to Hill Cleaning Equipment, Inc.

(8) The cost of supplies used was determined to be $60.

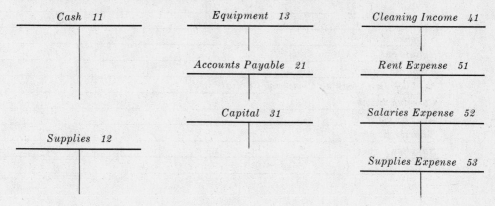

SOLUTION

Cash 11	
(1) 12,000	220 (2)
(5) 1,850	1,500 (3)
	425 (4)
	375 (6)
	500 (7)

Supplies 12	
(2) 220	60 (8)

Equipment 13	
(3) 3,500	

Accounts Payable 21	
(7) 500	2,000 (3)

Capital 31	
	12,000 (1)

Cleaning Income 41	
	1,850 (5)

Rent Expense 51	
(4) 425	

Salaries Expense 52	
(6) 375	

Supplies Expense 53	
(8) 60	

3.14. Prepare a trial balance as of November 30 for the Nu-Look Dry Cleaning Company, using the account balances in Problem 3.13.

Nu-Look Dry Cleaning Company		
Trial Balance		
November 30		
Cash		
Supplies		
Equipment		
Accounts Payable		
Nu-Look Dry Cleaning Company, Capital		
Cleaning Income		
Rent Expense		
Salaries Expense		
Supplies Expense		

SOLUTION

Nu-Look Dry Cleaning Company		
Trial Balance		
November 30		
Cash	$10,830	
Supplies	160	
Equipment	3,500	
Accounts Payable		$ 1,500
Nu-Look Dry Cleaning Company, Capital		12,000
Cleaning Income		1,850
Rent Expense	425	
Salaries Expense	375	
Supplies Expense	60	
	$15,350	$15,350

Examination I

Chapters 1-3

1. What is meant by the accounting cycle?

2. Define the following terms and give an example of each: (a) assets, (b) liabilities, (c) capital.

3. Define (a) revenue, (b) expense, (c) net income.

4. (a) What is an account? (b) What is a chart of accounts?

5. Distinguish between temporary and permanent accounts.

6. What is meant by the double-entry system of accounting?

7. What does the balance in the supplies account at the end of the period represent?

8. Prepare the capital statement for the year ended December 31 of the Grant Company, given:

Capital, January 1	$72,400
Net Income for Period	27,600
Withdrawals by the proprietor	12,000

9. (a) Prepare the capital statement for the year ended December 31 for the Mary Tyler Company given:

Capital January 1	$86,240
Net Income for Period	12,000
Withdrawals by Ms. Tyler	18,000

   (b) If there were a net loss of $12,000 instead of net income, find the new capital as of December 31.

10. On January 1, Anita Accord began business by investing $5,000 in her firm. During the month, she had the following income and expenditures:

Income from Services	$12,600	Supplies Expense	$ 75
Rent Expense	200	Utilities Expense	125
Salaries Expense	150	Repairs and Maintenance Expense	400
Commission Expense	100	Miscellaneous Expense	225

   Present the income statement for January.

11. Below are the account balances of the State-Rite Cleaning Company as of December 31, 19X2. Prepare (a) an income statement, (b) a capital statement, (c) a balance sheet.

Accounts Payable	$11,600	Miscellaneous Expense	$ 3,000
Cleaning Income	39,500	Notes Payable	2,800
Capital (beginning)	14,300	Rent Expense	12,600
Cash	9,300	Salaries Expense	9,200
Drawing	4,800	Supplies	5,300
Equipment	19,200	Supplies Expense	2,400
Repairs and Maintenance Expense	2,400		

12. For each numbered transaction below, indicate the account to be debited and the account to be credited by placing the letter representing the account in the appropriate column. Accounts Payable (*a*); Capital (*b*); Cash (*c*); Drawing (*d*); Equipment (*e*); Fees Income (*f*); Notes Payable (*g*); Rent Expense (*h*); Salaries Expense (*i*); Supplies (*j*); Supplies Expense (*k*).

		Debit	Credit
(1)	Invested cash in the firm.	(*c*)	(*b*)
(2)	Received cash for services rendered.		
(3)	Paid salaries for the week.		
(4)	Bought equipment on account.		
(5)	Bought supplies on account.		
(6)	Gave a note in settlement of the equipment on account.		
(7)	Borrowed money from the bank.		
(8)	Withdrew cash for personal use.		
(9)	A count showed that approximately 3/4 of the supplies inventory had been used during the year.		
(10)	Paid rent for the month.		

13. The Sullivan Residence Club established business on January 1, 19X2, and invested $15,000 cash and a $22,000 building in their club. A summary of transactions for January follows.

    (1)   Collected rents for the month of January $ 2,400

    (2)   Check was written for insurance   850

    (3)   Paid the electric bill   240

    (4)   Paid the January salary of the maintenance person   350

    (5)   Bought supplies on account   800

    (6)   Borrowed $15,000 from the bank for additions to the building   15,000

    (7)   Withdrew $300 for personal use   300

    (8)   Supplies on hand at the end of the month   500

Record the above information in the appropriate "T" accounts.

14. The "T" accounts below were taken from the ledger of the Utility Service Company. Prepare a trial balance from these accounts.

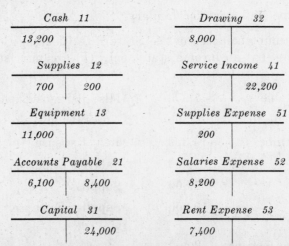

Answers to Examination I

1. The accounting cycle is the sequence of procedures repeated each accounting period. The steps are: (1) recording transactions in journals; (2) classifying data by posting to ledger; (3) summarizing data by classification; (4) adjusting and correcting recorded data; (5) preparing statements.

2. (a) Property of value owned by a business; Cash.

   (b) Amounts owed by the business to outsiders; Accounts Payable.

   (c) The investment by the owner(s) and the earnings retained in the business (also called *proprietorship* or *owners' equity*); J. Smith, Capital.

3. (a) The inflow of cash and receivables for an accounting period, resulting from the delivery of goods or the rendering of services.

   (b) The cost of goods and services used up or consumed in the process of obtaining revenue.

   (c) The increase in capital resulting from profitable operation of a business. Alternatively, the excess of revenues over expenses for the particular period.

4. (a) The account is a form used to record changes in a particular asset, liabiltiy, or item of capital, revenue, or expense. It is used to classify and summarize transactions.

   (b) The chart of accounts is a listing of the account titles showing the sequence of the accounts in the ledger and the number assigned to each account. It is a systematic method of identifying and locating each account.

5. Revenue and expense accounts are designated as temporary or nominal accounts because the increase in capital resulting from revenue is subject to reduction by expenses in the same period. These accounts are closed out at the end of the accounting period and the net balance transferred to the capital account. Permanent or real account balances — assets, liabilities, and capital — are not closed out at the end of the accounting period.

6. In the double-entry system, the recording of each transaction must be such that the total debits equal the total credits. In most cases, there will be only one debit and one credit account affected, and thus the dollar amounts will be equal.

7. Amount on hand at the beginning of the period, plus purchases during the period, minus consumption during the period.

8.

Grant Company
Capital Statement
Year Ended December 31

Capital, January 1		$72,400
Net Income for Period	$27,600	
Less: Drawing	12,000	
Increase in Capital		15,600
Capital, December 31		$88,000

9.

Mary Tyler Company
Capital Statement
Year Ended December 31

(a) Capital, January 1		$86,240
Net Income for Period	$12,000	
Less: Drawing	18,000	
Decrease in Capital		(6,000)
Capital, December 31		$80,240
(b) Capital, January 1		$86,240
Net Loss for Period	12,000	
Add: Drawing	18,000	
Decrease in Capital		(30,000)
Capital, December 31		$56,240

10.

Anita Accord
Income Statement
Month Ended January 31

Income from Services		$12,600
Expenses		
Repairs and Maintenance Expense	$400	
Rent Expense	200	
Salaries Expense	150	
Utilities Expense	125	
Commission Expense	100	
Supplies Expense	75	
Miscellaneous Expense	225	
Total Expenses		1,275
Net Income		$11,325

Note: The investment of $5,000 has nothing to do with the income statement presentation.

11. **(a)**

State-Rite Cleaning Company
Income Statement
Year Ended December 31, 19X2

Cleaning Income		$39,500
Expenses		
Rent Expense	$12,600	
Salaries Expense	9,200	
Repairs and Maintenance Expense	2,400	
Supplies Expense	2,400	
Miscellaneous Expense	3,000	
Total Expenses		29,600
Net Income		$ 9,900

(b)

State-Rite Cleaning Company
Capital Statement
Year Ended December 31, 19X2

Capital, January 1, 19X2		$14,300
Net Income for Period	$9,900	
Less: Drawing	4,800	
Increase in Capital		5,100
Capital, December 31, 19X2		$19,400

(c)

State-Rite Cleaning Company
Balance Sheet
December 31, 19X2

ASSETS

Cash	$ 9,300	
Supplies	5,300	
Equipment	19,200	
Total Assets		$33,800

LIABILITIES AND CAPITAL

Accounts Payable	$11,600	
Notes Payable	2,800	
Total Liabilities		$14,400
Capital, December 31, 19X2		19,400
Total Liabilities and Capital		$33,800

12.

	Debit	Credit
(1)	(c)	(b)
(2)	(c)	(f)
(3)	(i)	(c)
(4)	(e)	(a)
(5)	(j)	(a)
(6)	(a)	(g)
(7)	(c)	(g)
(8)	(d)	(c)
(9)	(k)	(j)
(10)	(h)	(c)

13.

Cash

Bal. 15,000		850	(2)
(1) 2,400		240	(3)
(6) 15,000		350	(4)
		300	(7)

Supplies 12

(5) 800		300	(8)

Drawing 32

(7) 300	

Capital 31

	Bal. 37,000

Supplies Expense 54

(8) 300	

Salaries Expense 51

(4) 350	

Building 13

Bal. 22,000	

Insurance Expense 52

(2) 850	

Accounts Payable 21

	800 (5)

Rent Income 41

	2,400 (1)

Utilities Expense 53

(3) 240	

Notes Payable 22

	15,000 (6)

14.

Utility Service Company
Trial Balance

Cash	$13,200	
Supplies	500	
Equipment	11,000	
Accounts Payable		$ 2,300
Capital		24,000
Drawing	8,000	
Service Income		22,200
Supplies Expense	200	
Salaries Expense	8,200	
Rent Expense	7,400	
	$48,500	$48,500

Chapter 4

Recording Transactions

4.1 INTRODUCTION

In the preceding chapters we discussed the nature of business transactions and the manner in which they are analyzed and classified. The primary emphasis was the *why* rather than the *how* of accounting operations; we aimed at an understanding of the *reason* for making the entry in a particular way. We showed the effects of transactions by making entries in "T" accounts. However, these entries do not provide the necessary data for a particular transaction nor do they provide a chronological record of transactions. The missing information is furnished by the journal.

4.2 THE JOURNAL

The journal, or day book, is the book of original entry for accounting data. Subsequently the data is transferred or *posted* to the ledger, the book of subsequent or *secondary* entry. The various transactions are evidenced by sales tickets, purchase invoices, check stubs, etc. On the basis of this evidence the transactions are entered in chronological order in the journal. The process is called *journalizing*.

There are a number of different journals that may be used in a business. For our purposes they may be grouped into (1) general journals and (2) specialized journals. The latter type, which are used in businesses with a large number of repetitive transactions, are described in Chapter 5. To illustrate journalizing, we here use the general journal whose standard form is shown below.

GENERAL JOURNAL   *Page*

Date (1)	Description (2)	P. R. (3)	Debit (4)	Credit (5)
19X2				
Oct. 7	Cash	11	*10,000*	
	John Hennessy, Capital	31		*10,000*
	(6) Invested cash in the business			

4.3 JOURNALIZING

We describe the entries in the general journal according to the numbering above.

(1) **Date.** The year, month, and day of the entry are written in the date column. The year and month do not have to be repeated for the additional entries until a new month occurs or a new page is needed.

(2) **Description.** The account title to be debited is entered on the first line, next to the date column. The name of the account to be credited is entered on the line below and indented.

(3) **P.R. (Posting Reference).** Nothing is entered in this column until the particular entry is posted; that is, until the amounts are transferred to the related ledger accounts. The posting process will be described in Sec. 4.4.

(4) **Debit.** The debit amount for each account is entered in this column. Generally there is only one item, but there could be two or more separate items.

(5) **Credit.** The credit amount for each account is entered in this column. Here again, there is generally only one account, but there could be two or more accounts involved with different amounts.

(6) **Explanation.** A brief description of the transaction is usually made on the line below the credit. Generally a blank line is left between the explanation and the next entry.

EXAMPLE 1.

To help in understanding the operation of the general journal, let us journalize the transactions previously described for Mr. Bagon's business (see page 37).

	P. R.	Debit	Credit
Transaction (1). **Invested in business**			
19X2			
Jan. 4 *Cash*		*5,000*	
A. Bagon, Capital			*5,000*
Investment in law practice			
Transaction (2). **Bought supplies**			
4 *Supplies*		*300*	
Cash			*300*
Bought supplies for cash			
Transaction (3). **Bought equipment on account**			
4 *Equipment*		*2,500*	
Accounts Payable			*2,500*
Bought equipment from Altway			
Transaction (4). **Fees earned**			
15 *Cash*		*2,000*	
Fees Income			*2,000*
Received payment for services			
Transaction (5). **Rent paid**			
30 *Rent Expense*		*500*	
Cash			*500*
Paid rent for month			
Transaction (6). **Paid salaries**			
30 *Salaries Expense*		*200*	
Cash			*200*
Paid salaries of part-time help			
Transaction (7). **Payment on account**			
31 *Accounts Payable*		*1,000*	
Cash			*1,000*
Payment on account to Altway			
Transaction (8). **Count of supplies**			
31 *Supplies Expense*		*200*	
Supplies			*200*
Supplies used during the month			
Transaction (9). **Withdrawal for personal use**			
31 *A. Bagon, Drawing*		*300*	
Cash			*300*
Personal withdrawal			

4.4 POSTING

The process of transferring information from the journal to the ledger for the purpose of summarizing is called *posting*. Primarily a clerical task, posting is ordinarily carried out in the following steps:

(1) ***Record the amount and date.*** The date and the amounts of the debits and credits are entered in the appropriate accounts.

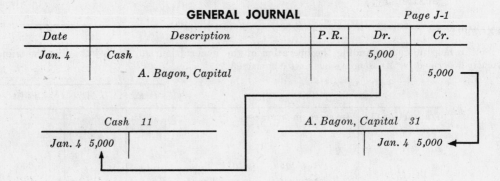

(2) ***Record the posting reference in the account.*** The number of the journal page is entered in the account (broken arrows below).

(3) ***Record the posting in the journal.*** For cross-referencing, the code number of the account is now entered in the P.R. column of the journal (solid arrows).

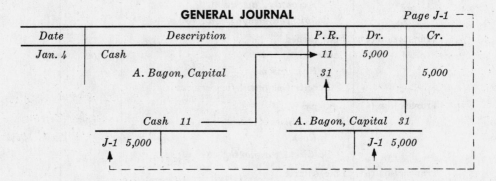

EXAMPLE 2.

The results of the posting from the journal of A. Bagon (see page 57) appear below.

ASSETS	=	LIABILITIES	+	CAPITAL

Cash 11		**Accounts Payable 21**		**A. Bagon, Capital 31**	
(1) 5,000	300 (2)	(7) 1,000	2,500 (3)		5,000 (1)
(4) 2,000	500 (5)				
	200 (6)			**A. Bagon, Drawing 32**	
	1,000 (7)			(9) 300	
	300 (9)				

| ASSETS | = | LIABILITIES | + | CAPITAL |

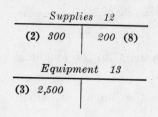

ASSETS

Supplies 12
| (2) 300 | 200 (8) |

Equipment 13
| (3) 2,500 | |

CAPITAL

Fees Income 41
| | 2,000 (4) |

Rent Expense 51
| (5) 500 | |

Salaries Expense 52
| (6) 200 | |

Supplies Expense 53
| (8) 200 | |

A. Bagon, Lawyer
Trial Balance
January 31, 19X2

	Debit	Credit
Cash	$4,700	
Supplies	100	
Equipment	2,500	
Accounts Payable		$1,500
A. Bagon, Capital		5,000
A. Bagon, Drawing	300	
Fees Income		2,000
Rent Expense	500	
Salaries Expense	200	
Supplies Expense	200	
	$8,500	$8,500

A. Bagon, Lawyer
Income Statement
Month Ended January 31, 19X2

Fees Income		$2,000
Expenses		
Rent Expense	$500	
Salaries Expense	200	
Supplies Expense	200	
Total Expenses		900
Net Income		$1,100

A. Bagon, Lawyer
Capital Statement
Month Ended January 31, 19X2

Capital, January 1		$5,000
Add: Net Income	$1,100	
Less: Drawing	300	
Increase in Capital		800
Capital, January 31		$5,800

A. Bagon, Lawyer
Balance Sheet
January 31, 19X2

ASSETS

Current Assets		
Cash	$4,700	
Supplies	100	
Total Current Assets		$4,800
Fixed Assets		
Equipment		2,500
Total Assets		$7,300

LIABILITIES AND CAPITAL

Accounts Payable	$1,500

CAPITAL

Capital, January 31	5,800
Total Liabilities and Capital	$7,300

Summary

(1) The initial book for recording all transactions is known as the _____.

(2) Another name and description of the journal is _____.

(3) The process of transferring information from the journal to the ledger is known as _____.

(4) The list of code numbers that identify the entries in the journal is called the _____.

(5) Asset account numbers begin with the number _____, while liabilities begin with ____.

(6) All capital account numbers begin with the number _____.

(7) All income account numbers begin with _____, while expense account numbers begin with _____.

(8) The process of recording transactions in the journal is termed _____.

(9) The complete process of accounting is called the _____.

Answers:

(1) journal	(4) chart of accounts	(7) 4, 5
(2) book of original entry	(5) 1, 2	(8) journalizing
(3) posting	(6) 3	(9) accounting cycle

Solved Problems

4.1. What is a compound journal entry?

SOLUTION

An entry having more than one debit or more than one credit is called a compound entry. For example, land was bought (debit for $10,000, with a down payment of cash (credit) of $4,000 and a mortgage (credit) of $6,000.

4.2. How does the incorrect posting of a debit as a credit affect the trial balance?

SOLUTION

The trial balance will be out of balance by twice the amount incorrectly posted. For example, if a $200 debit to cash is posted as a credit, there will be $400 in credits and 0 in debits, making a net difference of $400.

4.3. In the shaded space below each entry, write a brief explanation of the transaction that might appear in the general journal.

(a)	Equipment	8,000	
	Cash		2,000
	Accounts Payable, William Smith		6,000
(b)	Accounts Payable, William Smith	2,000	
	Cash		2,000
(c)	Accounts Payable, William Smith	4,000	
	Notes Payable		4,000

SOLUTION

(a)	Equipment	8,000	
	Cash		2,000
	Accounts Payable, William Smith		6,000
	Purchase of equipment, 25% for cash, balance on account		
(b)	Accounts Payable, William Smith	2,000	
	Cash		2,000
	Partial payment of the accounts payable		
(c)	Accounts Payable, William Smith	4,000	
	Notes Payable		4,000
	Notes payable in settlement of account payable		

4.4. Dr. Jane Voity, Dentist, began her practice, investing in the business the following assets:

Cash	$ 2,600
Supplies	1,400
Equipment	12,500
Furniture	3,000

Record the opening entry in the journal.

	Debit	Credit

SOLUTION

	Debit	Credit
Cash	2,600	
Supplies	1,400	
Equipment	12,500	
Furniture	3,000	
Jane Voity, Capital		19,500

4.5. If in Problem 4.4 Dr. Voity owed a balance on the equipment of $3,500, what would the opening entry then be?

	Debit	Credit

SOLUTION

	Debit	Credit
Cash	2,600	
Supplies	1,400	
Equipment	12,500	
Furniture	3,000	
Accounts Payable		3,500
Jane Voity, Capital		16,000

4.6. Record the following entries in the general journal for the Acom Cleaning Company.

    (a) Invested $12,000 cash in the business.
    (b) Paid $1,000 for office furniture.
    (c) Bought equipment costing $8,000, on account.
    (d) Received $2,200 in cleaning income.
    (e) Paid 1/5 of the amount owed on the equipment.

		Debit	Credit
(a)			
(b)			
(c)			
(d)			
(e)			

SOLUTION

		Debit	Credit
(a)	Cash	12,000	
	Acom, Capital		12,000
(b)	Office Furniture	1,000	
	Cash		1,000
(c)	Equipment	8,000	
	Accounts Payable		8,000
(d)	Cash	2,200	
	Cleaning Income		2,200
(e)	Accounts Payable	1,600	
	Cash		1,600

4.7. Record the following entries in the general journal for the Tusten Medical Group.

    (*a*) Invested $18,000 in cash, $4,800 in supplies, and $12,200 in equipment to begin the Tusten Medical Group.

    (*b*) Received $2,400 from cash patients for the week.

    (*c*) Invested additional cash of $5,000 in the firm.

		Debit	*Credit*
(*a*)			
(*b*)			
(*c*)			

SOLUTION

		Debit	*Credit*
(*a*)	Cash	18,000	
	Supplies	4,800	
	Equipment	12,200	
	Tusten, Capital		35,000
(*b*)	Cash	2,400	
	Fees Income		2,400
(*c*)	Cash	5,000	
	Tusten, Capital		5,000

4.8. If, in Problem 4.7, the Tusten Medical Group billed patients for the month for $1,600, present the necessary journal entry.

SOLUTION

Accounts Receivable	1,600	
Fees Income		1,600
To record services rendered on account		

4.9. If the Medical Group (see Problems 4.7 and 4.8) received $545 from patients who were billed last month, what entry would be necessary to record this information?

SOLUTION

Cash	545	
Accounts Receivable		545
Received cash on account		

4.10. Refer to Problems 4.8 and 4.9. When payment is received from billed patients (accounts receivable), why isn't the income account credited?

SOLUTION

      Fees Income had been recorded in the previous month, when the service had been rendered. On the accrual basis, income, as well as expense, is recorded in the period of service or use, not in the period of payment.

4.11. Post the following journal entries for the Canny Taxi Company to the "T" accounts below. Disregard folio numbers at this time.

		P. R.	Debit	Credit
(a)	Cash		6,000	
	Canny, Capital			6,000
(b)	Equipment		4,000	
	Accounts Payable			3,000
	Cash			1,000
(c)	Accounts Payable		3,000	
	Cash			3,000
(d)	Cash		1,500	
	Fares Income			1,500
(e)	Salaries Expense		600	
	Cash			600

```
      Cash   11              Equipment   12            Accounts Payable   21
_____         _____         _____
       |                          |                          |
       |                          |                          |


   Canny, Capital   31          Fares Income   41         Salaries Expense   42
_____         _____         _____
       |                          |                          |
       |                          |                          |
```

SOLUTION

```
      Cash   11                   Equipment   12            Accounts Payable   21
_____     _____     _____
 (a) 6,000 | (b) 1,000          (b) 4,000 |                   (c) 3,000 | (b) 3,000
 (d) 1,500 | (c) 3,000                    |
           | (e)   600          Fares Income   41            Salaries Expense   42
                             _____     _____
                                        | (d) 1,500          (e) 600 |

   Canny, Capital   31
_____
           | (a) 6,000
```

4.12. Use the balances of the "T" accounts in Problem 4.11 to prepare a trial balance.

Canny Taxi Company		
Trial Balance		
Cash		
Equipment		
Accounts Payable		
Capital		
Fares Income		
Salaries Expense		

SOLUTION

Canny Taxi Company		
Trial Balance		
Cash	$2,900	
Equipment	4,000	
Accounts Payable		
Capital		$6,000
Fares Income		1,500
Salaries Expense	600	
	$7,500	$7,500

4.13. Journalize the following transactions: (*a*) Larry Abrams opened a dry cleaning store on March 1, 19X2, investing $12,000 cash, $6,000 in equipment, and $4,000 worth of supplies; (*b*) bought $2,600 worth of equipment on account from J. Laym, Inc., Invoice 101; (*c*) received $2,800 from cash sales for the month; (*d*) paid rent, $200; (*e*) paid salaries, $600; (*f*) paid $1,600 on account to J. Laym, Inc.; (*g*) withdrew $500 for personal use; (*h*) used $1,000 worth of supplies during the month.

GENERAL JOURNAL   *J-1*

	Debit	Credit
(*a*)		
(*b*)		
(*c*)		
(*d*)		
(*e*)		
(*f*)		
(*g*)		
(*h*)		

SOLUTION   **GENERAL JOURNAL**   *J-1*

		Debit	Credit
(a)	Cash	12,000	
	Supplies	4,000	
	Equipment	6,000	
	L. Abrams, Capital		22,000
	Investment in business		
(b)	Equipment	2,600	
	Accounts Payable		2,600
	J. Laym, Inc. Invoice 101		
(c)	Cash	2,800	
	Cleaning Income		2,800
	Sales for month		
(d)	Rent Expense	200	
	Cash		200
	Rent for month		
(e)	Salaries Expense	600	
	Cash		600
	Salaries for month		
(f)	Accounts Payable	1,600	
	Cash		1,600
	Paid J. Laym, Inc. on account		
(g)	L. Abrams, Drawing	500	
	Cash		500
	Personal withdrawal		
(h)	Supplies Expense	1,000	
	Supplies		1,000
	Supplies used during month		

4.14. Post from the journal in Problem 4.13 to the following accounts:

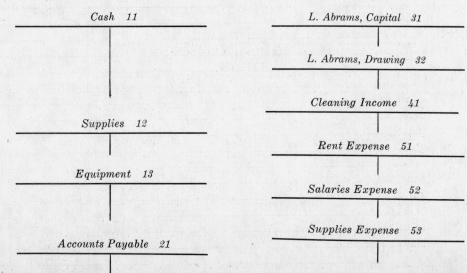

SOLUTION

Cash 11			
(a) J-1 12,000		(d) J-1	200
(c) J-1 2,800		(e) J-1	600
		(f) J-1	1,600
		(g) J-1	500

L. Abrams, Capital 31	
	(a) J-1 22,000

L. Abrams, Drawing 32	
(g) J-1 500	

Supplies 12		
(a) J-1 4,000	(h) J-1	1,000

Cleaning Income 41	
	(c) J-1 2,800

Equipment 13	
(a) J-1 6,000	
(b) J-1 2,600	

Rent Expense 51	
(d) J-1 200	

Accounts Payable 21	
(f) J-1 1,600	(b) J-1 2,600

Salaries Expense 52	
(e) J-1 600	

Supplies Expense 53	
(h) J-1 1,000	

4.15. From the information obtained in Problem 4.14, prepare a trial balance for Abrams Dry Cleaning Company.

Abrams Dry Cleaning Company		
Trial Balance		
Cash		
Supplies		
Equipment		
Accounts Payable		
L. Abrams, Capital		
L. Abrams, Drawing		
Cleaning Income		
Rent Expense		
Salaries Expense		
Supplies Expense		

SOLUTION

Abrams Dry Cleaning Company		
Trial Balance		
Cash	$11,900	
Supplies	3,000	
Equipment	8,600	
Accounts Payable		$ 1,000
L. Abrams, Capital		22,000
L. Abrams, Drawing	500	
Cleaning Income		2,800
Rent Expense	200	
Salaries Expense	600	
Supplies Expense	1,000	
	$25,800	$25,800

4.16. The trial balance for Vanguard Playhouse on October 31, 19X2, was as follows.

Vanguard Playhouse
Trial Balance
October 31, 19X2

Cash	$ 2,400	
Accounts Receivable	1,500	
Supplies	350	
Equipment	11,200	
Building	10,000	
Accounts Payable		$ 9,450
Notes Payable		12,000
Vanguard Playhouse, Capital		4,000
	$25,450	$25,450

Selected transactions for November were as follows:

(a) Nov. 2: Paid $1,000 due on the notes payable

(b) Nov. 8: Paid $3,000 on account

(c) Nov. 15: Receipts for the two-week period totaled $8,400

(d) Nov. 22: Bought an additional projector at a cost of $15,500 with a cash down payment of $5,000, the balance to be paid within one year

(e) Nov. 30: Paid salaries of $1,600

Using this data, transfer the October 31 balances to the ledger accounts below, prepare journal entries for the month of November, and post to the ledger accounts.

		JOURNAL			Page J-6
Date	Description		P.R.	Debit	Credit

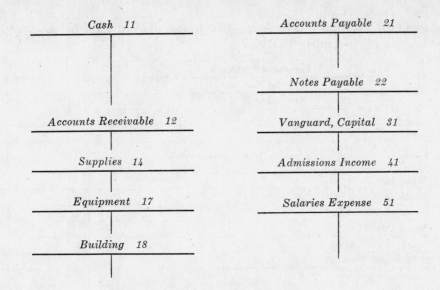

SOLUTION

JOURNAL   *J-6*

	Date	Description	P. R.	Debit	Credit
	19X2				
(a)	Nov. 2	Notes Payable	22	1,000	
		Cash	11		1,000
		Payment of installment note			
(b)	Nov. 8	Accounts Payable	21	3,000	
		Cash	11		3,000
		Payment on outstanding accounts			
(c)	Nov. 15	Cash	11	8,400	
		Admissions Income	41		8,400
		Receipts for the two-week period to date			
(d)	Nov. 22	Equipment	17	15,500	
		Cash	11		5,000
		Accounts Payable	21		10,500
		Purchase of a projector with cash payment,			
		balance due in one year			
(e)	Nov. 30	Salaries Expense	51	1,600	
		Cash	11		1,600
		Salaries paid to employees			

Cash 11

Bal. 2,400	(a) J-6 1,000		
(c) J-6 8,400	(b) J-6 3,000		
	(d) J-6 5,000		
	(e) J-6 1,600		

Accounts Receivable 12

Bal. 1,500

Supplies 14

Bal. 350

Equipment 17

Bal. 11,200	
(d) J-6 15,500	

Building 18

Bal. 10,000

Accounts Payable 21

(b) J-6 3,000	Bal. 9,450
	(d) J-6 10,500

Notes Payable 22

(a) J-6 1,000	Bal. 12,000

Vanguard, Capital 31

	Bal. 4,000

Admissions Income 41

	(c) J-6 8,400

Salaries Expense 51

(e) J-6 1,600

4.17. For Vanguard Playhouse (Problem 4.16), prepare (*a*) a trial balance and (*b*) a balance sheet as of November 30, 19X2.

(a)

Vanguard Playhouse		
Trial Balance		
November 30, 19X2		
Cash		
Accounts Receivable		
Supplies		
Equipment		
Building		
Accounts Payable		
Notes Payable		
Vanguard, Capital		
Admissions Income		
Salaries Expense		

(b)

Vanguard Playhouse		
Balance Sheet		
November 30, 19X2		
ASSETS		
Current Assets		
Total Current Assets		
Fixed Assets		
Total Fixed Assets		
Total Assets		
LIABILITIES AND CAPITAL		
Current Liabilities		
Total Current Liabilities		
*Vanguard, Capital, November 30, 19X2		
Total Liabilities and Capital		
*(Additional space to compute Capital)		

SOLUTION

(a)

Vanguard Playhouse		
Trial Balance		
November 30, 197–		
Cash	$ 200	
Accounts Receivable	1,500	
Supplies	350	
Equipment	26,700	
Building	10,000	
Accounts Payable		$16,950
Notes Payable		11,000
Vanguard, Capital		4,000
Admissions Income		8,400
Salaries Expense	1,600	
	$40,350	$40,350

(b)

Vanguard Playhouse		
Balance Sheet		
November 30, 19X2		
ASSETS		
Current Assets		
Cash	$ 200	
Accounts Receivable	1,500	
Supplies	350	
Total Current Assets		$ 2,050
Fixed Assets		
Equipment	26,700	
Building	10,000	
Total Fixed Assets		36,700
Total Assets		$38,750
LIABILITIES AND CAPITAL		
Current Liabilities		
Accounts Payable	$16,950	
Notes Payable	11,000	
Total Current Liabilities		$27,950
*Vanguard, Capital, November 30, 19X2		10,800
Total Liabilities and Capital		$38,750
* To obtain the capital balance as of November 30, first determine		
the net income for the period (income statement)		
Admissions Income	$ 8,400	
Less: Salaries Expense	1,600	
Net Income	$ 6,800	
Since there is no drawing involved, add the net income to the		
beginning capital:		
Capital, November 1	$ 4,000	
Add: Net Income	6,800	
Capital, November 30	$10,800	

Chapter 5

Repetitive Transactions

5.1 INTRODUCTION

In earlier sections, the accounting principles discussed were illustrated in terms of small businesses having relatively few transactions. Each transaction was recorded by means of an entry in the general journal, then posted to the related account in the general ledger.

Such a simple system becomes altogether too slow and cumbersome when transactions of various categories occur by the hundreds or thousands monthly. In that case, it is more practical to group the repetitive transactions according to type (sales, purchases, cash, etc.) and to provide a separate *special journal* for each type. Entries not of a repetitive nature, such as corrections, adjusting entries, and closing entries, will still be entered in the general journal.

5.2 ADVANTAGES OF SPECIAL JOURNALS

The advantages of using special journals where there are numerous repetitive transactions may be summarized as follows:

(1) *Reduces detailed recording.* In the special journal, each transaction is entered on a single line which is designed to provide all necessary information. For example, a sales transaction is recorded on a single line indicating a debit to the customer's account and giving the customer's name, the date, the amount, and any other desired data (such as the invoice number). Under the special-journal concept, individual posting is eliminated. Only one posting for the total amount is made to the appropriate ledger account at the end of the month. Thus, if a firm had 1,000 sales on account during the month, the sales account would be credited once, not 1,000 times.

(2) *Permits better division of labor.* Each special journal can be handled by a different person, who will become more familiar with the special work and therefore more efficient. Just as important: journalizing can now be done by a number of people working simultaneously, rather than consecutively.

(3) *Permits better internal control.* Having separate journals allows the work to be arranged in such a way that no one person has conflicting responsibilities; for example, the receipt and the recording of cash. Thus, no employee can steal received cash and then make a journal entry to conceal the theft.

5.3 SPECIAL LEDGERS (SUBSIDIARY LEDGERS)

Further simplification of the general ledger is brought about by the use of subsidiary ledgers. In particular, for those businesses which sell goods on credit and find it necessary to maintain a separate account with each customer and with each creditor, a special *accounts receivable ledger* and an *accounts payable ledger* eliminate multiple entries in the general ledger.

The advantages of special or subsidiary ledgers are similar to those of special journals. These are:

(1) **Reduces ledger detail.** Most of the information will be in the subsidiary ledger, and the general ledger will be reserved chiefly for summary or total figures. Therefore, it will be easier to prepare the financial statements.

(2) **Permits better division of labor.** Here again, each special or subsidiary ledger may be handled by a different person. Therefore, one person may work on the general ledger accounts while another person may simultaneously work on the subsidiary ledger.

(3) **Permits a different sequence of accounts.** In the general ledger, it is desirable to have the accounts in the same sequence as in the balance sheet and income statement. As a further aid, it is desirable to use numbers to locate and reference the accounts, as explained in Sec. 3.5. However, in connection with accounts receivable or accounts payable, which involve names of customers or companies, it is preferable to have the accounts in *alphabetical* sequence.

(4) **Permits better internal control.** Better control is maintained if a person other than the person responsible for the general ledger is responsible for the subsidiary ledger. For example, the accounts receivable or customers' ledger trial balance should agree with the balance of the accounts receivable account in the general ledger. The general ledger account acts as a *controlling account*, and the subsidiary ledger must agree with the control. No unauthorized entry could be made in the subsidiary ledger, as it would immediately put that record out of balance with the control account.

The idea of control accounts introduced above is an important one in accounting. Any group of similar accounts may be removed from the general ledger and a controlling account substituted for it. Not only is another level of error-protection thereby provided, but the time needed to prepare the general ledger trial balance and the financial statements becomes further reduced.

5.4   USE OF SPECIAL JOURNALS

The principal special journals are the sales journal, purchases journal, cash receipts journal, and cash disbursements journal.

We shall describe each and illustrate the relationship between the special journal and the general ledger, on the one hand, and, on the other hand, the relationship between the special journal and the subsidiary ledger. Also, it is desirable to point out in each case the relationship of the controlling account to the subsidiary ledger.

SALES JOURNAL

The entry for the individual sale on account is a debit to Accounts Receivable (and to the customer's account) and a credit to Sales. Only sales on account are recorded in the sales journal. Cash sales ordinarily do not require the customer's name and are recorded in the cash receipts journal, usually in daily total.

Referring to Example 1 below, we have the following procedure for recording and posting the sales journal:

1. Record the sale on account in the sales journal.
2. Post from the sales journal to the individual accounts in the subsidiary ledger.
3. Record the posting of the individual accounts in the post reference (P.R.) column. A check mark indicates that the posting has been made.
4. At the end of the month, total the amount of sales made on account. This total is posted in the general ledger to the accounts receivable account (12) as a debit and to the sales account (41) as a credit. In the general ledger the source of the entry (S-1) is entered in each account.

EXAMPLE 1.

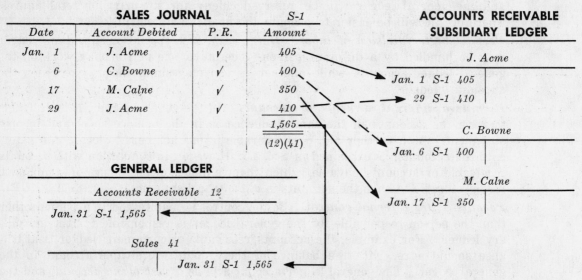

The balances in the accounts receivable ledger may be summarized by listing each customer and the amount he owes. The accounts receivable trial balance known as a "Schedule of Accounts Receivable" should agree with the controlling account.

EXAMPLE 2.

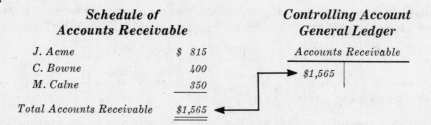

Schedule of Accounts Receivable		Controlling Account General Ledger
		Accounts Receivable
J. Acme	$ 815	$1,565
C. Bowne	400	
M. Calne	350	
Total Accounts Receivable	$1,565	

PURCHASES JOURNAL

In most businesses, purchases are made regularly and are evidenced by purchase invoices issued to creditors. In previous chapters the entry to record the purchase of goods on account had the following form:

Purchases   (Debit)
    Accounts Payable   (Credit)

Where there are many transactions for purchases of merchandise for resale, for supplies to be used in the business, for equipment, etc., the labor-saving features of a special purchases journal may be utilized. The basic principles that apply to the sales journal also apply to the purchases journal. However, because of the variety of items that are purchased, more columns are needed in the purchases journal.

For the sales journal (see Example 2) the Schedule of Accounts Receivable total equaled the controlling account in the general ledger. In the purchases journal the individual transactions with creditors (accounts payable) are posted to the creditor's account in the subsidiary ledger, while the total is posted to the controlling account, Accounts Payable.

EXAMPLE 3.

January 2:   Purchased merchandise on account from Altman Company, $2,000
January 8:   Purchased supplies on account from Bay Company, $600
January 15:   Purchased equipment on account from Calloway Company, $5,000

January 15:   Purchased land from J. Smith on account, $1,000

January 21:   Purchased additional supplies on account from Bay Company, $200

January 28:   Purchased additional merchandise on account from Altman Company, $1,000

PURCHASES JOURNAL   P-1 (1)

Date	Account Credited	P. R.	Acct. Pay. Cr.	Purch. Dr.	Supp. Dr.	Sundry		
						Accounts Debited	P. R.	Amt.
Jan. 2	(2) Altman Company	√	2,000	2,000				
8	Bay Company	√	600		600			
15	Calloway Company	√	5,000			Equipment	18	5,000
15	J. Smith	√	1,000			Land	17	1,000
21	Bay Company	√	,200		200	(4)		
28	Altman Company	√	1,000	1,000				
		(3)	9,800	3,000	800			6,000
			(21)	(51)	(14)			(√)

NOTES: (1) P-1 denotes the page number (1) of the purchases journal.

(2) The individual amounts will be posted as credits to their respective accounts in the accounts payable subsidiary ledger. The check marks in the purchases journal indicate such postings.

(3) Accounts Payable, Purchases, and Supplies are posted to the respective accounts in the general ledger as totals only.

(4) The sundry amount of $6,000 is not posted as a total; instead, the individual amounts are posted, as many different accounts may be affected each month.

GENERAL LEDGER

Supplies 14		Accounts Payable 21	
Jan. 31 P-1 800			Jan. 31 P-1 9,800

Land 17	
Jan. 15 P-1 1,000	

Equipment 18		Purchases 51	
Jan. 15 P-1 5,000		Jan. 31 P-1 3,000	

ACCOUNTS PAYABLE SUBSIDIARY LEDGER

Altman Company		Bay Company	
	Jan. 2 P-1 2,000		Jan. 8 P-1 600
	28 P-1 1,000		21 P-1 200

Calloway Company		J. Smith	
	Jan. 15 P-1 5,000		Jan. 15 P-1 1,000

To prove that the accounts payable ledger is in balance, the total owed to the four companies must agree with the balance in the accounts payable control account.

Schedule of Accounts Payable

Altman Company	$3,000		Accounts Payable
Bay Company	800		P-1 $9,800 ◀
Calloway Company	5,000		
J. Smith	1,000		
Total	$9,800 ◀		

CASH RECEIPTS JOURNAL

Transactions involving cash are recorded in either the cash receipts or the cash disbursements journal. Items that increase cash position are recorded in the cash receipts journal. Increases in cash may come from such sources as collections from customers, receipts from cash sales, investments, and collection of interest and principal on notes held by the firm (notes receivable).

The procedure for recording and posting the cash receipts journal is described below and illustrated in Example 4.

1. The total of the cash column is posted as a debit to the cash account.
2. Each amount is posted to the individual customer's account. The total is posted as a credit to the accounts receivable account in the general ledger.
3. The total of the sales credit column is posted as a credit to the sales account.
4. Each item in the sundry account is posted individually to the general ledger. The total of the sundry account is not posted.
5. The accuracy of the journal (that is, the equality of debits and credits) is verified by adding the three credit columns and comparing the total with the debit column.

EXAMPLE 4.

The month of February saw the following cash-increasing transactions.

February 2:   Received $600 from J. Acme in partial settlement of his bill
February 5:   Returned defective merchandise bought for cash and received $80 in settlement
February 14:   Cash sales for the first half of the month, $3,800
February 24:   Received a check from C. Bowne in full settlement of his account, $400
February 28:   Cash sales for the second half of the month, $3,720

As shown in Example 2, there are balances in Mr. Acme's and Mr. Bowne's accounts of $815 and $400, respectively.

CASH RECEIPTS JOURNAL   *CR-1*

Date	Account Credited	P.R.	Cash Dr.	Acct. Rec. Cr.	Sales Cr.	Sundry Cr.
February 2	J. Acme	✓	600	600		
5	Purchase Returns	52	80			80
14	Sales	✓	3,800		3,800	
24	C. Bowne	✓	400	400		
28	Sales	✓	3,720		3,720	
			8,600	1,000	7,520	80
			(11)	(12)	(41)	(✓)

GENERAL LEDGER

Cash 11

February 28   CR-1   8,600

Sales 41

February 28   CR-1   7,520

Accounts Receivable 12

Bal. 1,215 | February 28   CR-1   1,000

Purchase Returns 52

February 5   CR-1   80

ACCOUNTS RECEIVABLE SUBSIDIARY LEDGER

J. Acme

Bal. 815 | February 2   CR-1   600

C. Bowne

Bal. 400 | February 24   CR-1   400

CASH DISBURSEMENTS JOURNAL

The cash disbursements journal is used to record all transactions that *reduce* cash. These transactions may arise from payments to creditors, cash purchases (of supplies, equipment, or merchandise), the payment of expenses, (salary, rent, insurance, etc.), as well as from personal withdrawals.

The procedure for recording and posting the cash disbursements journal parallels that for the cash receipts journal:

1. A check is written each time a payment is made; the check numbers provide a convenient reference, and they help in controlling cash and in reconciling the bank account.

2. The cash credit column is posted in total to the general ledger at the end of the month.

3. Debits to Accounts Payable represent cash paid to creditors. These individual amounts will be posted to the creditors' accounts in the accounts payable subsidiary ledger. At the end of the month the total of the accounts payable column is posted to the general ledger.

4. The sundry column is used to record debits for any account that cannot be entered in the other special columns. These would include cash purchases of equipment and inventory, payment of expenses, and cash withdrawals. Each item is posted separately to the general ledger. The total of the sundry column is not posted.

EXAMPLE 5.

CASH DISBURSEMENTS JOURNAL   CD-1

Date	Check No.	Account Debited	P.R.	Cash Cr.	Acct. Pay. Dr.	Sundry Dr.
Feb. 2	1	Bay Company	√	600	600	
8	2	Rent Expense	52	220		220
15	3	Salaries Expense	53	1,900		1,900
21	4	Purchases	51	1,600		1,600
24	5	Salaries Expense	53	1,900		1,900
				6,220	600	5,620
				(11)	(21)	(√)

GENERAL LEDGER

Cash 11	
Bal. 8,600*	Feb. 28 CD-1 6,220

Accounts Payable 21	
Feb. 28 CD-1 600	Bal. 9,800**

Purchases 51	
Feb. 21 CD-1 1,600	

Rent Expense 52	
Feb. 8 CD-1 220	

Salaries Expense 53	
Feb. 15 CD-1 1,900	
24 CD-1 1,900	

ACCOUNTS PAYABLE SUBSIDIARY LEDGER

Bay Company	
Feb. 2 CD-1 600	Bal. 800**

* From the cash receipts journal, Example 4.
** From the purchases journal, Example 3.

5.5 DISCOUNTS

To induce a buyer to make payment before the amount is due, the seller may allow the buyer to deduct a certain percent of the bill. If payment is due within a stated number of days after the date of invoice, the number of days will usually be preceded by the letter "n", signifying net. For example, bills due in 30 days would be indicated by n/30.

A two-percent discount offered if payment is made within ten days would be indicated by 2/10. If the buyer has a choice of either paying the amount less 2% within the ten-day period or paying the entire bill within 30 days, the terms would be written as 2/10, n/30.

EXAMPLE 6.

A sales invoice totaling $800 and dated January 2 has discount terms of 2/10, n/30. If the purchaser pays on or before January 12 (10 days after the date of purchase), he may deduct $16 ($800 × 2%) from the bill and pay only $784. If he chooses not to pay within the discount period, he is obligated to pay the entire amount of $800 by February 1.

From the point of view of the seller, the discount is a sales discount; the purchaser would consider it a purchase discount. If a business experiences a great number of sales and purchase discounts, then special columns would be added in the cash receipts and cash disbursements journals respectively.

Sales Discount appears as a reduction of Sales in the income statement. Purchase Discount appears as a reduction of Purchases in the Cost of Goods Sold section of the income statement.

5.6 RETURN OF MERCHANDISE

Many factors in business will cause a return of merchandise: damaged goods, incorrect size or style, or a price not agreed upon. Returns associated with purchases are recorded as purchase returns and allowances, and those associated with sales are recorded as sales returns and allowances.

PURCHASE RETURNS AND ALLOWANCES

If a firm has many purchase returns, a purchase returns and allowances journal should be used. However, for illustrative purposes, entries for the return of purchases (bought on account) are here made in the general journal:

	P. R.	Debit	Credit
Accounts Payable, Smith and Company	√ 21	420	
Purchase Returns and Allowances	52		420

The debit portion of the accounts payable is posted to the accounts payable account in the general ledger (21), and also to the accounts payable subsidiary ledger (√). Because the controlling account and the customer's account are both debited, a diagonal line is needed in the post reference column to show both postings. For items involving a return for cash, the cash receipts journal is used.

ACCOUNTS PAYABLE LEDGER		GENERAL LEDGER		
Smith and Company		*Accounts Payable 21*		*Purchase Returns 52*
J-1 420	Bal. 800	J-1 420	Bal. 800	J-1 420

Purchase Returns and Allowances appears in the income statement as a reduction of Purchases.

SALES RETURNS AND ALLOWANCES

If many transactions occur during the year, in which customers return goods bought on account, a special journal known as the sales returns and allowances journal would be used. However, where sales returns are infrequent the general journal is sufficient.

The entry to record returns of sales on account in the general journal would be:

	P.R.	Debit	Credit
Sales Returns and Allowances	42	600	
Accounts Receivable, Murphey Company	√ 12		600

The accounts receivable account, which is credited, is posted both in the accounts receivable controlling account (12) and in the accounts receivable ledger (√).

ACCOUNTS RECEIVABLE LEDGER   **GENERAL LEDGER**

Murphey Company		Accounts Receivable 12		Sales Returns 42	
Bal. 900	J-1 600	Bal. 900	J-1 600	J-1 600	

If the sales returns involve the payment of cash, it would appear in the cash disbursements journal.

Sales Returns and Allowances appears in the income statement as a reduction of Sales Income.

5.7 TYPES OF LEDGER ACCOUNT FORMS

The "T" account has been used for most illustrations of accounts thus far. The disadvantage of the "T" account is that it requires totaling the debit and the credit columns in order to find the balance. As it is necessary to have the balance of a customer's or creditor's account available at any given moment, an alternate form of the ledger, the three-column account, may be used. The advantage of the form is that an extra column, "Balance," is provided, so that the amount the customer owes is always shown. As each transaction is recorded, the balance is updated. Below is an illustration of an accounts receivable ledger account using this form.

A. Lapinsky

Date	P.R.	Debit	Credit	Balance
Jan. 2	S-1	650		650
4	S-1	409		1,059
8	CD-1		500	559

Summary

(1) The journal used to record sales of merchandise on account is known as the _____ journal.

(2) The sale of merchandise for cash would appear in the _____ journal.

(3) It is common practice to divide the ledger in a large business into three separate ledgers, known as the _____ , _____ , and _____ ledgers.

(4) The total of the sales journal is posted at the end of the month as a debit to Accounts Receivable and a credit to _____ .

(5) The only column in the purchases journal that will not be posted in total at the end of the month is the _____ column.

(6) Sales Discount and Purchase Discount appear in the _____ statement as reductions of Sales and of Purchases, respectively.

(7) Terms of 2/10, n/30 on a $750 purchase of January 4, paid within the discount period, would provide a discount of $ ____ .

(8) Accounts Receivable and Accounts Payable in the general ledger may be classified as _____ .

Answers: (1) sales;   (2) cash receipts;   (3) general, accounts receivable, accounts payable;   (4) Sales;   (5) sundry;   (6) income;   (7) 15;   (8) controlling accounts

Solved Problems

5.1.   For each of the following transactions, indicate with a check mark the journal in which it should be recorded.

(a) Purchase of merchandise on account

(b) Purchase of merchandise for cash

(c) Receipt of cash from a customer in settlement of an account

(d) Cash sales for the month

(e) Payment of salaries

(f) Sales of merchandise for cash

(g) Sales of merchandise on account

(h) Cash refunded to customer

(i) Sale of a fixed asset for cash

(j) Notes payable sent to creditor in settlement of an account

	Cash Receipts Journal	Cash Disburs. Journal	Sales Journal	Purchases Journal	General Journal
(a)					
(b)					
(c)					
(d)					
(e)					
(f)					
(g)					
(h)					
(i)					
(j)					

SOLUTION

	Cash Receipts Journal	Cash Disburs. Journal	Sales Journal	Purchases Journal	General Journal
(a)				√	
(b)		√			
(c)	√				
(d)	√				
(e)		√			
(f)	√				
(g)			√		
(h)		√			
(i)	√				
(j)					√

5.2.   Record the following transactions in the sales journal.

January   1:   Sold merchandise on account to Fleischer Company, $550

January   4:   Sold merchandise on account to Gerard Company, $650

January 18:   Sold merchandise on account to Harke Company, $300

January 29:   Sold additional merchandise on account to Harke Company, $100

SALES JOURNAL   *S-1*

Date	Account Debited	P. R.	Amount

SOLUTION

SALES JOURNAL   *S-1*

Date	Account Debited	P. R.	Amount
Jan. 1	Fleischer Company	√	550
4	Gerard Company	√	650
18	Harke Company	√	300
29	Harke Company	√	100
			1,600

5.3.   Post the customers' accounts in Problem 5.2 to the accounts receivable subsidiary ledger and prepare a schedule of accounts receivable.

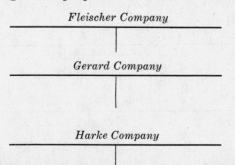

Fleischer Company

Gerard Company

Harke Company

SCHEDULE OF ACCOUNTS RECEIVABLE

Fleischer Company	
Gerard Company	
Harke Company	

SOLUTION

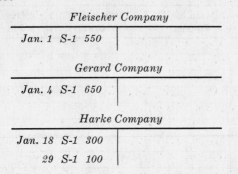

Fleischer Company

Jan. 1 S-1 550

Gerard Company

Jan. 4 S-1 650

Harke Company

Jan. 18 S-1 300
    29 S-1 100

SCHEDULE OF ACCOUNTS RECEIVABLE

Fleischer Company	550
Gerard Company	650
Harke Company	400
	1,600

5.4. For Problem 5.2, make the entries needed to record the sales for the month.

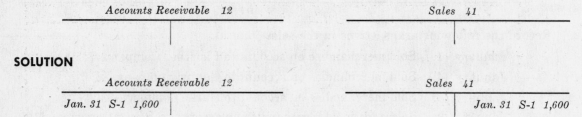

Accounts Receivable 12

Sales 41

SOLUTION

Accounts Receivable 12

Jan. 31 S-1 1,600

Sales 41

Jan. 31 S-1 1,600

5.5. Based on the following Sales Journal, post each transaction to its respective accounts receivable account.

SALES JOURNAL   S-4

Date	Account Debited	P.R.	Amount
Jan. 5	J. Kotin	√	350
7	R. Glatt	√	600
9	L. Harmin	√	450
15	J. Kotin	√	250
20	R. Glatt	√	500
26	R. Glatt	√	100
31			2,250

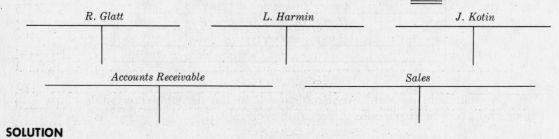

R. Glatt   *L. Harmin*   *J. Kotin*

Accounts Receivable   *Sales*

SOLUTION

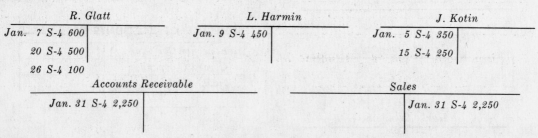

R. Glatt

Jan. 7 S-4 600
    20 S-4 500
    26 S-4 100

L. Harmin

Jan. 9 S-4 450

J. Kotin

Jan. 5 S-4 350
    15 S-4 250

Accounts Receivable

Jan. 31 S-4 2,250

Sales

Jan. 31 S-4 2,250

NOTE: $2,250 is the total of all transactions involving the sale of goods on account.

5.6. Vitman Company was established in December of the current year. Its sales of merchandise on account and related returns and allowances during the remainder of the month are described below.

Dec. 15　Sold merchandise on account to Acme Co., $850
　　　19　Sold merchandise on account to Balt Corp., $800
　　　20　Sold merchandise on account to Conway Inc., $1,200
　　　22　Issued Credit Memorandum for $40 to Balt Corp. for merchandise returned
　　　24　Sold merchandise on account to Davy Company, $1,650
　　　25　Sold additional merchandise on account to Balt Corp., $900
　　　26　Issued Credit Memorandum for $25 to Acme Co. for merchandise returned
　　　27　Sold additional merchandise on account to Conway, Inc., $1,600

Record the transactions for December in the sales journal and general journal below.

SALES JOURNAL S-6

Date	Account Debited	P.R.	Amount

GENERAL JOURNAL J-8

Date	Description	P.R.	Dr.	Cr.

SOLUTION

SALES JOURNAL S-6

Date	Account Debited	P.R.	Amount
Dec. 15	Acme Co.		$ 850
19	Balt Corp.		800
20	Conway, Inc.		1,200
24	Davy Company		1,650
25	Balt Corp.		900
27	Conway, Inc.		1,600
			$7,000

GENERAL JOURNAL J-8

Date	Description	P.R.	Dr.	Cr.
Dec. 22	Sales Returns		40	
	Accounts Receivable — Balt Corp.			40
26	Sales Returns		25	
	Accounts Receivable — Acme Co.			25

5.7. Based on the information in Problem 5.6, post to the customers' accounts.

Acme Co.

Conway, Inc.

Balt Corp.

Davy Company

SOLUTION

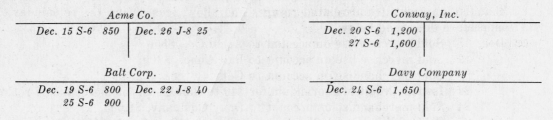

5.8. Post the General Journal and the Sales Journal to the three accounts below using the data supplied in Problem 5.6. What is the sum of the balances of the accounts in the subsidiary ledger (Problem 5.7)? What is the balance of the controlling account?

SOLUTION

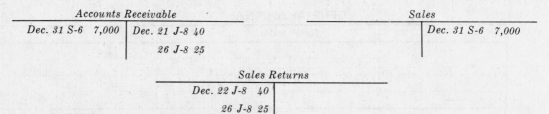

The balance in the subsidiary ledger $6,935 and the balance in the accounts receivable account (control) $6,935 is the same.

5.9. What are the net proceeds of goods sold on March 10 for $750, terms 2/10, n/30, if payment is made (a) on March 18? (b) on March 22?

SOLUTION

(a) $750 × 2% = $15   (b) $750 (the discount period ended March 20)
     $750 − $15 = $735

5.10. What entries are needed for parts (a) and (b) of Problem 5.9?

SOLUTION

(a)	Cash	735	
	Sales Discount	15	
	Accounts Receivable		750

(b)	Cash	750	
	Accounts Receivable		750

5.11. Assuming Problem 5.9 involved cash payments rather than cash receipts, what entries would be needed to record parts (*a*) and (*b*)?

SOLUTION

(a)			
	Accounts Payable	750	
	Purchase Discount		15
	Cash		735

(b)			
	Accounts Payable	750	
	Cash		750

5.12. Record the following transactions in general journal form.

May 1: Sold goods on account to Kay Munoz, $600, terms 2/10, n/30

6: Mrs. Munoz returned $100 of the merchandise because of damages

10: Received a check from Kay Munoz for the amount owed

SOLUTION

		Dr.	Cr.
May 1	Accounts Receivable, Kay Munoz	600	
	Sales		600
May 6	Sales Returns	100	
	Accounts Receivable, K. Munoz		100
May 10	Cash	490	
	Sales Discount	10*	
	Accounts Receivable, K. Munoz		500

* ($600 − $100 × 2%)

5.13. Record the following transactions in the purchases journal.

April. 2: Purchased merchandise on account from Kane Company, $450

April 5: Purchased supplies on account from Lane Supply House, $180

April 20: Purchased merchandise on account from Hanson Company, $400

April 24: Purchased additional supplies on account from Lane Supply House, $50

April 29: Purchased equipment on account from Olin Equipment, $1,600

PURCHASES JOURNAL   *P-1*

Date	Account Credited	P.R.	Acct. Pay. Cr.	Purch. Dr.	Supp. Dr.	Sundry		
						Acct. Dr.	P.R.	Amt.

SOLUTION

PURCHASES JOURNAL   *P-1*

Date	Account Credited	P.R.	Acct. Pay. Cr.	Purch. Dr.	Supp. Dr.	Sundry		
						Acct. Dr.	P.R.	Amt.
Apr. 2	Kane Company		450	450				
5	Lane Supply House		180		180			
20	Hanson Company		400	400				
24	Lane Supply House		50		50			
29	Olin Equipment		1,600			Equipment		1,600
			2,680	850	230			1,600

5.14. Post the information from Problem 5.13 into the accounts payable subsidiary ledger and prepare a schedule of accounts payable.

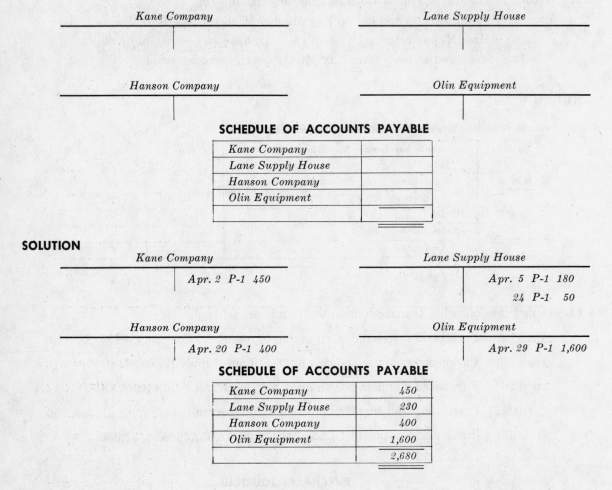

Kane Company   Lane Supply House

Hanson Company   Olin Equipment

SCHEDULE OF ACCOUNTS PAYABLE

Kane Company	
Lane Supply House	
Hanson Company	
Olin Equipment	

SOLUTION

Kane Company   Lane Supply House

Apr. 2 P-1 450   Apr. 5 P-1 180
                                                   24 P-1   50

Hanson Company   Olin Equipment

Apr. 20 P-1 400   Apr. 29 P-1 1,600

SCHEDULE OF ACCOUNTS PAYABLE

Kane Company	450
Lane Supply House	230
Hanson Company	400
Olin Equipment	1,600
	2,680

5.15. Post the purchases journal totals from Problem 5.13 to the accounts in the general ledger.

GENERAL LEDGER

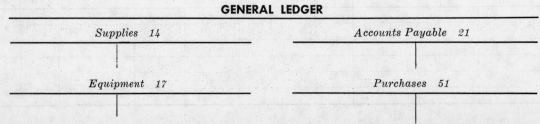

Supplies   14   Accounts Payable   21

Equipment   17   Purchases   51

SOLUTION

GENERAL LEDGER

Supplies 14		Accounts Payable 21	
Apr. 30 P-1 230			Apr. 30 P-1 2,680

Equipment 17		Purchases 51	
Apr. 29 P-1 1,600		Apr. 30 P-1 850	

5.16. Record the following transactions in the cash receipts journal.

January 2: Received $510 from L. Harmon in full settlement of his account

January 10: Received $615 from B. Elder in settlement of his account

January 14: Cash sales for the past two weeks, $3,400

January 20: Sold $200 of office supplies [not a merchandise item] to Smith Company as a service

January 24: The owner made an additional investment of $1,500

January 30: Cash sales for the last two weeks, $2,620

CASH RECEIPTS JOURNAL   CR-1

Date	Account Cr.	P. R.	Cash Dr.	Acct. Rec. Cr.	Sales Cr.	Sundry Cr.

SOLUTION

CASH RECEIPTS JOURNAL   CR-1

Date	Account Cr.	P. R.	Cash Dr.	Acct. Rec. Cr.	Sales Cr.	Sundry Cr.
Jan. 2	L. Harmon		510	510		
10	B. Elder		615	615		
14	Sales		3,400		3,400	
20	Office Supplies		200			200
24	Capital		1,500			1,500
30	Sales		2,620		2,620	
			8,845	1,125	6,020	1,700

5.17. Post the information from Problem 5.16 into the accounts receivable subsidiary ledger.

ACCOUNTS RECEIVABLE LEDGER

L. Harmon		B. Elder	
Bal. 510		Bal. 615	

SOLUTION

ACCOUNTS RECEIVABLE LEDGER

L. Harmon		B. Elder	
Bal. 510	Jan. 2 CR-1 510	Bal. 615	Jan. 10 CR-1 615

5.18. Post the cash receipts journal totals from Problem 5.16 to the accounts in the general ledger.

GENERAL LEDGER

Cash 11		Capital 31	
			Bal. 6,500

Accounts Receivable 12			
Bal. 3,000			

Office Supplies 15		Sales 41	
Bal. 3,500			

SOLUTION

GENERAL LEDGER

Cash 11		Capital 31	
Jan. 31 CR-1 8,845			Bal. 6,500
			Jan. 24 CR-1 1,500

Accounts Receivable 12		Sales 41	
Bal. 3,000	Jan. 31 CR-1 1,125		Jan. 31 CR-1 6,020

Office Supplies 15			
Bal. 3,500	Jan. 20 CR-1 200		

5.19. Record the following transactions in the cash disbursements journal.

March 1: Paid rent for the month, $320 (Check #16)

March 7: Paid J. Becker $615 for his February invoice (Check #17)

March 10: Bought store supplies for cash, $110 (Check #18)

March 15: Paid salaries for the two-week period, $685 (Check #19)

March 23: Paid B. Cone for February invoice, $600 (Check #20)

March 30: Paid salaries for the second half of the month, $714 (Check #21)

CASH DISBURSEMENTS JOURNAL   CD-1

Date	Check No.	Account Dr.	P. R.	Cash Cr.	Acct. Pay. Dr.	Sundry Dr.

SOLUTION

CASH DISBURSEMENTS JOURNAL

CD-1

Date	Check No.	Account Dr.	P.R.	Cash Cr.	Acct. Pay. Dr.	Sundry Dr.
Mar. 1	16	Rent Expense		320		320
7	17	J. Becker		615	615	
10	18	Store Supplies		110		110
15	19	Salaries Expense		685		685
23	20	B. Cone		600	600	
30	21	Salaries Expense		714		714
				3,044	1,215	1,829

5.20. Post the information from Problem 5.19 into the accounts payable subsidiary ledger.

ACCOUNTS PAYABLE LEDGER

J. Becker		B. Cone	
	Bal. 615		Bal. 600

SOLUTION

ACCOUNTS PAYABLE LEDGER

J. Becker		B. Cone	
Mar. 7 CD-1 615	Bal. 615	Mar. 23 CD-1 600	Bal. 600

5.21. Post the cash disbursements journal from Problem 5.19 to the accounts in the general ledger.

GENERAL LEDGER

Cash 11		Rent Expense 51	
Bal. 4,200			

Store Supplies 15		Salaries Expense 52	

Accounts Payable 21	
	Bal. 1,840

SOLUTION

GENERAL LEDGER

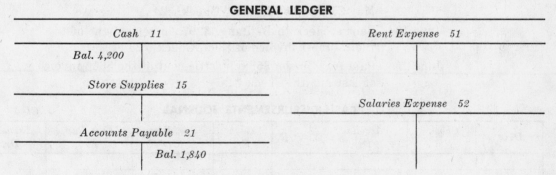

Cash 11		Rent Expense 51	
Bal. 4,200	Mar. 31 CD-1 3,044	Mar. 1 CD-1 320	

Store Supplies 15		Salaries Expense 52	
Mar. 10 CD-1 110		Mar. 15 CD-1 685	
		30 CD-1 714	

Accounts Payable 21	
Mar. 31 CD-1 1,215	Bal. 1,840

5.22. The cash receipts journal below utilizes a special column for sales discount. Record the following cash transactions in the journal.

> May 2: Received a check for $588 from A. Banks in settlement of his $600 April 25 bill
>
> May 12: Received $686 in settlement of the May 3 invoice of $700 from J. Johnson
>
> May 26: Received a check for $495 in settlement of B. Simpson's May 17 bill of $500

CASH RECEIPTS JOURNAL   CR-1

Date	Account Cr.	P.R.	Cash Dr.	Sales Disc. Dr.	Acct. Rec. Cr.	Sundry Cr.

SOLUTION

CASH RECEIPTS JOURNAL   CR-1

Date	Account Cr.	P.R.	Cash Dr.	Sales Disc. Dr.	Acct. Rec. Cr.	Sundry Cr.
May 2	A. Banks		588	12	600	
12	J. Johnson		686	14	700	
26	B. Simpson		495	5	500	
			1,769	31	1,800	

5.23. The cash disbursements journal below utilizes the special column Purchases Discount. Record the following cash transactions in the cash disbursements journal.

> June 2: Paid J. Thompson $490 in settlement of their May 25 invoice for $500, Check #24
>
> June 10: Sent a check to B. Rang, $297, in settlement of their June 1 invoice of $300, Check #25
>
> June 21: Paid A. Johnson $588 in settlement of the $600 invoice of last month, Check #26

CASH DISBURSEMENTS JOURNAL   CD-1

Date	Check No.	Account Dr.	P.R.	Cash Cr.	Pur. Disc. Cr.	Acct. Pay. Dr.	Sundry Dr.

SOLUTION

CASH DISBURSEMENTS JOURNAL   CD-1

Date	Check No.	Account Dr.	P.R.	Cash Cr.	Pur. Disc. Cr.	Acct. Pay. Dr.	Sundry Dr.
June 2	24	J. Thompson		490	10	500	
10	25	B. Rang		297	3	300	
21	26	A. Johnson		588	12	600	
				1,375	25	1,400	

5.24. All transactions affecting the cash account of Park Company for the month of January, 19X2, are presented below.

January 1:   Received cash from Alden Company for the balance due on
              their account, $1,600, less 2% discount
January 5:   Received payment from Walk Company on account, $1,550
January 8:   Paid rent for the month, $650, Check #165
January 10:   Purchased supplies for cash, $614, Check #166
January 14:   Cash sales for the first half of the month, $5,280
January 15:   Paid bi-weekly salaries, $1,600, Check #167
January 19:   Received $406 in settlement of a $400 note receivable plus interest
January 19:   Received payment from J. Cork of $500, less 1% discount
January 20:   Paid B. Simmons $686 in settlement of their $700 invoice, Check #168
January 24:   Paid $450 on account to L. Hann, Check #169
January 27:   Paid H. Hiram $800, less 2%, on account, Check #170
January 30:   Paid bi-weekly salaries, $1,680, Check #171

Record the above transactions in both the cash receipts and cash disbursements journals.

CASH RECEIPTS JOURNAL   CR-1

Date	Account Cr.	P. R.	Cash Dr.	Sales Disc. Dr.	Sales Cr.	Acct. Rec. Cr.	Sundry Cr.

CASH DISBURSEMENTS JOURNAL   CD-1

Date	Check No.	Account Dr.	P. R.	Cash Cr.	Pur. Disc. Cr.	Acct. Pay. Dr.	Sundry Dr.

SOLUTION

CASH RECEIPTS JOURNAL   CR-1

Date	Account Cr.	P. R.	Cash Dr.	Sales Disc. Dr.	Sales Cr.	Acct. Rec. Cr.	Sundry Cr.
Jan. 1	Alden Co.	√	1,568	32		1,600	
5	Walk Co.	√	1,550			1,550	
14	Sales	√	5,280		5,280		
19	Notes Rec.						400
19	Interest Inc.		406				6
19	J. Cork	√	495	5		500	
			9,299	37	5,280	3,650	406

CASH DISBURSEMENTS JOURNAL   CD-1

Date	Check No.	Account Dr.	P.R.	Cash Cr.	Pur. Disc. Cr.	Acct. Pay. Dr.	Sundry Dr.
Jan. 8	165	Rent Exp.		650			650
10	166	Supplies		614			614
15	167	Salaries Exp.		1,600			1,600
20	168	B. Simmons	√	686	14	700	
24	169	L. Hann	√	450		450	
27	170	H. Hiram	√	784	16	800	
30	171	Salaries Exp.		1,680			1,680
				6,464	30	1,950	4,544

5.25. The Johnston Company transactions involving purchases and sales for the month of January are presented below.   All purchases and sales are made on account.

January 3:   Sold merchandise to Acme Supply Company, $440

January 5:   Purchased merchandise from Balfour Corporation, $7,200

January 10:   Sold merchandise to Mennon Company, $345

January 10:   Sold merchandise to Blant Company, $2,400

January 14:   Purchased from Wyde Equipment $750 worth of equipment

January 17:   Purchased office supplies from Gold Supply, $850

January 21:   Purchased merchandise from Caldon Company, $6,240

January 28:   Returned damaged merchandise purchased from Balfour Corporation, receiving credit of $300

January 30:   Issued credit of $60 to Acme Supply Company for defective goods returned to us

Record the transactions in the sales, purchases, and general journals.

SALES JOURNAL   S-1

Date	Account Debited	P.R.	Amount
January			

PURCHASES JOURNAL   P-1

Date	Account Cr.	P.R.	Acct. Pay Cr.	Pur. Dr.	Supp. Dr.	Sundry		
						Acct. Dr.	P.R.	Amount

GENERAL JOURNAL   J-1

Date	Description	P.R.	Debit	Credit

SOLUTION

SALES JOURNAL　　　　　　S-1

Date	Account Debited	P.R.	Amount
Jan. 3	Acme Supply Company	√	440
10	Mennon Company	√	345
10	Blant Company	√	2,400
			3,185

PURCHASES JOURNAL　　　　　　P-1

Date	Account Cr.	P.R.	Acct. Pay. Cr.	Pur. Dr.	Supp. Dr.	Sundry Account Dr.	P.R.	Amount
Jan. 5	Balfour Corp.	√	7,200	7,200				
14	Wyde Equipment		750			Equipment		750
17	Gold Supply		850		850			
21	Caldon Company	√	6,240	6,240				
			15,040	13,440	850			750

GENERAL JOURNAL　　　　　　J-1

Date	Description	P.R.	Debit	Credit
Jan. 28	Accounts Payable, Balfour Corporation		300	
	Purchase Returns			300
Jan. 30	Sales Returns		60	
	Accounts Receivable, Acme Supply Company			60

5.26. William Drew began business on March 1. The transactions completed by the Drew Company for the month of March are listed below. Record these transactions, using the various journals provided.

March 1: Deposited $14,000 in a bank account for the operation of Drew Company

March 2: Paid rent for the month, $600, Check #1

March 4: Purchased equipment on account from Andon Equipment, $10,000

March 7: Purchased merchandise on account from Baily Company, $1,200

March 7: Cash sales for the week, $1,650

March 10: Issued Check #2 for $150, for store supplies

March 11: Sold merchandise on account to Manny Company, $600

March 12: Sold merchandise on account to Nant Company, $350

March 14: Paid bi-weekly salaries of $740, Check #3

March 14: Cash sales for the week, $1,800

March 16: Purchased merchandise on account from Cotin Company, $1,100

March 17: Issued Check #4 to Baily Company for March 7 purchase, less 2%

March 18: Bought $250 worth of store supplies from Salio Supply House on account

March 19: Returned defective merchandise of $200 to Cotin Company and received credit

March 19: Sold merchandise on account to Olin Company, $645

March 21: Issued Check #5 to Andon Equipment for $500, in part payment of equipment purchase

March 22:	Received check from Nant Company in settlement of their March 12 purchase, less 2% discount
March 22:	Purchased merchandise from Canny Corporation for cash, $750, Check #6
March 23:	Cash sales for the week, $1,845
March 24:	Purchased merchandise on account from Daily Corporation, $850
March 25:	Sold merchandise on account to Pallit Corporation, $740
March 26:	Purchased additional supplies, $325, from Salio Supply House on account
March 27:	Received check from Manny Company in settlement of their account, less 1% discount
March 30:	Cash sales for the week, $1,920
March 30:	Received $300 on account from Olin Company
March 31:	Paid bi-weekly salaries, $810, Check #7

GENERAL JOURNAL   J-1

Date	Description	P. R.	Debit	Credit

CASH RECEIPTS JOURNAL   CR-1

Date	Account Cr.	P. R.	Cash Dr.	Sales Disc. Dr.	Acct. Rec. Cr.	Sales Cr.	Sundry Cr.

CASH DISBURSEMENTS JOURNAL   CD-1

Date	Check No.	Account Dr.	P. R.	Cash Cr.	Pur. Disc. Cr.	Acct. Pay. Dr.	Sundry Dr.

PURCHASES JOURNAL

P-1

Date	Account Cr.	P.R.	Acct. Pay. Cr.	Pur. Dr.	Store Supp. Dr.	Office Supp. Dr.	Sundry Acct. Dr.		
							Acct.	P.R.	Amount

SALES JOURNAL

S-1

Date	Account Debited	P.R.	Accounts Receivable Dr. Sales Cr.

SOLUTION

GENERAL JOURNAL

J-1

Date	Description	P.R.	Debit	Credit
Mar. 19	Accounts Payable, Cotin Co.	√ / 21	200	
	Purchase Returns and Allowances	52		200
	Defective goods			

CASH RECEIPTS JOURNAL

CR-1

Date	Account Credited	P.R.	Cash Dr.	Sales Disc. Dr.	Acct. Rec. Cr.	Sales Cr.	Sundry Cr.
Mar. 1	Drew Company, Capital	31	14,000				14,000
7	Sales	√	1,650			1,650	
14	Sales	√	1,800			1,800	
22	Nant Company	√	343	7	350		
23	Sales	√	1,845			1,845	
27	Manny Company	√	594	6	600		
27	Sales	√	1,920			1,920	
30	Olin Company	√	300		300		
			22,452	13	1,250	7,215	14,000
			(11)	(42)	(12)	(41)	(√)

CASH DISBURSEMENTS JOURNAL

CD-1

Date	Check No.	Account Debited	P.R.	Cash Cr.	Pur. Disc. Cr.	Acct. Pay. Dr.	Sundry Dr.
Mar. 2	1	Rent Expense	54	600			600
10	2	Store Supplies	14	150			150
14	3	Salaries Expense	55	740			740
17	4	Baily Company	√	1,176	24	1,200	
21	5	Andon Equipment	√	500		500	
22	6	Purchases	51	750			750
31	7	Salaries Expense	55	810			810
				4,726	24	1,700	3,050
				(11)	(53)	(21)	(√)

PURCHASES JOURNAL   P-1

Date	Account Cr.	P. R.	Acct. Pay. Cr.	Pur. Dr.	Store Supp. Dr.	Office Supp. Dr.	Sundry Acct. Dr.		
							Acct.	P. R.	Amount
Mar. 4	Andon Equipment	√	10,000				Equip.	19	10,000
7	Baily Company	√	1,200	1,200					
16	Cotin Company	√	1,100	1,100					
18	Salio Supply House	√	250		250				
24	Daily Corporation	√	850	850					
26	Salio Supply House	√	325		325				
			13,725	3,150	575				10,000
			(21)	(51)	(14)				(√)

SALES JOURNAL   S-1

Date	Account Debited	P. R.	Accounts Receivable Dr. Sales Cr.
Mar. 11	Manny Company	√	600
12	Nant Company	√	350
19	Olin Company	√	645
25	Pallit Corporation	√	740
			2,335
			(12)(41)

5.27. Based upon the work in Problem 5.26, post all transactions to the appropriate accounts in the general ledger, the accounts receivable ledger, and the accounts payable ledger.

GENERAL LEDGER

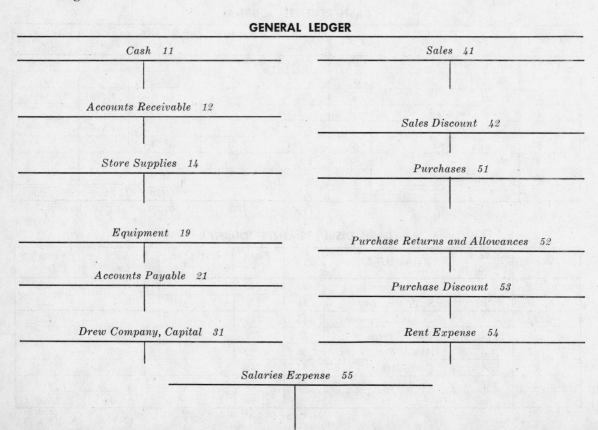

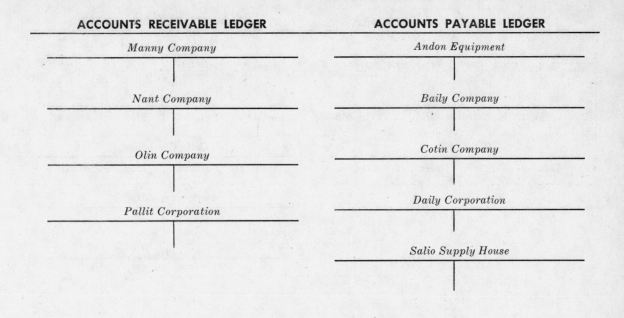

ACCOUNTS RECEIVABLE LEDGER

Manny Company

Nant Company

Olin Company

Pallit Corporation

ACCOUNTS PAYABLE LEDGER

Andon Equipment

Baily Company

Cotin Company

Daily Corporation

Salio Supply House

SOLUTION

GENERAL LEDGER

Cash   11

Mar. 31 CR-1 22,452	Mar. 31 CD-1 4,726
17,726	

Accounts Receivable   12

Mar. 31 S-1 2,335	Mar. 31 CR-1 1,250
1,085	

Store Supplies   14

Mar. 10 CD-1 150	
31 P-1 575	
725	

Equipment   19

Mar. 4 P-1 10,000	

Accounts Payable   21

Mar. 19 J-1 200	Mar. 31 P-1 13,725
31 CD-1 1,700	11,825

Drew Company, Capital   31

	Mar. 1 CR-1 14,000

Sales   41

	Mar. 31 S-1 2,335
	31 CR-1 7,215
	9,550

Sales Discount   42

Mar. 31 CR-1 13	

Purchases   51

Mar. 22 CD-1 750	
31 P-1 3,150	
3,900	

Purchase Returns and Allowances   52

	Mar. 19 J-1 200

Purchase Discount   53

	Mar. 31 CD-1 24

Rent Expense   54

Mar. 2 CD-1 600	

Salaries Expense   55

Mar. 14 CD-1 740	
31 CD-1 810	
1,550	

ACCOUNTS RECEIVABLE LEDGER			ACCOUNTS PAYABLE LEDGER	

Manny Company

Mar. 11 S-1 600	Mar. 27 CR-1 600

Nant Company

Mar. 12 S-1 350	Mar. 22 CR-1 350

Olin Company

Mar. 19 S-1 645	Mar. 30 CR-1 300

Pallit Corporation

Mar. 25 S-1 740	

Andon Equipment

Mar. 21 CD-1 500	Mar. 4 P-1 10,000

Baily Company

Mar. 17 CD-1 1,200	Mar. 7 P-1 1,200

Cotin Company

Mar. 19 J-1 200	Mar. 16 P-1 1,100

Daily Corporation

	Mar. 24 P-1 850

Salio Supply House

	Mar. 18 P-1 250
	26 P-1 325

5.28. Based upon the information in Problems 5.26 and 5.27, prepare (a) a schedule of accounts receivable, (b) a schedule of accounts payable, (c) a trial balance.

(a)

Drew Company
Schedule of Accounts Receivable
March 31, 19X2

Olin Company
Pallit Corporation

(b)

Drew Company
Schedule of Accounts Payable
March 31, 19X2

Andon Equipment
Cotin Equipment
Daily Corporation
Salio Supply House

(c)

Drew Company
Trial Balance
March 31, 19X2

Cash		
Accounts Receivable		
Store Supplies		
Equipment		
Accounts Payable		
Drew Company, Capital		
Sales		
Sales Discount		
Purchases		
Purchase Returns and Allowances		
Purchase Discount		
Rent Expense		
Salaries Expense		

SOLUTION

(a)

Drew Company
Schedule of Accounts Receivable
March 31, 19X2

Olin Company	$ 345
Pallit Corporation	740
	$1,085

(b)

Drew Company
Schedule of Accounts Payable
March 31, 19X2

Andon Equipment	$ 9,500
Cotin Company	900
Daily Corporation	850
Salio Supply House	575
	$11,825

(c)

Drew Company
Trial Balance
March 31, 19X2

Cash	$17,726	
Accounts Receivable	1,085	
Store Supplies	725	
Equipment	10,000	
Accounts Payable		$11,825
Drew Company, Capital		14,000
Sales		9,550
Sales Discount	13	
Purchases	3,900	
Purchase Returns and Allowances		200
Purchase Discount		24
Rent Expense	600	
Salaries Expense	1,550	
	$35,599	$35,599

Chapter 6

Adjusting and Closing Procedures

6.1 INTRODUCTION: THE ACCRUAL BASIS OF ACCOUNTING

As mentioned in Chapter 2, accounting records are kept on the *accrual basis*, except in the case of very small businesses. This means that *revenue is recognized when earned, regardless of when cash is actually collected, and expense is matched to the revenue, regardless of when cash is paid out.* Most revenue is earned when goods or services are delivered. At this time title to the goods or services is transferred and there is created a legal obligation to pay for such goods or services. Some revenue is recognized on a time basis, such as rental income, and is earned when the specified period of time has passed. The accrual concept demands that expenses be kept in step with revenue, so that each month sees only that month's expenses applied against the revenue for that month. The necessary matching is brought about through a type of journal entry. In this chapter we shall discuss these *adjusting entries*, and also the *closing entries* through which the adjusted balances are ultimately transferred to balance sheet accounts at the end of the fiscal year.

6.2 ADJUSTING ENTRIES COVERING RECORDED DATA

To adjust expense or income items that have already been recorded, only a reclassification is required; that is, amounts have only to be transferred from one of the Prepaid Expenses accounts (e.g., Prepaid Insurance) to another (Insurance Expense). The following seven examples will show how adjusting entries are made for the principal types of *recorded expenses*.

EXAMPLE 1. Prepaid Insurance.

Assume that a business paid a $1,200 premium on April 1 for one year's insurance in advance. This represents an increase in one asset (prepaid expense) and a decrease in another asset (cash). Thus, the entry would be:

Prepaid Insurance	*1,200*	
Cash		*1,200*

At the end of April, 1/12 of the $1,200, or $100, had expired or been used up. Therefore, an adjustment has to be made, decreasing or crediting Prepaid Insurance and increasing or debiting Insurance Expense. The entry would be:

Insurance Expense	*100*	
Prepaid Insurance		*100*

Thus, $100 would be shown as Insurance Expense in the income statement for April and the balance of $1,100 would be shown as part of Prepaid Expense in the balance sheet.

EXAMPLE 2. Prepaid Taxes.

Assume that on April 1 a business made the quarterly property tax payment of $600. At that time the transaction would be recorded with a debit to Prepaid Taxes, and a credit to Cash, for $600. Since the payment covers 3 months, the tax expense will be $200 per month. The entries would be as follows:

April 1	*Prepaid Property Taxes*	*600*	
	Cash		*600*
April 30	*Property Tax Expense*	*200*	
	Prepaid Property Taxes		*200*

The balance to be shown on the balance sheet of April 30 for Prepaid Property Taxes would be $400.

EXAMPLE 3.   Prepaid Rent.

Assume that on April 1 a business paid $1,800 to cover rent for the balance of the year. The full amount would have been recorded as a prepaid expense in April. Since there is a 9-month period involved, the rent expense each month is $200. The balance of Prepaid Rent would be $1,600 at the beginning of May. The adjusting entry for April would be:

Rent Expense	*200*	
Prepaid Rent		*200*

EXAMPLE 4.   Prepaid Interest.

Assume that the business found it necessary to take a loan of $5,000 from the local bank on April 1. The period of the loan was 2 months, with interest of 6% a year.   When interest is deducted in advance, or discounted, there is prepaid interest involved. On April 1 the entry would be:

Cash	*4,950*	
Prepaid Interest	*50*	
Notes Payable		*5,000*

The prepaid interest, an asset, was computed as follows:

$$\$5,000 \times 6\% \text{ per year} \times 1/6 \text{ year} = \$50$$

At the end of April the adjusting entry would be:

Interest Expense	*25*	
Prepaid Interest		*25*

EXAMPLE 5.   Supplies.

A type of prepayment which is somewhat different from those previously described is the payment for office or factory supplies. Assume that on April 1, $400 worth of supplies were purchased on credit. There were none on hand before. This would increase assets and also increase liabilities. At the end of April, when expense and revenue are to be matched and statements prepared, a count of the amount on hand will be made. Assume that the inventory count shows that $250 of supplies are still on hand. Then the amount consumed during April was $150 ($400 − $250). The two entries would be as follows:

April 1	*Supplies*	*400*	
	Accounts Payable		*400*
April 30	*Supplies Expense*	*150*	
	Supplies		*150*

Supplies Expense of $150 will be included in the April income statement; Supplies of $250 will be included as an asset on the balance sheet of April 30.

In each of the above examples the net effect of the adjusting entry is to credit the same account as was originally debited.

EXAMPLE 6.   Accumulated Depreciation.

This is a valuation or offset account, which means that the balance is offset against the related asset account. In the case of property, plant, and equipment it is desirable to know the original cost as well as the value after depreciation. Assume that machinery costing $15,000 was purchased on February 1 of the current year and was expected to last 10 years. With the straight-line method of accounting (i.e., equal charges each period), the depreciation would be $1,500 a year, or $125 a month. The adjusting entry would be as follows:

Depreciation Expense	*125*	
Accumulated Depreciation		*125*

At the end of April, Accumulated Depreciation would have a balance of $375, representing three months' accumulated depreciation. The account would be shown in the balance sheet as follows:

Machinery	*15,000*	
Less: Accumulated Depreciation	*375*	*14,625*

Adjustment of *recorded revenue* (unearned income) takes place as in the following two examples. Note that unearned income represents a liability, since something remains to be done before the revenue is actually earned.

EXAMPLE 7.   Unearned Rent.

Assume that rent of $400 was received on March 15, for April rent. The following entries would be made:

March 15	*Cash*	*400*	
	*Unearned Rent**		*400*

At the end of April, when the rent had been earned, Unearned Rent would be debited.

April 30	*Unearned Rent**	*400*	
	Rent Income		*400*

* The account, Unearned Rent, is a liability.

EXAMPLE 8.   Unearned Commissions.

Assume that $300 was received on April 1, for commissions for 3 months. At the end of April, Unearned Commissions would be debited, and Earned Commissions Income would be credited, for $100. The entries would be as follows:

April 1	*Cash*	*300*	
	Unearned Commissions		*300*
April 30	*Unearned Commissions*	*100*	
	Earned Commissions Income		*100*

6.3   ADJUSTING ENTRIES COVERING UNRECORDED DATA

In the previous section we discussed various kinds of adjustments to accounts to which entries had already been made. Now we consider those instances in which an expense has been incurred or an income earned but the applicable amount has not been recorded during the month. For example, if salaries are paid on a weekly basis, the last week of the month may apply to two months. If April ends on a Tuesday, then the first two days of the week will apply to April and be an April expense, while the last three days will be a May expense.

To arrive at the proper total for salaries for the month of April, we must include along with the April payrolls that were paid in April, the two days' salary that was not paid until May. Thus, we make an entry to *accrue* the two days' salary. To accrue means to collect or accumulate.

The following two examples show adjusting entries for the most important types of *unrecorded expenses* (accrued expenses).

EXAMPLE 9.   Accrued Salaries.

Assume that April 30 falls on Tuesday for the last weekly payroll period. Then, two days of that week will apply to April, three days to May. The payroll for the week amounted to $2,500, of which $1,000 applied to April and $1,500 to May. The entries would be as follows:

April 30	*Salaries Expense*	*1,000*	
	Salaries Payable		*1,000*

When the payment of the payroll is made — say, on May 8 — the entry would be as follows:

May 8	Salaries Expense	1,500	
	Salaries Payable	1,000	
	Cash		2,500

As can be seen above, $1,000 was charged to expense in April and $1,500 in May. The debit to Accrued Salaries Payable of $1,000 in May merely canceled the credit entry made in April, when the liability was set up for the April salaries expense.

EXAMPLE 10.   Interest Payable.

At the end of the accounting period the interest accrued on any business liabilities should be recognized in the accounts. Assume that instead of interest being prepaid on the $5,000 loan described in Example 4, the interest is due when the loan is due. In that case, there would be accrued interest for April of $25, and the following adjusting entry would be required for April:

April 30	Interest Expense	25	
	Interest Payable		25

Most businesses would have some *unrecorded revenue* (accrued income); that is, income earned but not yet received. Generally, this would be interest earned on notes from customers, rent earned on premises rented to a tenant, or various other items for which income had been earned but had not yet been collected.

EXAMPLE 11.   Interest Receivable.

A business holds a note receivable from a customer for $10,000. The note, due in 3 months, bears interest at 6% and was issued on March 1. The total interest would be $150 ($10,000 × 6% per year × 1/4 year). By the end of April, interest for two months had been earned. The following adjusting entry would be required for April:

April 30	Interest Receivable	50	
	Interest Income		50

When the note is settled by the customer in May, he would pay the principal plus the interest, as shown below:

May 31	Cash	10,150	
	Note Receivable		10,000
	Interest Receivable		100
	Interest Income		50

As can be seen, the interest earned was $50 a month. Therefore, Interest Receivable was debited $50 for March and $50 for April. The same entry was not necessary for May, since the note was settled at the end of May.

6.4   CLOSING ENTRIES

The information for the month-to-month adjusting entries and the related financial statements can be obtained from the work sheet, whose use will be fully described in Chapter 7. After the income statement and balance sheet have been prepared from the worksheet for the last month in the fiscal year, a summary account — variously known as Expense and Income Summary, Profit and Loss Summary, etc. — is set up. Then, by means of *closing entries*, each expense account is credited so as to produce a zero balance, and the total amount for the closed-out accounts is debited to Expense and Income Summary.

Similarly, the individual revenue accounts are closed out by debiting, and the total amount is credited to the summary account. Thus, the new fiscal year starts with zero balances in the income and expense accounts, while the Expense and Income Summary balance gives the net income or the net loss for the old year.

EXAMPLE 12.

To illustrate closing procedure, we refer to the accounts of Alan Bagon.

Alan Bagon
Trial Balance
April 30, 19X2

Cash	$4,700	
Supplies	100	
Equipment	2,500	
Accounts Payable		$1,500
Alan Bagon, Capital		5,000
Alan Bagon, Drawing	300	
Fees Income		2,000
Rent Expense	500	
Salaries Expense	200	
Supplies Expense	200	
	$8,500	$8,500

The closing entries are as follows.

(1) **Close out revenue accounts.** Debit the individual revenue accounts and credit the total to Expense and Income Summary. Here, there is only one income account.

April 30 Fees Income	2,000	
Expense and Income Summary		2,000

(2) **Close out expense accounts.** Credit the individual expense accounts and debit the total to Expense and Income Summary.

April 30 Expense and Income Summary	900	
Rent Expense		500
Salaries Expense		200
Supplies Expense		200

(3) **Close out the Expense and Income Summary account.** If there is a profit, the credit made for total income in (1) above will exceed the debit made for total expense in (2) above. Therefore, to close out the balance to zero, a debit entry will be made to Expense and Income Summary. A credit will be made to the capital account to transfer the net income for the period. If expenses exceed income, then a loss has been sustained and a credit would be made to Expense and Income Summary and a debit to the capital account. Based on the information given, the entry is:

April 30 Expense and Income Summary	1,100	
Alan Bagon, Capital		1,100

(4) **Close out the drawing account.** The drawing account would be credited for the total amount of the drawings for the period and the capital account debited for that amount. The difference between net income and drawing for the period represents the net change in the capital account for the period. The net income of $1,100, less drawings of $300, results in a net increase of $800 in the capital account. The closing entry for the drawing account is:

April 30 Alan Bagon, Capital	300	
Alan Bagon, Drawing		300

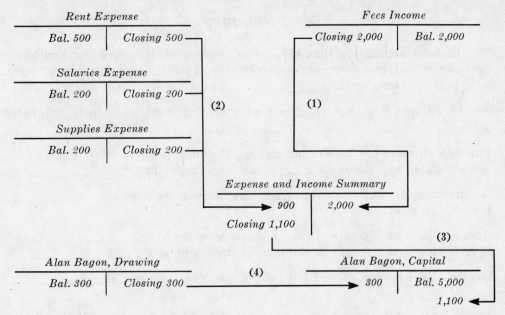

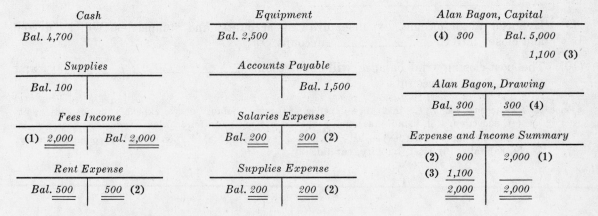

After the closing entries (1) through (4) are made, the various accounts will appear as below.   The income and expense accounts and the drawing account are ruled off or closed out, thus showing no balance. The net profit for the period and the drawing account balance were transferred to Alan Bagon, Capital, a balance sheet account.

6.5 POST-CLOSING TRIAL BALANCE

After the closing entries are made, only balance sheet accounts — assets, liabilities, and capital — remain open.   A trial balance of these accounts is thus a *post-closing trial balance.*

EXAMPLE 13.

Alan Bagon
Post-Closing Trial Balance
April 30, 19X2

Cash	$4,700	
Supplies	100	
Equipment	2,500	
Accounts Payable		$1,500
Alan Bagon, Capital		5,800
	$7,300	$7,300

Summary

(1) The basis of accounting that recognizes revenue when earned, regardless of when cash is received, and matches the expenses to the revenue, regardless of when cash is paid out, is known as the _____.

(2) An adjusting entry that records the expired amount of prepaid insurance would debit the _____ account.

(3) Supplies on hand is classified as an _____ and appears in the _____, while supplies expense is an _____ and appears in the _____.

(4) Accumulated Depreciation appears in the balance sheet as a _____ from the related asset.

(5) Accrued Salaries is treated in the balance sheet as a _____, while Salaries Expense appears in the income statement as an _____.

(6) Income that has been earned but not yet received is known as _____ _____.

(7) Expenses that have been incurred but not yet paid for are known as _____ _____.

(8) The revenue and expense accounts are closed out to the summary account known as _____.

(9) Eventually, all income, expense, drawing accounts, and summaries, will be netted and closed into the _____ account.

(10) The post-closing trial balance will involve only _____ , _____ , and _____ accounts.

Answers: (1) accrual basis; (2) insurance expense; (3) asset, balance sheet, expense, income statement; (4) deduction; (5) liability account, expense account; (6) unrecorded revenue or accrued income; (7) unrecorded expenses or accrued expenses; (8) Expense and Income Summary; (9) capital; (10) asset, liability, capital.

Solved Problems

6.1 An insurance policy covering a two-year period was purchased on November 1 for $600. The amount was debited to Prepaid Insurance. Show the adjusting entry for the two-month period ending December 31.

SOLUTION

Insurance Expense		50*	
Prepaid Insurance			50

$$* \frac{\$600}{2 \text{ yrs.}} \times \frac{2 \text{ months}}{12 \text{ months}} = \$50$$

6.2. Taxes of $900 were debited to Prepaid Taxes representing payment made for a six-month period beginning December 1. What adjustment is needed on December 31?

SOLUTION

Tax expense		150*	
Prepaid Taxes			150

* $900 × 1/6

6.3. Based on Problem 6.2, explain the balances of each of the two accounts.

SOLUTION

Tax Expense: The balance of $150 represents the amount of the expense for one month and would appear in the Income Statement as a General Expense.

Prepaid Taxes: The balance of $750 represents future payments for the next five months and would appear as a current asset in the Balance Sheet.

6.4. $2,400 was paid on September 1 and represented an advance payment for six months rent of a new factory office. The account Prepaid Rent was debited for this transaction. (*a*) What adjusting entry is necessary in order to show the true value of the accounts at the end of the year? (*b*) What amount will appear as an asset in the Balance Sheet as of the end of the year?

SOLUTION

(a)	Rent Expense		1,600*	
	Prepaid Rent			1,600

* $2,400 ÷ 6 × 4 months

(*b*) The amount of Prepaid Rent, appearing in the current asset section of the Balance Sheet, will be $800 ($2,400 − $1,600) representing future payments for the two months, January and February of the following year.

6.5. A purchase of $900 was debited to Office Supplies. A count of the supplies at the end of the period showed $500 still on hand. Make the adjusting entry at the end of the period.

SOLUTION

Office Supplies Expense	400	
Office Supplies		400

6.6. Below is the opening balance of the Store Supplies account at the beginning of the year. After taking an inventory count of the remaining supplies, it was discovered that $750 had been used during the year. (a) Post the adjusting entry. (b) In what statements will the account balances be reflected?

Store Supplies		Store Supplies Expense	
Bal. 2,250			

SOLUTION

	Store Supplies		Store Supplies Expense	
(a)	Bal. 2,250	750 ← →	750	

(b) Store Supplies: Appears in the Balance Sheet as a current asset with a balance of $1,500.

Store Supplies Expense: Appears in the Income Statement as an operating expense of $750.

6.7. Machinery costing $12,000, purchased November 30, is being depreciated at the rate of 10% per year. Show the adjusting entry for December 31.

SOLUTION

Depreciation Expense, Machinery	100*	
Accumulated Depreciation, Machinery		100

* $12,000 \times 10\%$ per year $\times \frac{1}{12}$ year $= \$100$

6.8. Based on Problem 6.7, how would the information stated above be presented in the Balance Sheet?

SOLUTION

Fixed Assets:

Machinery	12,000	
Less: Accumulated Depreciation – Machinery	100	11,900

6.9. The business received $6,000 as an advance payment for work to be done for a customer. At the end of the year, $4,000 of the services had been performed. (*a*) Prepare the adjusting entry if the original amount had been credited to Unearned Income. (*b*) What type of account is Unearned Income?

SOLUTION

(*a*)

Unearned Income	4,000	
Service Income		4,000

(*b*)   It is unrealized income and therefore a liability.

6.10. A business pays weekly salaries of $10,000 on Friday for a five-day week. Show the adjusting entry when the fiscal period ends on (*a*) Tuesday; (*b*) Thursday.

(*a*)

(*b*)

SOLUTION

(*a*)

Salaries Expense	4,000*	
Salaries Payable		4,000

(*b*)

Salaries Expense	8,000*	
Salaries Payable		8,000

* ($10,000 ÷ 5 days) = $2,000 per day. Tuesday = $2,000 × 2.
Thursday = $2,000 × 4.

6.11. On September 1 Mary Somner borrowed $8,000 for 6 months at 9% interest from the First National Bank. What is the necessary adjusting entry to record the accrued interest as of December 31, the end of the fiscal year?

SOLUTION

Interest Expense	240*	
Interest Payable		240

* Interest is calculated for 4 months, September 1–December 31

$$\$8,000 \times \frac{9}{100} \times \frac{4\ \text{months}}{12\ \text{months}} = \$240$$

6.12. The Willet Wilkinson Company's before-closing trial balance shows service revenue of $10,000 and interest income of $2,000. The expenses are: salaries, $6,000; rent, $2,000; depreciation, $1,500; and interest, $500. Give the closing entries to be made to Expense and Income Summary for (*a*) income and (*b*) expense.

(a)

(b)

SOLUTION

(a)

Service Income	10,000	
Interest Income	2,000	
Expense and Income Summary		12,000

(b)

Expense and Income Summary	10,000	
Salaries Expense		6,000
Rent Expense		2,000
Depreciation Expense		1,500
Interest Expense		500

6.13. Using Problem 6.12(a) and (b), prepare the closing entry for net income, and (c) post the transactions to the Expense and Income Summary and to the capital account. Finally, close out the applicable account.

Expense and Income Summary		Willet Wilkinson, Capital
(b) 10,000 (a) 12,000		Bal. 20,000
(c) ?		

SOLUTION

Expense and Income Summary	2,000	
Willet Wilkinson, Capital		2,000

Expense and Income Summary		Willet Wilkinson, Capital
(b) 10,000 (a) 12,000		Bal. 20,000
(c) 2,000		(c) 2,000
12,000 12,000		

6.14. If all the revenue and expense accounts have been closed at the end of the fiscal year, what do the debit and credit figures in the account below indicate? What is the net profit or loss?

Expense and Income Summary	
98,000	102,000

SOLUTION

The debit amount represents $98,000 of expenses while the credit amount of $102,000 depicts income for the period. The net balance of the account, $4,000 ($102,000 − $98,000) shows the net income for the period and will be closed out to the capital account.

6.15. After all revenue and expense accounts were closed at the end of the fiscal year, the Expense and Income Summary had a debit total of $100,000 and a credit total of $150,000. The drawing account for William Whyte had a debit balance of $35,000. Journalize the closing entries.

SOLUTION

Expense and Income Summary	50,000	
William Whyte, Capital		50,000
William Whyte, Capital	35,000	
William Whyte, Drawing		35,000

6.16. Based upon the balances below, prepare entries to close out (a) revenue accounts, (b) expense accounts, (c) Expense and Income Summary, (d) drawing account.

P. Silver, Capital		22,000
P. Silver, Drawing	6,000	
Service Income		12,000
Interest Income		1,500
Salaries Expense	8,000	
Rent Expense	4,000	
Depreciation Expense	3,000	
Interest Expense	2,000	

(a)

(b)

(c)

(d)

SOLUTION

(a)	Service Income	12,000	
	Interest Income	1,500	
	Expense and Income Summary		13,500
(b)	Expense and Income Summary	17,000	
	Salaries Expense		8,000
	Rent Expense		4,000
	Depreciation Expense		3,000
	Interest Expense		2,000
(c)	P. Silver, Capital	3,500*	
	Expense and Income Summary		3,500
(d)	P. Silver, Capital	6,000	
	P. Silver, Drawing		6,000

* 3,500 represents a net loss and is debited to the capital account

6.17. Post the transactions shown in Problem 6.16.

Capital	
	Bal. 22,000

Salaries Expense	
Bal. 8,000	

Drawing	
Bal. 6,000	

Rent Expense	
Bal. 4,000	

Service Income	
	Bal. 12,000

Depreciation Expense	
Bal. 3,000	

Interest Income	
	Bal. 1,500

Interest Expense	
Bal. 2,000	

Expense and Income Summary	

SOLUTION

Capital	
(c) 3,500	Bal. 22,000
(d) 6,000	

Salaries Expense	
Bal. 8,000	(b) 8,000

Drawing	
Bal. 6,000	(d) 6,000

Rent Expense	
Bal. 4,000	(b) 4,000

Service Income	
(a) 12,000	Bal. 12,000

Depreciation Expense	
Bal. 3,000	(b) 3,000

Interest Income	
(a) 1,500	Bal. 1,500

Interest Expense	
Bal. 2,000	(b) 2,000

Expense and Income Summary	
(b) 17,000	(a) 13,500
	(c) 3,500
17,000	17,000

Note that all income and expense accounts have been closed out. No balances exist in the above accounts with the exception of Capital which now has a balance of $12,500.

Examination II
Chapters 4-6

1. Contrast the journal and the ledger.

2. What effect does the incorrect posting of a debit as a credit have on the trial balance?

3. Distinguish between prepaid expenses and accrued expenses.

4. What are adjusting entries? Closing entries?

5. Interpret the balance in the Supplies account at the end of the accounting period (a) before adjustment; (b) after adjustment.

6. In the table below, indicate in which of the five journals each transaction is to be recorded.

		Cash Payments	Cash Receipts	Sales	Purchases	General
(1)	Sale of merchandise for cash		(✓)			
(2)	Sale of merchandise on account					
(3)	Cash refunded to a customer					
(4)	Receipt of cash from a customer in settlement of an account					
(5)	Purchase of merchandise for cash					
(6)	Purchase of merchandise on account					
(7)	Payment of salaries					
(8)	Note payable sent to a creditor in settlement of an account					
(9)	Payment of interest on the mortgage					
(10)	Received a note in settlement of a customer's account					

7. The balances of the accounts of the Judith Playhouse, as of November 30, were as follows:

Judith Playhouse
Trial Balance
November 30

Cash	$10,000	
Accounts Receivable	2,100	
Supplies	600	
Equipment	12,000	
Building	9,000	
Accounts Payable		$ 6,500
Notes Payable		12,000
Judith Playhouse, Capital		15,200
	$33,700	$33,700

Selected transactions for the month of December were:

(a)   Dec. 1:   Bought new theatrical equipment for $3,000, paying
                    half in cash and giving our note for the balance
(b)   Dec. 10:   Paid $1,000 due on the notes payable
(c)   Dec. 14:   Receipts for the two-week period (admissions income)
                    totaled $9,600
(d)   Dec. 20:   Paid utilities, $150
(e)   Dec. 24:   Paid $1,000 for five-year insurance policy on the theatre
(f)   Dec. 28:   Paid monthly salaries, $1,250

Journalize the transactions.

8. (a) Weekly salaries of $8,000 are payable on Friday, for a five-day week. What is the
        adjusting entry if the fiscal period ends on Wednesday?

    (b) An insurance policy covering a four-year period was purchased on February 1,
        for $1,200. What is the adjusting entry on December 31?

    (c) Office supplies of $700 were debited to Office Supplies. At the end of the month,
        the account shows $300 worth still on hand. Prepare the adjusting entry.

9. In the following assume a fiscal year extending from January 1 through December 31.

    (a) A machine costing $8,000 was purchased on October 31 and is being depreciated
        at the rate of 10% per year. What amount will appear as the adjusting entry on
        December 31?

    (b) An insurance policy covering a six-year period was purchased on March 1 for
        $1,800. What amount will appear as an expense on the income statement at the
        end of the year? What amount will appear on the balance sheet as an asset?

10. After all revenue and expense accounts of the Gold Silver Company were closed at the
    end of the year, the expense and income summary had a debit balance of $125,000 and
    a credit balance of $190,000. The capital account had a credit balance of $72,000, while
    the drawing account had a debit balance of $12,000. Journalize the closing entries.

11. Prepare an income statement, capital statement, and balance sheet based on the fol-
    lowing data:

    On January 1, 19X2, the Mary Moore Co. had capital of $15,200. On December 31, the
    end of the fiscal year, the balances of assets, liabilities, revenue, and expenses were
    as follows:

Accounts Payable	$ 3,100
Accumulated Depreciation	500
Cash	14,800
Depreciation Expense	500
Drawing	2,600
Equipment	14,400
Fees Income	37,700
Insurance Expense	800
Miscellaneous Expense	1,850
Prepaid Insurance	830
Prepaid Rent	500
Rent Expense	3,000
Salaries Expense	16,500
Salaries Payable	200
Supplies	570
Supplies Expense	350

Answers to Examination II

1. The journal is a book of original entry which contains a *chronological* record of transactions. Each transaction is recorded first in the journal, which specifies the accounts to be debited and credited, along with a brief explanation of the transaction. The ledger is the complete set of accounts. It takes various physical forms, depending on whether the accounting is manual or machine.

2. The trial balance will be out of balance by twice the amount of incorrect posting.

3. Prepaid expenses are those paid in advance of consumption; accrued expenses are those for which the consumption precedes the payment.

4. *Adjusting entries* are those required at the end of the accounting period to make the accounts properly reflect the results of operations for the period and the financial position at the end of the period. *Closing entries* are those which summarize the activities of the period, matching the inflow of income with the outflow of expenses to arrive at the net increase or decrease in owners' equity for the period. They separate the operations of one period from those of another. The accounts that are closed are the nominal or temporary accounts, which are really only extensions of the capital accounts.

5. (a) The balance before adjustment is the balance at the beginning of the period plus the amount purchased during the period. It includes both the amount on hand and the amount used.

   (b) The balance after adjustment includes only the inventory of supplies on hand at the end of the period. The amount used has been transferred to the supplies expense account.

6.

	Cash Payments	Cash Receipts	Sales	Purchases	General
(1)		✓			
(2)			✓		
(3)	✓				
(4)		✓			
(5)	✓				
(6)				✓	
(7)	✓				
(8)					✓
(9)	✓				
(10)					✓

7. (a) Equipment   3,000
          Cash   1,500
          Notes Payable   1,500

   (b) Notes Payable   1,000
          Cash   1,000

   (c) Cash   9,600
          Admissions Income   9,600

   (d) Utilities Expense   150
          Cash   150

   (e) Prepaid Insurance   1,000
          Cash   1,000

   (f) Salaries Expense   1,250
          Cash   1,250

8. (a) Salaries Expense   4,800
          Salaries Payable   4,800
       $[3 \times (8,000/5) = 4,800]$

   (b) Insurance Expense   275
          Prepaid Insurance   275
       $[1,200 \div 4 = 300; \ 11/12 \times 300 = 275]$

   (c) Supplies Expense   400
          Supplies   400

9. (a) $133.33 $[\$8,000 \times 10\% = \$800; \ 1/6 \times \$800 = \$133.33]$

   (b) Expense: $ 250 $[\$1,800 \div 6 = \$300; \ 5/6 \times \$300 = \$250]$
       Asset: $1,550 $[\$1,800 - \$250 = \$1,550]$

10.   Expense and Income Summary   65,000
            Capital   65,000

        Capital   12,000
            Drawing   12,000

11.   **Mary Moore Company**
                            Income Statement
                      Year Ended December 31, 19X2

Fees Income $37,700
Operating Expenses
    Salaries Expense $16,500
    Rent Expense   3,000
    Insurance Expense   800
    Depreciation Expense   500
    Supplies Expense   350
    Miscellaneous Expense   1,850
Total Operating Expense   23,000
Net Income $14,700

                        Mary Moore Company
                         Capital Statement
                   Year Ended December 31, 19X2

Capital, January 1 $15,200
Net Income for the year $14,700
Less: Withdrawals   2,600
    Increase in Capital   12,100
Capital, December 31 $27,300

                        Mary Moore Company
                          Balance Sheet
                        December 31, 19X2

ASSETS
Current Assets
    Cash $14,800
    Supplies   570
    Prepaid Insurance   830
    Prepaid Rent   500
Total Current Assets $16,700
Fixed Assets
    Equipment $14,400
    Less: Accumulated Depreciation   500   13,900
Total Assets $30,600

LIABILITIES AND CAPITAL
Current Liabilities
    Accounts Payable $3,100
    Salaries Payable   200
Total Current Liabilities $ 3,300
Capital, December 31   27,300
Total Liabilities and Capital $30,600

Chapter 7

Summarizing and Reporting
via the
Service Business Work Sheet

7.1 INTRODUCTION

The recording of transactions and the adjusting and closing procedures have been discussed in previous chapters. It is reasonable to expect that among the hundreds of computations and clerical tasks involved some errors will occur, such as posting a debit as a credit. Today many financial records are maintained on the computer or on mechanical bookkeeping systems. The use of machine time to correct errors can be very costly and can bring painful questions from high financial executives.

One of the best ways yet developed of avoiding errors in the permanent accounting records, and also of simplifying the work at the end of the period, is to make use of an informal record called the *work sheet*.

7.2 WORK SHEET PROCEDURES FOR A SERVICE BUSINESS

We are already familiar with the types of accounts found in a service business — i.e. a business in which revenue comes from services rendered — so we shall first discuss the work sheet for such a business.

The work sheet is usually prepared in pencil on a large sheet of accounting stationery called analysis paper. On the work sheet the ledger accounts are adjusted, balanced, and arranged in proper form for preparing the financial statements. All procedures can be reviewed quickly and the adjusting and closing entries can be made in the formal records with less chance of error. Moreover, with the data for the income statement and balance sheet already proved out on the work sheet, these statements can be prepared more quickly.

For a typical service business we may suppose the work sheet to have 8 money columns; namely, a debit and a credit column for four groups of figures: (1) Trial Balance, (2) Adjustments, (3) Income Statement, and (4) Balance Sheet. The steps in completing the work sheet are then:

1. Enter the trial balance figures from the ledger.
2. Enter the adjustments.
3. Extend the adjusted figures to either the income statement or balance sheet columns.
4. Total the income statement columns and the balance sheet columns.
5. Enter the net income or net loss.

EXAMPLE 1.

Prepare the work sheet for the Thomas Company, whose ledger balances appear on the following page.

117

Thomas Company
Trial Balance
December 31, 19X2

Cash	$ 3,510	
Accounts Receivable	3,010	
Supplies	1,050	
Prepaid Rent	400	
Equipment	18,000	
Accumulated Depreciation		$ 3,000
Notes Payable		4,000
Accounts Payable		2,380
Taxes Payable		400
Jane Thomas, Capital		13,690
Jane Thomas, Drawing	3,000	
Service Fees Income		10,500
Salaries Expense	4,600	
Miscellaneous Expense	400	
	$33,970	$33,970

1. **Enter the trial balance figures.** The balance of each general ledger account is entered in the appropriate trial balance column of the work sheet (see Fig. 7-1). The balances summarize all the transactions for the year ending December 31 before any adjusting entries have been applied.

Thomas Company
Work Sheet
Year Ending December 31, 19X2

Account Title	Trial Balance Debit	Trial Balance Credit	Adjustments Debit	Adjustments Credit	Income Statement Debit	Income Statement Credit	Balance Sheet Debit	Balance Sheet Credit
Cash	3,510						3,510	
Accounts Receivable	3,010						3,010	
Supplies	1,050			(a) 500			550	
Prepaid Rent	400			(b) 100			300	
Equipment	18,000						18,000	
Accumulated Deprec.		3,000		(c) 1,800				4,800
Notes Payable		4,000						4,000
Accounts Payable		2,380						2,380
Taxes Payable		400						400
Jane Thomas, Capital		13,690						13,690
Jane Thomas, Drawing	3,000						3,000	
Service Fees Income		10,500				10,500		
Salaries Expense	4,600		(d) 200		4,800			
Misc. Expense	400				400			
	33,970	33,970						
Supplies Expense			(a) 500		500			
Rent Expense			(b) 100		100			
Depreciation Expense			(c) 1,800		1,800			
Salaries Payable				(d) 200				200
Interest Expense			(e) 20		20			
Interest Payable				(e) 20				20
			2,620	2,620	7,620	10,500	28,370	25,490
Net Income					2,880			2,880
					10,500	10,500	28,370	28,370

Fig. 7-1

2. Enter the adjustments. After the trial balance figures have been entered and the totals are in agreement, the adjusting entries should be entered in the second pair of columns. The related debits and credits are keyed by letters so that they may be rechecked quickly for any errors. The letters should be in proper sequence, beginning with asset accounts at the top of the page.

(*a*) *Supplies.* In order to determine the amount of supplies used, it is necessary to make a count of the amount on hand on December 31. The amount was found to be $550. The balance at the beginning of the year plus purchases amounted to $1,050. Therefore, $1,050 − $550 = $500 worth of supplies that have been used. There is no account for supplies expense, so the account name must be listed at the bottom of the work sheet. The adjusting entry is:

Supplies Expense	500	
Supplies		500

(*b*) *Rent.* Rent of $400 for 4 months was paid in advance on December 1. Therefore, the original amount charged to Prepaid Rent must be reduced by $100, the amount of rent for December. The account name, Rent Expense, should be listed at the bottom of the work sheet. The adjusting entry for December is as follows:

Rent Expense	100	
Prepaid Rent		100

(*c*) *Depreciation.* The equipment is being written off over a 10-year period using the straight-line method. Thus, $1,800 a year ($18,000 ÷ 10) is being charged to expense. The title Depreciation Expense will also have to be written in at the bottom of the work sheet. The entry will be:

Depreciation Expense	1,800	
Accumulated Depreciation		1,800

(*d*) *Salaries.* The salaries amount in the trial balance column would include only the payments which have been recorded and paid during the year. The portion which was earned in December but paid in January, because the weekly pay period ended in January, would not be included. If the amount is $200, the accrued entry would be:

Salaries Expense	200	
Salaries Payable		200

The account title Salaries Payable will also have to be listed on the work sheet.

(*e*) *Interest.* On the notes payable, there is accrued interest for one month. Assuming that the note bears 6% interest, the accrued interest would be $20 ($4,000 × 6% × 1/12). The entry will be:

Interest Expense	20	
Interest Payable		20

3. Extend the adjusted figures to either the income statement or balance sheet columns. The process of extending the balances horizontally should begin with the account at the top of the sheet. The revenue and expense accounts should be extended to the income statement columns; the assets, liabilities, and capital to the balance sheet columns. Each figure is extended to only one of the columns.

4. Total the income statement columns and the balance sheet columns. The difference between the debit and credit totals in both sets of columns should be the same amount, which represents net income or net loss for the period.

	Income Statement		Balance Sheet	
	Dr.	*Cr.*	*Dr.*	*Cr.*
Total	7,620	10,500	28,370	25,490
Net Income	2,880			2,880
	10,500	10,500	28,370	28,370

5. Enter the net income or net loss. The credit column total in the income statement is $10,500, the debit column total is $7,620. The credit column, or income side, is the larger, representing a net income of $2,880. Since net income increases capital, the net income figure should go on the credit side of the balance sheet. The balance sheet credit column total of $25,490 plus net income of $2,880 totals $28,370, which equals the debit column total. Since both the income statement columns and balance sheet columns are in agreement, it is a simple matter to prepare the formal income statement and balance sheet.

If there had been a loss, the debit or expense column in the income statement would have been the larger and the loss amount would have been entered in the credit column in order to balance the two columns. As a loss would decrease the capital, it would be entered in the balance sheet debit column.

After the work sheet has been completed, financial statements should be made. Based on the work sheet in Fig. 7-1, the following statements are prepared:

Thomas Company
Income Statement
Year Ending December 31, 19X2

Service Fees Income		$10,500
Expenses		
Salaries Expense	$4,800	
Miscellaneous Expense	400	
Supplies Expense	500	
Rent Expense	100	
Depreciation Expense	1,800	
Interest Expense	20	
Total Expenses		7,620
Net Income		$ 2,880

Thomas Company
Capital Statement
Year Ending December 31, 19X2

Capital, January 1		$13,690
Net Income, 19X2	$2,880	
Drawing, 19X2	3,000	
Decrease in Capital		(120)
Capital, December 31		$13,570

Thomas Company
Balance Sheet
December 31, 19X2

ASSETS

Current Assets		
Cash	$3,510	
Accounts Receivable	3,010	
Supplies	550	
Prepaid Rent	300	
Total Current Assets		$7,370
Fixed Assets		
Equipment	$18,000	
Less Accumulated Depreciation	4,800	13,200
Total Assets		$20,570

LIABILITIES

Notes Payable	$4,000	
Accounts Payable	2,380	
Taxes Payable	400	
Salaries Payable	200	
Interest Payable	20	
Total Liabilities		7,000
Capital, December 31		13,570
Total Liabilities and Capital		$20,570

Summary

(1)   One of the best accounting methods for avoiding errors in the permanent accounting records and also of simplifying the work at the end of the period is to make use of the _____ .

(2)   The work sheet is an _____ accounting record, usually prepared in _____ .

(3)   On the work sheet, the ledger accounts are _____ , _____ , and _____ in proper form for preparing the financial statements.

(4)   The balances of the accounts appearing in the work sheet in the first two columns are obtained from the _____ .

(5)   If the total of the debit column of the income statement in the work sheet is larger than the total of the credit column of the income statement, the balance is said to be a _____ for the period.

(6)   The account that is used to show the amount of depreciation for the fiscal year is titled _____ while the account that gives the total depreciation to date is called _____ .

(7)   The amount of salaries in the trial balance includes payments which have been recorded and paid _____ .

Answers: (1) work sheet; (2) informal, pencil; (3) adjusted, balanced, arranged; (4) ledger; (5) net loss; (6) depreciation expense, accumulated depreciation; (7) during the year.

Solved Problems

7.1.   (*a*) Supplies inventory at the beginning of the month was $745.   At the end of the month, there remained a balance of $325. Prepare the adjusting entry needed to reflect the above data.

(*b*) Supplies inventory at the beginning of the month was $745.   At the end of the month it was determined that $325 had been used. Prepare the adjusting entry needed to reflect the above data.

		Dr.	Cr.
(*a*)			

		Dr.	Cr.
(*b*)			

SOLUTION

		Dr.	Cr.
(*a*)	Supplies Expense	420	
	Supplies		420
(*b*)	Supplies Expense	325	
	Supplies		325

7.2. A truck bought on January 5, 19X2 for $14,000 has an estimated life of seven years.

(*a*) What is the entry to record the depreciation expense as of December 31, 19X2?

(*b*) How would this information be presented on the Balance Sheet at the end of the year?

		Dr.	Cr.
(*a*)			
(*b*)			

SOLUTION

		Dr.	Cr.
(*a*)	Depreciation Expense	2,000	
	Accumulated Depreciation ($14,000 ÷ 7)		2,000
(*b*)	Truck	14,000	
	Less: Accumulated Depreciation	2,000	12,000

Note: The book value of the truck on December 31 would be $12,000.

7.3. Assume the same information as in Problem 7.2 except that the truck was purchased on October 1, 19X2.

(*a*) Present the adjusting entry needed to record the information.

(*b*) Based on part (*a*), how would this information be presented on the balance sheet as of December 31, 19X3, one full year later?

(*a*)			
(*b*)			

SOLUTION

(*a*)	Depreciation Expense	500*	
	Accumulated Depreciation		500
	($14,000 ÷ 7 years − $2,000)		

$$* \ \frac{3 \text{ months}}{12 \text{ months}} \times \$2,000 = \$500$$

(*b*)	Truck	14,000	
	Less: Accumulated Depreciation	2,500*	11,500

* $ 500 for 19X2
  2,000 for 19X3
 $2,500 Accumulated

7.4. An $8,000 note payable written on November 1 for 180 days bears interest at 6%. What is the adjusting entry as of December 31?

SOLUTION

Interest Expense	80	
Interest Payable		80

Note: The amount of interest expense in 19X2 from November 1–December 31 (60 days) is computed as follows:

$$\$8,000 \times 6\% \times 60/360$$

or

$$\frac{\$8,000}{1} \times \frac{6}{100} \times \frac{1}{6} = \$80$$

7.5. Journalize the following adjusting entries at December 31:

(a) Supplies on hand, January 1, $950; December 31, $460.

(b) The Prepaid Rent account has a balance of $3,000, representing rent for one year paid in advance on March 1.

(c) Depreciation on equipment during the year, $450.

(d) Salaries accrued but not paid at December 31, $280.

		Dr.	Cr.
(a)			
(b)			
(c)			
(d)			

SOLUTION

		Dr.	Cr.
(a)	Supplies Expense	490	
	Supplies		490
(b)	Rent Expense	2,500*	
	Prepaid Rent		2,500
(c)	Depreciation Expense	450	
	Accumulated Depreciation		450
(d)	Salaries Expense	280	
	Salaries Payable		280

* Rent expense for expired 10 months of the year.
$$10/12 \times \$3,000 = 2,500$$

7.6. The following selected accounts are taken from the ledger of C. Gold Co. Place check marks in the appropriate columns to which the accounts will be extended in the work sheet.

Title	Income Statement		Balance Sheet	
	Dr.	Cr.	Dr.	Cr.
1. Cash				
2. Accounts Receivable				
3. Notes Receivable				
4. Accounts Payable				
5. C. Gold, Drawing				
6. C. Gold, Capital				
7. Sales				
8. Depreciation Expense				
9. Salaries Payable				

SOLUTION

Title	Income Statement		Balance Sheet	
	Dr.	Cr.	Dr.	Cr.
1. Cash			✓	
2. Accounts Receivable			✓	
3. Notes Receivable			✓	
4. Accounts Payable				✓
5. C. Gold, Drawing			✓	
6. C. Gold, Capital				✓
7. Sales		✓		
8. Depreciation Expense	✓			
9. Salaries Payable				✓

7.7. From the partial view of the work sheet below, determine the net income or loss.

Income Statement		Balance Sheet	
Dr.	Cr.	Dr.	Cr.
29,500	36,200	52,400	45,700

SOLUTION

36,200 (total credits of income statement)
− 29,500 (total debits of income statement)
6,700 (net income)

	Income Statement		Balance Sheet	
	Dr.	Cr.	Dr.	Cr.
	29,500	36,200	52,400	45,700
Net Income 6,700				6,700
	36,200	36,200	52,400	52,400

7.8. Complete the work sheet below. What do the following items tell the reader?

Income Statement		Balance Sheet	
Dr.	Cr.	Dr.	Cr.
46,200	42,000	65,600	69.800
	?	?	
?	?	?	?

SOLUTION

Income Statement		Balance Sheet	
Dr.	Cr.	Dr.	Cr.
46,200	42,000	65,600	69.800
Net Loss	4,200	4,200	
46,200	46,200	69,800	69,800

The above figures show that the firm has experienced a net loss of $4,200. This is because more expenses ($46,200) have been reported than income ($42,000). As a loss decreased capital, it would be entered in the balance sheet debit column.

7.9. Below is the work sheet for the Juaz Company. Prepare adjusting entries on the work sheet based on the year end data.

Juaz Company
Work Sheet
Year Ending December 31, 19X2

Account Title	Trial Balance		Adjustments	
	Dr.	Cr.	Dr.	Cr.
Cash	18,000			
Supplies	4,000			
Prepaid Insurance	900			
Equipment	11,000			
Accumulated Depreciation		2,000		
Accounts Payable		7,000		
Juaz, Capital		20,900		
Juaz, Drawing	1,000			
Service Income		22,000		
Rent Expense	2,000			
Salaries Expense	9,000			
General Expense	6,000			
	51,900	51,900		

Year End Data:

   (*a*) Supplies on hand, $3,000

   (*b*) Insurance expired during the year, $600

   (*c*) Depreciation on equipment, $1,500

   (*d*) Salaries accrued, $1,000

SOLUTION

Juaz Company
Work Sheet
Year Ending December 31, 19X2

Account Title	Trial Balance Dr.	Cr.	Adjustments Dr.	Cr.
Cash	18,000			
Supplies	4,000			(a) 1,000
Prepaid Insurance	900			(b) 600
Equipment	11,000			
Accumulated Depreciation		2,000		(c) 1,500
Accounts Payable		7,000		
Juaz, Capital		20,900		
Juaz, Drawing	1,000			
Service Income		22,000		
Rent Expense	2,000			
Salaries Expense	9,000		(d) 1,000	
General Expense	6,000			
	51,900	51,900		
Supplies Expense			(a) 1,000	
Insurance Expense			(b) 600	
Depreciation Expense			(c) 1,500	
Salaries Payable				(d) 1,000
			4,100	4,100

7.10. Based on the data in Problem 7-9, extend the work sheet figures to both the Income Statement and Balance Sheet.

Juaz Company
Work Sheet
Year Ending December 31, 19X2

Account Title	Trial Balance Dr.	Cr.	Adjustments Dr.	Cr.	Income Statement Dr.	Cr.	Balance Sheet Dr.	Cr.
Cash	18,000							
Supplies	4,000			(a) 1,000				
Prepaid Insurance	900			(b) 600				
Equipment	11,000							
Accumulated Depreciation		2,000		(c) 1,500				
Accounts Payable		7,000						
Juaz, Capital		20,900						
Juaz, Drawing	1,000							
Service Income		22,000						
Rent Expense	2,000							
Salaries Expense	9,000		(d) 1,000					
General Expense	6,000							
	51,900	51,900						
Supplies Expense			(a) 1,000					
Insurance Expense			(b) 600					
Depreciation Expense			(c) 1,500					
Salaries Payable				(d) 1,000				
			4,100	4,100				
Net Income								

SOLUTION

Juaz Company
Work Sheet
Year Ending December 31, 19X2

Account Title	Trial Balance Dr.	Trial Balance Cr.	Adjustments Dr.	Adjustments Cr.	Income Statement Dr.	Income Statement Cr.	Balance Sheet Dr.	Balance Sheet Cr.
Cash	18,000						18,000	
Supplies	4,000			(a) 1,000			3,000	
Prepaid Insurance	900			(b) 600			300	
Equipment	11,000						11,000	
Accumulated Depreciation		2,000		(c) 1,500				3,500
Accounts Payable		7,000						7,000
Juaz, Capital		20,900						20,900
Juaz, Drawing	1,000						1,000	
Service Income		22,000				22,000		
Rent Expense	2,000				2,000			
Salaries Expense	9,000		(d) 1,000		10,000			
General Expense	6,000				6,000			
	51,900	51,900						
Supplies Expense			(a) 1,000		1,000			
Insurance Expense			(b) 600		600			
Depreciation Expense			(c) 1,500		1,500			
Salaries Payable				(d) 1,000				1,000
			4,100	4,100	21,100	22,000	33,300	32,400
Net Income					900			900
					22,000	22,000	33,300	33,300

7.11. Prepare an 8-column work sheet using adjustments: (a) rent expired for year, $1,200, (b) supplies on hand, $200, and (c) salaries accrued, $400.

P. C. Silver Company
Work Sheet
Year Ending December 31, 19X2

Account Title	Trial Balance Dr.	Trial Balance Cr.	Adjustments Dr.	Adjustments Cr.	Income Statement Dr.	Income Statement Cr.	Balance Sheet Dr.	Balance Sheet Cr.
Cash	7,000							
Accounts Receivable	3,500							
Prepaid Rent	3,000							
Supplies	800							
Equipment	6,200							
Accounts Payable		4,500						
P. C. Silver, Capital		12,000						
Fees Income		10,000						
Salaries Expense	4,600							
General Expense	1,400							
	26,500	26,500						

SOLUTION

P. C. Silver Company
Work Sheet
Year Ending December 31, 19X2

Account Title	Trial Balance		Adjustments		Income Statement		Balance Sheet	
	Dr.	Cr.	Dr.	Cr.	Dr.	Cr.	Dr.	Cr.
Cash	7,000						7,000	
Accounts Receivable	3,500						3,500	
Prepaid Rent	3,000			(a)1,200			1,800	
Supplies	800			(b) 600			200	
Equipment	6,200						6,200	
Accounts Payable		4,500						4,500
P.C. Silver, Capital		12,000						12,000
Fees Income		10,000				10,000		
Salaries Expense	4,600		(c) 400		5,000			
General Expense	1,400				1,400			
	26,500	26,500						
Rent Expense			(a) 1,200		1,200			
Supplies Expense			(b) 600		600			
Salaries Payable				(c) 400				400
			2,200	2,200	8,200	10,000	18,700	16,900
Net Income					1,800			1,800
					10,000	10,000	18,700	18,700

7.12. From the information in Problem 7.11, prepare all adjusting and closing entries.

ADJUSTING ENTRIES

(a)

(b)

(c)

CLOSING ENTRIES

(a)

(b)

(c)

SOLUTION

ADJUSTING ENTRIES

(a)	Rent Expense	1,200	
	Prepaid Rent		1,200
(b)	Supplies Expense	600	
	Supplies		600
(c)	Salaries Expense	400	
	Salaries Payable		400

CLOSING ENTRIES

(a)	Fees Income	10,000	
	Expense and Income Summary		10,000
(b)	Expense and Income Summary	8,200	
	Salaries Expense		5,000
	General Expense		1,400
	Rent Expense		1,200
	Supplies Expense		600
(c)	Expense and Income Summary	1,800	
	P. C. Silver, Capital		1,800

7.13. From the data of Problem 7.11, prepare the income statement and balance sheet.

P. C. Silver Company		
Income Statement		
Year Ending December 31, 19X2		
Fees Income		
Expenses		
Salaries Expense		
General Expense		
Rent Expense		
Supplies Expense		
Total Expenses		
Net Income		

P. C. Silver Company
Balance Sheet
December 31, 19X2

ASSETS		LIABILITIES AND CAPITAL	
Current Assets		Liabilities	
Cash		Accounts Payable	
Accounts Receivable		Salaries Payable	
Prepaid Rent		Total Liabilities	
Supplies		Capital	
Total Current Assets		Capital, January 1, 19X2	
Fixed Assets		Add: Net Income	
Equipment		Capital, December 31, 19X2	
Total Assets		Total Liabilities and Capital	

SOLUTION

P. C. Silver Company Income Statement Year Ending December 31, 19X2		
Fees Income		$10,000
Expenses		
Salaries Expense	$5,000	
General Expense	1,400	
Rent Expense	1,200	
Supplies Expense	600	
Total Expenses		8,200
Net Income		$ 1,800

P. C. Silver Company Balance Sheet December 31, 19X2			

ASSETS   **LIABILITIES AND CAPITAL**

Current Assets		Liabilities		
Cash	$ 7,000	Accounts Payable		$ 4,500
Accounts Receivable	3,500	Salaries Payable		400
Prepaid Rent	1,800	Total Liabilities		$ 4,900
Supplies	200	Capital		
Total Current Assets	$12,500	Capital, January 1, 19X2	$12,000	
Fixed Assets		Add: Net Income	1,800	
Equipment	6,200	Capital, December 31, 19X2		13,800
Total Assets	$18,700	Total Liabilities and Capital		$18,700

7.14. Based on the following information:

    (a) Rent expired $2,100

    (b) Insurance expired   700

    (c) Supplies on hand, December 31   300

    (d) Depreciation on Equipment   900

    (e) Salaries accrued   100

Complete the work sheet on page 131.

Perez Company
Work Sheet
Year Ending December 31, 19X2

Account Title	Trial Balance Dr.	Trial Balance Cr.	Adjustments Dr.	Adjustments Cr.	Income Statement Dr.	Income Statement Cr.	Balance Sheet Dr.	Balance Sheet Cr.
Cash	12,000							
Accounts Receivable	11,300							
Prepaid Rent	3,100							
Prepaid Insurance	1,600							
Supplies	800							
Equipment	11,500							
Accumulated Deprec.		900						
Accounts Payable		6,400						
J. Perez, Capital		15,200						
J. Perez, Drawing	8,000							
Fees Income		42,500						
Salaries Expense	14,000							
Misc. Expense	2,700							
	65,000	65,000						
Rent Expense								
Insurance Expense								
Supplies Expense								
Depreciation Expense								
Salaries Payable								

SOLUTION

Perez Company
Work Sheet
Year Ending December 31, 19X2

Account Title	Trial Balance Dr.	Trial Balance Cr.	Adjustments Dr.	Adjustments Cr.	Income Statement Dr.	Income Statement Cr.	Balance Sheet Dr.	Balance Sheet Cr.
Cash	12,000						12,000	
Accounts Receivable	11,300						11,300	
Prepaid Rent	3,100			(a) 2,100			1,000	
Prepaid Insurance	1,600			(b) 700			900	
Supplies	800			(c) 500			300	
Equipment	11,500						11,500	
Accumulated Deprec.		900		(d) 900				1,800
Accounts Payable		6,400						6,400
J. Perez, Capital		15,200						15,200
J. Perez, Drawing	8,000						8,000	
Fees Income		42,500				42,500		
Salaries Expense	14,000		(e) 100		14,100			
Misc. Expense	2,700				2,700			
	65,000	65,000						
Rent Expense			(a) 2,100		2,100			
Insurance Expense			(b) 700		700			
Supplies Expense			(c) 500		500			
Depreciation Expense			(d) 900		900			
Salaries Payable				(e) 100				100
			4,300	4,300	21,000	42,500	45,000	23,500
Net Income					21,500			21,500
					42,500	42,500	45,000	45,000

7.15. Based on the information in Problem 7.14, prepare the adjusting and closing entries.

ADJUSTING ENTRIES

(a)			
(b)			
(c)			
(d)			
(e)			

CLOSING ENTRIES

(a)			
(b)			
(c)			
(d)			

SOLUTION

ADJUSTING ENTRIES

(a)	Rent Expense	2,100	
	Prepaid Rent		2,100
(b)	Insurance Expense	700	
	Prepaid Insurance		700
(c)	Supplies Expense	500	
	Supplies		500
(d)	Depreciation Expense	900	
	Accumulated Depreciation		900
(e)	Salaries Expense	100	
	Salaries Payable		100

CLOSING ENTRIES

(a)	Fees Income	42,500	
	Expense and Income Summary		42,500
(b)	Expense and Income Summary	21,000	
	Salaries Expense		14,100
	Misc. Expense		2,700
	Rent Expense		2,100
	Insurance Expense		700
	Supplies Expense		500
	Depreciation Expense		900
(c)	Expense and Income Summary	21,500	
	J. Perez, Capital		21,500
(d)	J. Perez, Capital	8,000	
	J. Perez, Drawing		8,000

7.16. Prepare an Income Statement, Capital Statement, and Balance Sheet based on the information in Problem 7.14.

Perez Company		
Income Statement		
Year Ending December 31, 19X2		

Perez Company		
Capital Statement		
Year Ending December 31, 19X2		

Perez Company		
Balance Sheet		
December 31, 19X2		

SOLUTION

Perez Company		
Income Statement		
Year Ending December 31, 19X2		
Revenue		
Fees Income		$42,500
Expenses		
Salaries Expense	$14,100	
Rent Expense	2,100	
Depreciation Expense	900	
Insurance Expense	700	
Supplies Expense	500	
Miscellaneous Expense	2,700	
Total Expenses		21,000
Net Income		$21,500

Perez Company		
Capital Statement		
Year Ending December 31, 19X2		
Capital, January 1		15,200
Net Income for the year	21,500	
Less: Withdrawals	8,000	
Increase in Capital		13,500
Capital, December 31		$28,700

Perez Company		
Balance Sheet		
December 31, 19X2		
ASSETS		
Current Assets		
Cash	$12,000	
Accounts Receivable	11,300	
Prepaid Rent	1,000	
Prepaid Insurance	900	
Supplies	300	
Total Current Assets		$25,500
Fixed Assets		
Equipment	11,500	
Less: Accumulated Depreciation	1,800	
Net Fixed Assets		9,700
Total Assets		$35,200
LIABILITIES AND CAPITAL		
Current Liabilities		
Accounts Payable	6,400	
Salaries Payable	100	
Total Liabilities		6,500
J. Perez, Capital		28,700
Total Liabilities and Capital		$35,200

Chapter 8

Summarizing and Reporting
via the
Merchandising Business Work Sheet

8.1   WORK SHEET PROCEDURES FOR A MERCHANDISING BUSINESS

Merchandising (trading) businesses are those whose income derives largely from buying or selling goods rather than from rendering services. In addition to the accounts discussed in Chapter 7, the work sheet for a merchandising business will carry: Inventory, Cost of Goods Sold, and Purchases. Let us discuss these new accounts separately, and then illustrate their handling on the work sheet.

8.2   INVENTORY AND PURCHASES TREATMENT

Inventory represents the value of goods on hand either at the beginning or the end of the accounting period. The beginning balance would be the same amount as the ending balance of the previous period. Generally, not all purchases of merchandise are sold in the same period; so unsold merchandise must be counted and priced, and the total recorded in the ledger as Ending Inventory. The amount of this inventory will be shown as an asset in the balance sheet. The amount of goods sold during the period will be shown as Cost of Goods Sold in the income summary. (See Sec. 8.4.)

EXAMPLE 1.

Assume that the January 1 (beginning) inventory is $20,000 and the December 31 (ending) inventory is $26,000. Two entries are required to show the replacement of the old by the new inventory:

Entry 1	Expense and Income Summary	20,000	
	Merchandise Inventory		20,000
Entry 2	Merchandise Inventory	26,000	
	Expense and Income Summary		26,000

The effect on the inventory and the expense and income balances is as follows:

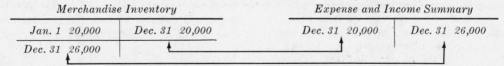

On the work sheet (Fig. 8-1) the $20,000 balance of the inventory account that appears in the trial balance represents the inventory at the beginning of the year. This amount will be transferred to Expense and Income Summary as Entry (a).

| (a) | Expense and Income Summary | 20,000 | |
| | Merchandise Inventory | | 20,000 |

The inventory at the end of the current year, $26,000, is an asset and will be adjusted on the work sheet as (b).

| (b) | Merchandise Inventory | 26,000 | |
| | Expense and Income Summary | | 26,000 |

135

Thomas Company
Work Sheet
Year Ending December 31, 19X2

Account Title	Trial Balance Dr.	Trial Balance Cr.	Adjustments Dr.	Adjustments Cr.	Income Statement Dr.	Income Statement Cr.	Balance Sheet Dr.	Balance Sheet Cr.
Cash	3,510						3,510	
Accounts Receivable	3,010						3,010	
Merchandise Inventory	20,000		(b) 26,000	(a) 20,000			26,000	
Supplies	1,050			(c) 500			550	
Prepaid Rent	400			(d) 100			300	
Equipment	18,000						18,000	
Accumulated Depreciation		3,000		(e) 1,800				4,800
Notes Payable		4,000						4,000
Accounts Payable		2,380						2,380
Taxes Payable		400						400
Jane Thomas, Capital		38,690						38,690
Jane Thomas, Drawing	3,000						3,000	
Sales		30,500				30,500		
Purchases	25,000				25,000			
Salaries Expense	4,600		(f) 200		4,800			
Misc. Expense	400				400			
	78,970	78,970						
Expense and Income Summary			(a) 20,000	(b) 26,000	20,000	26,000		
Supplies Expense			(c) 500		500			
Rent Expense			(d) 100		100			
Depreciation Expense			(e) 1,800		1,800			
Salaries Payable				(f) 200				200
Interest Expense			(g) 20		20			
Interest Payable				(g) 20				20
			48,620	48,620	52,620	56,500	54,370	50,490
Net Income					3,880			3,880
					56,500	56,500	54,370	54,370

Fig. 8-1

Unlike the procedure for other accounts, both the debit and the credit amounts for Expense and Income Summary are extended to the income statement in Fig. 8-1. This is done because the amount of the debit adjustment (which represents the beginning inventory of $20,000) and of the credit adjustment (which represents the ending inventory of $26,000) are needed to prepare the income statement. It would not be practical to net the two items, as the single figure would not give enough information regarding the beginning and ending inventories. The merchandise inventory of $26,000 (ending) is extended to the debit column of the balance sheet.

Account Title	Trial Balance Dr.	Trial Balance Cr.	Adjustments Dr.	Adjustments Cr.	Income Statement Dr.	Income Statement Cr.	Balance Sheet Dr.	Balance Sheet Cr.
Merchandise Inventory	20,000		(b) 26,000	(a) 20,000			26,000	
Expense and Income Summary			(a) 20,000	(b) 26,000	20,000	26,000		

We have not said anything about how the inventory balance is actually computed. This important question forms the subject of Chapter 10.

PURCHASES

It is preferable for managerial purposes to maintain a separate account for purchases rather than including them in the inventory account. The account includes only merchandise purchased for retail and appears in the Income Statement; purchases of machinery, trucks, etc., to be used in the business are debited to the particular asset account.

The journal entry to record a merchandise purchase is as follows:

Purchases	7,000	
Accounts Payable (or Cash)		7,000

At the end of the period the total in the purchases account is closed to the expense and income summary account.

8.3 THE MERCHANDISING WORK SHEET

For simplicity, the Thomas Company's Trial Balance and work sheet (see pages 136 and 137) will be used with the addition of the Merchandise Inventory and Purchases account. This would have the effect of making the Thomas Company service industry (Chapter 7) a merchandising company.

Thomas Company
Trial Balance
December 31, 19X2

Cash	$ 3,510	
Accounts Receivable	3,010	
*Merchandise Inventory	20,000	
Supplies	1,050	
Prepaid Rent	400	
Equipment	18,000	
Accumulated Depreciation		3,000
Notes Payable		4,000
Accounts Payable		2,380
Taxes Payable		400
*Jane Thomas, Capital		38,690
Jane Thomas, Drawing	3,000	
*Sales		30,500
*Purchases	25,000	
Salaries Expense	4,600	
Misc. Expense	400	
	$78,970	$78,970

* New accounts or amounts.

Additional Data:
(a) Merchandise Inventory, Beginning of Year $20,000
(b) Merchandise Inventory End of Year   26,000
(c) Supplies on Hand   550
(d) Rent Expired   100
(e) Depreciation for Year   1,800
(f) Accrued Salaries   200
(g) Accrued Interest on Notes Payable   20

Note that with the exception of Merchandise Inventory, all adjustments are identical to the work sheet (see Fig. 7.1) in Chapter 7.

8.4   COST OF GOODS SOLD

Since we do not reflect purchases or sales of goods in the inventory account during the year (periodic method), we must determine the cost of the inventory remaining on hand at the end of the accounting period and make any adjustments necessary.   Ending inventory, or merchandise which has not been sold and is on hand at the end of the period, is an asset which appears on the balance sheet.   Cost of Goods Sold appears in the income statement as a deduction from Sales. This cost may be calculated by the following procedure:

(a)	*Inventory (beginning), January 1, 19X2*	*$20,000*
(b)	*Add: Purchases*	*25,000*
(c)	*Goods Available for Sale*	*45,000*
(d)	*Less: Inventory (ending), December 31, 19X2*	*26,000*
(e)	*Cost of Goods Sold*	*$ $19,000*

(a) **Inventory (beginning).** The amount to be used will be the same as the ending inventory of 19X2 (determined by counting and applying one of the methods of Sec. 10.3).

(b) **Purchases.**   This is the total amount of goods bought for resale during 19X2, minus any purchases returned to the seller and any discounts given (*net* purchases).

(c) **Goods Available for Sale.** Computed by adding the inventory at the beginning of the year to the net purchases during 19X2.

(d) **Inventory (ending).** Determined by taking a physical count of all goods remaining in the business on December 31, 19X2, and applying one of the methods of Sec. 10.3.

(e) **Cost of Goods Sold.** This is the difference between what was available for sale and what is left at the end of the year. The cost of goods sold will then be deducted from net sales to determine the gross profit.

Based upon the work sheet (see Fig. 8.1), the Cost of Goods Sold section of the Income Statement would appear as:

Cost of Goods Sold

Merchandise Inventory (beginning)	*$20,000*
Purchases	*25,000*
Goods Available for Sale	*$45,000*
Less: Merchandise Inventory (ending)	*26,000*
Cost of Goods Sold	*$19,000*

The Income Statement for the Merchandising business of Thomas Company would then be:

Sales		*$30,500*
Cost of Goods Sold (see above)		*19,000*
Gross Profit		*$11,500*
Operating Expenses		
Salaries Expense	*$4,800*	
Miscellaneous Expense	*400*	
Supplies Expense	*500*	
Rent Expense	*100*	
Depreciation Expense	*1,800*	
Interest Expense	*20*	
Total Expenses		*7,620*
Net Income		*$3,880*

Summary

(1) A business whose income is derived largely from buying or selling goods rather than rendering services is known as a _____ firm.

(2) The goods on hand at the beginning or the end of the accounting period is called _____ .

(3) The merchandise inventory that is on hand at the end of the period will appear in the _____ .

(4) The Purchases account is used only for goods for _____ . Purchases of trucks and equipment are debited to _____ accounts.

(5) Beginning inventory plus net purchases will equal _____ .

(6) In recording both beginning inventory and ending inventory as an adjusting entry, the _____ account is used.

(7) The difference between what was available for sale and what is left at the end of the year is known as the _____ .

Answers: (1) Merchandising; (2) Inventory; (3) balance sheet; (4) resale; asset; (5) Goods Available for Sale; (6) Expense and Income Summary; (7) Cost of Goods Sold.

Solved Problems

8.1. The Folk Company purchased merchandise costing $150,000. What is the cost of goods sold under each assumption below?

	Beginning Inventory	Ending Inventory
(a)	100,000	60,000
(b)	75,000	50,000
(c)	50,000	30,000
(d)	0	10,000

SOLUTION

	Beginning Inventory	+ Purchases	− Ending Inventory	= Cost of Goods Sold
(a)	100,000	150,000	60,000	190,000
(b)	75,000	150,000	50,000	175,000
(c)	50,000	150,000	30,000	170,000
(d)	0	150,000	10,000	140,000

8.2. Compute the cost of goods sold from the following information: Beginning Inventory, $20,000; Purchases, $70,000; Ending Inventory, $34,000.

SOLUTION

Beginning Inventory	$20,000	
Purchases	70,000	
Total Available for Sale	90,000	
Less: Ending Inventory	34,000	
Cost of Goods Sold	$56,000	

8.3. For each situation below, determine the missing figures.

	Beginning Inventory	Purchases During Period	Ending Inventory	Cost of Goods Sold
(a)	$18,000	$40,000	_____	$35,000
(b)	_____	41,000	$15,000	42,000
(c)	21,000	37,000	20,000	_____
(d)	27,000	_____	25,000	38,000

SOLUTION

(a) $23,000; (b) $16,000; (c) $38,000; (d) $36,000

8.4 Journalize the following data:

(a) Merchandise inventory, January 1, $31,800; December 31, $38,500.

(b) Prepaid insurance before adjustment $1,540. It was found that $460 had expired during the year.

(c) Office supplies physically counted on December 31 were worth $120. The original balance of Supplies was $750.

(d) Office salaries for a five-day week ending on Friday average $2,500. The last payday was on Friday, December 27.

	Dr.	Cr.
(a)		
(b)		
(c)		
(d)		

SOLUTION

		Dr.	Cr.
(a)	Expense and Income Summary	31,800	
	Merchandise Inventory		31,800
	Merchandise Inventory	38,500	
	Expense and Income Summary		38,500
(b)	Insurance Expense	460	
	Prepaid Insurance		460
(c)	Office Supplies Expense	630	
	Office Supplies		630
(d)	Office Salaries Expense	1,000	
	Salaries Payable (December 30 and 31)		1,000

8.5. Journalize the adjusting entries, based on the following data:

(a) Merchandise Inventory: January 1, $31,700; December 31, $37,500.

(b) Office supplies Inventory on January 1, $1,200; office supplies on hand, December 31, $780.

(c) Sales Salaries average $3,000 for a 5-day work week ending on Friday. The last payday of the year was on Friday, December 26.

(d) Prepaid insurance before adjustments has a balance of $1,230. Analysis of the account shows that $750 has expired during the year.

SOLUTION

(a)	*Expense and Income Summary*	31,700	
	Merchandise Inventory		31,700
	Merchandise Inventory	37,500	
	Expense and Income Summary		37,500
(b)	*Office Supplies Expense*	420	
	Office Supplies		420
(c)	*Sales Salaries Expense*	1,800	
	Sales Salaries Payable (Dec. 29, 30, and 31)		1,800
(d)	*Insurance Expense*	750	
	Prepaid Insurance		750

8.6. The trial balance below includes the Merchandise Inventory balance of $12,400. At the end of the year, it was found that the Merchandise Inventory balance was $16,200. Post the needed entry directly to the work sheet columns below.

Trial Balance	*Adjustments*	
	Dr.	Cr.
Merchandise Inventory, 12,400		
Expense and Income Summary		

SOLUTION

Trial Balance	*Adjustments*	
	Dr.	Cr.
Merchandise Inventory, 12,400	*(a) 16,200*	*(b) 12,400*
Expense and Income Summary	*(b) 12,400*	*(a) 16,200*

8.7. Based on the above solution extend the figures to the appropriate columns.

	Income Statement		*Balance Sheet*	
	Dr.	Cr.	Dr.	Cr.
Merchandise Inventory				
Expense and Income Summary				

SOLUTION

	Income Statement		*Balance Sheet*	
	Dr.	Cr.	Dr.	Cr.
Merchandise Inventory			*16,200*	
Expense and Income Summary	*12,400*	*16,200*		

8.8. A section of the work sheet is presented below. Enter the adjustment required for Inventory, if it is assumed that Ending Inventory was $38,000.

Title	Trial Balance		Adjustments	
	Dr.	Cr.	Dr.	Cr.
Merchandise Inventory	32,400			
Expense and Income Summary				

SOLUTION

Title	Trial Balance		Adjustments	
	Dr.	Cr.	Dr.	Cr.
Merchandise Inventory	32,400		38,000	32,400
Expense and Income Summary			32,400	38,000

8.9. Using the information in Problem 8.8, extend the accounts in the work sheet. What does the debit balance in the balance sheet represent?

Title	Income Statement		Balance Sheet	
	Dr.	Cr.	Dr.	Cr.
Merchandise Inventory				
Expense and Income Summary				

SOLUTION

Title	Income Statement		Balance Sheet	
	Dr.	Cr.	Dr.	Cr.
Merchandise Inventory			38,000	
Expense and Income Summary	32,400	38,000		

The $38,000 represents inventory on hand at the end of the year.

8.10. Based on the work sheet's income statement columns below, prepare an income statement.

Expense and Income Summary	26,400	28,200
Sales		62,500
Purchases	31,400	
Rent Expense	6,000	
Salaries Expense	18,300	
Depreciation Expense	500	

SOLUTION

Sales		$62,500
Cost of Goods Sold		
Merchandise Inventory (beginning)	$26,400	
Purchases	31,400	
Goods Available for Sale	57,800	
Merchandise Inventory (ending)	28,200	
Cost of Goods Sold		29,600
Gross Profit		$32,900
Operating Expenses		
Rent Expense	$ 6,000	
Salaries Expense	18,300	
Depreciation Expense	500	
Total Expenses		24,800
Net Income		$ 8,100

8.11. From the trial balance of the J. C. Company prepare an eight-column work sheet.

J. C. Company
Trial Balance
June 30, 19X2

	Debit	Credit
Cash	$12,300	
Accounts Receivable	16,000	
Merchandise Inventory	2,700	
Supplies	450	
Prepaid Insurance	500	
Accounts Payable		$ 3,200
Notes Payable		7,100
J. C., Capital		14,750
Sales		39,800
Purchases	17,200	
Salaries Expense	11,400	
Advertising Expense	2,300	
General Expense	2,000	
	$64,850	$64,850

Use the following data for adjustments: (a) Merchandise Inventory, June 30, 19X2, $1,900; (b) Supplies on hand, $150; (c) Expired Insurance, $200.

J. C. Company
Work Sheet
Year Ending June 30, 19X2

Account Title	Trial Balance Dr.	Trial Balance Cr.	Adjustments Dr.	Adjustments Cr.	Income Statement Dr.	Income Statement Cr.	Balance Sheet Dr.	Balance Sheet Cr.
Cash	12,300							
Acct. Rec.	16,000							
Merch. Inv.	2,700							
Supplies	450							
Prepaid Ins.	500							
Acct. Pay.		3,200						
Notes Pay.		7,100						
J. C., Capital		14,750						
Sales		39,800						
Purchases	17,200							
Salaries Exp.	11,400							
Adv. Exp.	2,300							
Gen. Exp.	2,000							
	64,850	64,850						
Exp. & Inc. Sum.								
Supplies Exp.								
Ins. Exp.								
Net Income								

SOLUTION

J. C. Company
Work Sheet
Year Ending June 30, 19X2

Account Title	Trial Balance		Adjustments		Income Statement		Balance Sheet	
	Dr.	Cr.	Dr.	Cr.	Dr.	Cr.	Dr.	Cr.
Cash	12,300						12,300	
Acct. Rec.	16,000						16,000	
Merch. Inv.	2,700		(a) 1,900	(a) 2,700			1,900	
Supplies	450			(b) 300			150	
Prepaid Ins.	500			(c) 200			300	
Acct. Pay.		3,200						3,200
Notes Pay.		7,100						7,100
J. C., Capital		14,750						14,750
Sales		39,800				39,800		
Purchases	17,200				17,200			
Salaries Exp.	11,400				11,400			
Adv. Exp.	2,300				2,300			
Gen. Exp.	2,000				2,000			
	64,850	64,850						
Exp. & Inc. Sum.			(a) 2,700	(a) 1,900	2,700	1,900		
Supplies Exp.			(b) 300		300			
Ins. Exp.			(c) 200		200			
			5,100	5,100	36,100	41,700	30,650	25,050
Net Income					5,600			5,600
					41,700	41,700	30,650	30,650

8.12. The accounts and their balances in the M. Rothfeld Company ledger on December 31, the end of the fiscal year, are as follows:

Cash	$ 4,600
Accounts Receivable	6,900
Merchandise Inventory	28,300
Supplies	750
Prepaid Rent	1,800
Equipment	16,000
Accumulated Depreciation, Equipment	1,900
Accounts Payable	6,110
M. Rothfeld, Capital	48,200
M. Rothfeld, Drawing	12,900
Sales	128,000
Purchases	91,000
Advertising Expense	3,200
Salaries Expense	16,600
Miscellaneous Expense	2,160

Prepare an eight-column work sheet, with the following adjustments:

(a)	Merchandise inventory as of December 31	$33,400
(b)	Supplies on hand	250
(c)	Depreciation for the period	600
(d)	Accrued salaries	1,250

Account Title	Trial Balance		Adjustments		Income Statement		Balance Sheet	
	Dr.	Cr.	Dr.	Cr.	Dr.	Cr.	Dr.	Cr.
Cash	4,600							
Acct. Rec.	6,900							
Merch. Inv.	28,300							
Supplies	750							
Prepaid Rent	1,800							
Equipment	16,000							
Accum. Deprec.		1,900						
Accounts Pay.		6,110						
M. Rothfeld, Capital		48,200						
M. Rothfeld, Drawing	12,900							
Sales		128,000						
Purchases	91,000							
Adv. Exp.	3,200							
Salaries Exp.	16,600							
Misc. Exp.	2,160							
	184,210	184,210						
Exp. & Inc. Sum.								
Supplies Exp.								
Deprec. Exp.								
Salaries Pay.								
Net Income								

SOLUTION

Account Title	Trial Balance		Adjustments		Income Statement		Balance Sheet	
	Dr.	Cr.	Dr.	Cr.	Dr.	Cr.	Dr.	Cr.
Cash	4,600						4,600	
Acct. Rec.	6,900						6,900	
Merch. Inv.	28,300		(a) 33,400	(a) 28,300			33,400	
Supplies	750			(b) 500			250	
Prepaid Rent	1,800						1,800	
Equipment	16,000						16,000	
Accum. Deprec.		1,900		(c) 600				2,500
Accounts Pay.		6,110						6,110
M. Rothfeld, Capital		48,200						48,200
M. Rothfeld, Drawing	12,900						12,900	
Sales		128,000				128,000		
Purchases	91,000				91,000			
Adv. Exp.	3,200				3,200			
Salaries Exp.	16,600		(d) 1,250		17,850			
Misc. Exp.	2,160				2,160			
	184,210	184,210						
Exp. & Inc. Sum.			(a) 28,300	(a) 33,400	28,300	33,400		
Supplies Exp.			(b) 500		500			
Deprec. Exp.			(c) 600		600			
Salaries Pay.				(d) 1,250				1,250
			64,050	64,050	143,610	161,400	75,850	58,060
Net Income					17,790			17,790
					161,400	161,400	75,850	75,850

8.13. Based on the data in Problem 8.12 prepare:

    (*a*)   an income statement

    (*b*)   a capital statement

    (*c*)   a balance sheet

M. ROTHFELD COMPANY
INCOME STATEMENT

CAPITAL STATEMENT

BALANCE SHEET

SOLUTION

M. ROTHFELD COMPANY
INCOME STATEMENT

Sales		$128,000
Cost of Goods Sold		
Merchandise Inventory, January 1, 19X2	$ 28,300	
Purchases	91,000	
Goods Available for Sale	119,300	
Merchandise Inventory, December 31, 19X2	33,400	
Cost of Goods Sold		85,900
Gross Profit		$ 42,100
Expenses		
Advertising Expense	$ 3,200	
Salaries Expense	17,850	
Supplies Expense	500	
Depreciation Expense	600	
Miscellaneous Expense	2,160	
Total Expenses		24,310
Net Income		$ 17,790

CAPITAL STATEMENT

Capital, January 1, 19X2		$ 48,200
Net Income for year 19X2	$ 17,790	
Drawing for year 19X2	12,900	
Increase in Capital		4,890
Capital, December 31, 19X2		$ 53,090

BALANCE SHEET

ASSETS		
Current Assets		
Cash	$ 4,600	
Accounts Receivable	6,900	
Merchandise Inventory	33,400	
Supplies	250	
Prepaid Rent	1,800	
Total Current Assets		$ 46,950
Fixed Assets		
Equipment	$ 16,000	
Less: Accumulated Depreciation	2,500	13,500
Total Assets		$ 60,450
LIABILITIES AND CAPITAL		
Current Liabilities		
Accounts Payable	$ 6,110	
Salaries Payable	1,250	
Total Liabilities		$ 7,360
Capital		$ 53,090
Total Liabilities and Capital		$ 60,450

8.14. Shown are the balances for P. Widmann Co. on December 31, before adjustments.

Cash	Accounts Receivable	Merchandise Inventory
11,000	8,000	34,100

Supplies	Prepaid Insurance	Equipment
2,300	2,600	10,500

Accumulated Deprec.	Accounts Payable	P. Widmann, Capital
1,300	6,400	31,400

P. Widmann, Drawing	Sales	Purchases
8,000	112,100	57,500

Salaries Expense	Rent Expense	Misc. Expense
11,000	3,600	2,600

Using the additional data below, prepare an eight-column work sheet.

(a) Merchandise Inventory, December 31 $32,800
(b) Supplies Inventory, December 31   800
(c) Insurance expired during the year   1,400
(d) Depreciation for the year   900
(e) Accrued salaries, December 31   200

SOLUTION

P. Widmann Company
Work Sheet
Year Ending December 31, 19X2

Account Title	Trial Balance Dr.	Trial Balance Cr.	Adjustments Dr.	Adjustments Cr.	Income Statement Dr.	Income Statement Cr.	Balance Sheet Dr.	Balance Sheet Cr.
Cash	11,000						11,000	
Accounts Receivable	8,000						8,000	
Merchandise Inventory	34,100		(a) 32,800	(a) 34,100			32,800	
Supplies	2,300			(b) 1,500			800	
Prepaid Insurance	2,600			(c) 1,400			1,200	
Equipment	10,500						10,500	
Accumulated Deprec.		1,300		(d) 900				2,200
Accounts Payable		6,400						6,400
P. Widmann, Capital		31,400						31,400
P. Widmann, Drawing	8,000						8,000	
Sales		112,100				112,100		
Purchases	57,500				57,500			
Salaries Expense	11,000		(e) 200		11,200			
Rent Expense	3,600				3,600			
Misc. Expense	2,600				2,600			
	151,200	151,200						
Inc. & Exp. Summary			(a) 34,100	(a) 32,800	34,100	32,800		
Supplies Expense			(b) 1,500		1,500			
Insurance Expense			(c) 1,400		1,400			
Depreciation Expense			(d) 900		900			
Salaries Payable				(e) 200				200
			70,900	70,900	112,800	144,900	72,300	40,200
Net Income					32,100			32,100
					144,900	144,900	72,300	72,300

8.15. Based on the information in Problem 8.14, journalize the adjusting and closing entries.

SOLUTION

ADJUSTING ENTRIES

(a)	Merchandise Inventory	32,800	
	Expense and Income Summary		32,800
	Expense and Income Summary	34,100	
	Merchandise Inventory		34,100
(b)	Supplies Expense	1,500	
	Supplies		1,500
(c)	Insurance Expense	1,400	
	Prepaid Insurance		1,400
(d)	Depreciation Expense	900	
	Accumulated Depreciation		900
(e)	Salaries Expense	200	
	Salaries Payable		200

CLOSING ENTRIES

(a)	Sales	112,100	
	Expense and Income Summary		112,100
(b)	Expense and Income Summary	78,700	
	Purchases		57,500
	Salaries Expense		11,200
	Rent Expense		3,600
	Supplies Expense		1,500
	Insurance Expense		1,400
	Depreciation Expense		900
	Misc. Expense		2,600
(c)	Expense and Income Summary	32,100	
	P. Widmann, Capital		32,100
(d)	P. Widmann, Capital	8,000	
	P. Widmann, Drawing		8,000

8.16. Based on the information in Problem 8.14, prepare an income statement, capital statement, and balance sheet for 19X2.

P. Widmann Company		
Income Statement		
Year Ending December 31, 19X2		

P. Widmann Company		
Capital Statement		
Year Ending December 31, 19X2		

P. Widmann Company		
Balance Sheet		
December 31, 19X2		

SOLUTION

P. Widmann Company		
Income Statement		
Year Ending December 31, 19X2		
Sales		
Cost of Goods Sold		$112,100
Merchandise Inventory, Jan. 1	$34,100	
Purchases	57,500	
Goods Available for Sale	91,600	
Less: Merchandise Inventory, Dec. 31	32,800	
Cost of Goods Sold		58,800
Gross Profit		$53,300
Operating Expenses:		
Salaries Expense	11,200	
Rent Expense	3,600	
Supplies Expense	1,500	
Insurance Expense	1,400	
Depreciation Expense	900	
Misc. Expense	2,600	
Total Expenses		21,200
Net Income		32,100

P. Widmann Company		
Capital Statement		
Year Ending December 31, 19X2		
Capital, January 1, 19X2		$31,400
Net Income	$32,100	
Less Drawing	8,000	
Increase in Capital		24,100
Capital, December 31, 19X2		$55,500

P. Widmann Company		
Balance Sheet		
December 31, 19X2		
ASSETS		
Current Assets		
Cash	$11,000	
Accounts Receivable	8,000	
Merchandise Inventory	32,800	
Supplies	800	
Prepaid Insurance	1,200	
Total Current Assets		$53,800
Fixed Assets		
Equipment	$10,500	
Less Accumulated Depreciation	2,200	8,300
Total Assets		$62,100
LIABILITIES AND CAPITAL		
Current Liabilities		
Accounts Payable	$ 6,400	
Salaries Payable	200	
Total Current Liabilities		$ 6,600
Capital, December 31		55,500
Total Liabilities and Capital		$62,100

Chapter 9

Cash and Its Control

9.1 INTRODUCTION

In most firms transactions involving the receipt and disbursement of cash far outnumber any other kinds of transactions. Cash is, moreover, the most liquid asset and most subject to theft and fraud. It then becomes essential to have a system of accounting procedures and records that will maintain adequate control over cash.

9.2 CLASSIFICATION OF CASH

Roughly speaking, cash is anything that a bank will accept for deposit and will credit to the depositor's account. More precisely:

(1) *Cash is a medium of exchange.* Thus, such items as

      currency
      coin
      demand deposits
      savings deposits
      petty cash funds
      bank drafts
      cashier's checks
      personal checks
      money orders

qualify as cash. There are other items which are usually under the control of the company cashier, which are not cash, such as postage stamps, postdated checks, and IOUs. Postage is prepaid expense; postdated checks are receivables; and IOUs are receivables or prepaid expenses, depending on whether they are to be collected or applied against employee expenses.

(2) *Cash is immediately available for payment of current debts.* Certificates of deposit are temporary investments rather than cash, since they cannot be immediately withdrawn. (Technically, savings accounts may not be withdrawn without notice to the bank, but generally this requirement is not enforced; hence, savings deposits were listed above as cash.) Likewise, a sinking fund specifically established to pay bond requirements or a deposit with a manufacturer for purchase of equipment is not available to pay other current obligations and, therefore, is not cash. Such items are generally shown on the balance sheet as noncurrent assets, while cash is listed as a current asset.

9.3 CONTROLLING CASH RECEIPTS

In a very small business the owner-manager can maintain control through personal contact and supervision. This kind of direct intervention must, in a firm of any size, be replaced by a system of internal control, exercised through accounting reports and records. We have already encountered the guiding principle of internal control in Sec. 5.3; namely, the separation of duties. No person assigned to handle cash should, at the same time, be in a position to make entries in the records affecting his own activities.

The specific controls applied to cash receipts may be summarized as:

1. All receipts should be banked promptly.
2. Receipts from cash sales should be supported by sales tickets, cash register tapes, etc.
3. Accountability should be established each time cash is transferred.
4. Persons receiving cash should not make disbursements of cash, record cash transactions, or reconcile bank accounts.

9.4 CONTROLLING CASH DISBURSEMENTS

The main ideas here are that payments be made only by properly authorized persons, that equivalent value be received, and that documents adequately support the payment. Following are specific internal controls relating to cash disbursements.

1. All disbursements, except petty cash payments, should be made by prenumbered check.
2. Vouchers and supporting documents should be submitted for review when checks are signed.
3. Persons who sign checks should not have access to cash receipts, should not have custody of funds or record cash entries, and should not reconcile bank accounts.

It is seen that special procedures will be needed for petty cash; these will be treated in Sec. 9.8.

9.5 CONTROLLING CASH BALANCES

The basic principle of separation of duties is evident in the specific controls for cash balances:

1. Bank reconciliations should be prepared by persons who do not receive cash or sign checks.
2. Bank statements and paid checks should be received unopened by the person reconciling the account.
3. All cash funds on hand should be closely watched and surprise counts made at intervals.

If the rule of Sec. 9.3, requiring the banking of all cash receipts, is followed, then it is clear that the monthly bank statement can be made a powerful control over cash balances. Hence the importance of reconciling bank balances.

9.6 BANK STATEMENTS

CHECKS

A business opens a checking account to gain the privilege of placing its deposits in a safe place and the ability also to write checks. When an account is opened, each person who is authorized to write checks on that account must sign a signature card. The bank keeps the signature card on file and compares it when checks are submitted. The check becomes a written notice by the depositor directing the bank to deduct a specific sum of money from the checking account and to pay that amount to the person or company written on the check. A check involves three parties:

(1) **Drawer.** The one who writes the check.
(2) **Drawee.** The bank on which the check is drawn.
(3) **Payee.** The person or company to whom the check is to be paid.

Checks offer several advantages. The checkbook stubs provide a record of the cash paid out, while the cancelled checks provide proof that money has been paid to the person legally entitled to it. Also, the use of checks is the most convenient form of paying bills because checks can be sent safely through the mail. If a check is lost or stolen, the depositors can request the bank not to pay (a stop order).

ENDORSEMENTS

When a check is given to the bank for deposit, the depositor signs the check on the back to show that he or she accepts responsibility for the amount of that check. The depositor's signature is known as an endorsement. This endorsement transfers the ownership of the check and guarantees to the individual that the depositor will guarantee its payment. Different kinds of endorsements serve different needs.

(*1*) **Blank Endorsement.** This is an endorsement that consists only of the name of the endorser. Its disadvantage lies in the fact that a lost or stolen check with a blank endorsement may be cashed by the finder or thief. Therefore, this type of endorsement should not be used unless the depositor is at the bank ready to make a deposit (Fig. 9-1).

(*2*) **Endorsement in Full.** This type of endorsement states the check can be cashed or transferred only on the order of the person named in the endorsement (Fig. 9-2).

(*3*) **Restrictive Endorsement.** This type of endorsement limits the receiver of the check as to the use he or she can make of the funds collected. Usually this type of endorsement is done when checks are prepared for deposit (Fig. 9-3).

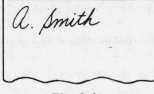

Fig. 9-1

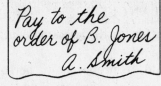

Fig. 9-2

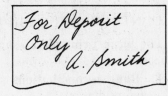

Fig. 9-3

9.7   RECONCILING THE BANK BALANCE

Each month, generally, the bank forwards to the depositor a statement of his account showing:

1. Beginning balance
2. Deposits made and other credits
3. Checks paid and other charges (debits)
4. Ending balance

Included in the envelope with the statement are the paid, or "canceled," checks and any other deductions or additions (debit or credit memoranda) to the account. A deduction may be a debit memorandum for bank service charges; an addition may be a credit memorandum for the proceeds of a note collected by the bank for the depositor.

Usually the balance of the bank statement and the balance of the depositor's account will not agree. To prove the accuracy of both records the reconciling differences have to be found and any necessary entries made. The reconciling items will fall into two broad groups: (1) those on the depositor's books but not recorded by the bank, and (2) those on the bank statement but not on the books.

ITEMS ON BOOKS BUT NOT ON BANK STATEMENT

Outstanding checks. These are checks issued by the depositor but not yet presented to the bank for payment. The total of these checks is to be *deducted* from the bank balance.

Deposits in transit. Cash receipts recorded by a company but too late to be deposited. The total of such deposits is to be *added* to the bank balance.

Bookkeeping errors. Errors in recording amounts of checks; for example, a transposition of figures. The item should be added to the bank balance if it was previously overstated on the books. If the item was previously understated on the books, the amount should be deducted.

ITEMS ON BANK STATEMENT BUT NOT ON BOOKS

Service charges. The bank generally deducts amounts for bank services. The exact amount is usually not known by the depositor until he receives the statement. The amount should be deducted from the book balance.

NSF (not sufficient funds) checks. Checks which have been deposited but cannot be collected because of insufficient funds in the account of the drawer of the check. The bank then issues a debit memorandum charging the depositor's account. The amount should be deducted from the book balance.

Collections. The bank collects notes and other items for a small fee. The bank then adds the proceeds to the account and issues a credit memorandum to the depositor. Often there are unrecorded amounts at the end of the month. These amounts should be added to the book balance.

Bank errors. Bank errors should not be entered on the books. They should be brought to the attention of the bank and corrected by the bank. Journal entries should be made for any adjustments to the book accounts. The statement used in accounting for the differences between the bank balance and the depositor's balance is known as a *bank reconciliation.*

EXAMPLE 1.

The following information was available when the John Hennessey Company began to reconcile its bank balance on May 31, 19X2: Balance per depositor's books, $1,640; Balance per bank statement, $2,420; Deposit in transit, $150; Checks outstanding—#650, $300 and #654, $240; Collection of $400 note plus interest of $8, $408; Collection fee for note, $10; Bank service charge, $8.

John Hennessey Company
Bank Reconciliation
May 31, 19X2

Balance per bank		$2,420	Balance per books		$1,640
Add: Deposit in transit		150	Add: Proceeds of note		408
		$2,570			$2,048
Less:			Less:		
Outstanding checks			Collection fee	$10	
#650	$300		Service charge	8	
#654	240	540			18
Adjusted balance		$2,030	Adjusted balance		$2,030

Only reconciling items in the depositor's section (right side above) are to be recorded on the books. The reconciling items in the bank section (left side above) have already been recorded on the books and merely have not yet reached the bank. They will normally be included in the next bank statement.

To complete the reconcilement, the following two journal entries will be needed.

Entry 1	Cash	408	
	Notes Receivable		400
	Interest Income		8
Entry 2	Service Charge Expense	18	
	Cash		18

9.8 PETTY CASH

Funds spent through the cash disbursements journal take the form of checks issued in payment of various liabilities. In addition, a business will have many expenditures of small amounts for which it is not practical to issue checks. Examples are postage, parcel post, delivery expense, and miscellaneous small items, which are paid for in cash through a petty cash fund.

Under the so-called *imprest system* a fund is established for a fixed petty cash amount, and this fund is periodically reimbursed by a single check for amounts expended. The steps in setting up and maintaining the petty cash fund are as follows:

(1) An estimate is made of the total of the small amounts likely to be disbursed over a short period, usually a month. A check is drawn for the estimated total and put into the fund. The only time an entry is made in the petty cash account is for the initial establishment of the fund, unless at some later time it is determined that this fund must be increased or decreased.

EXAMPLE 2.

Petty Cash	40		
Cash		40	

(2) The individual in charge of petty cash usually keeps the money in a locked box along with petty cash vouchers, such as illustrated below. The petty cash voucher, when signed by the recipient, acts as a receipt and provides information concerning the transaction. As each payment is made, the voucher is entered in the petty cash record and placed with the balance of money in the petty cash box.

PETTY CASH VOUCHER

No._____ Date _____

Paid To _____ Amount _____

Reason _____

Received By _____

EXAMPLE 3.

PETTY CASH RECORD

Date	Explanation	Voucher	Receipts	Payments	Postage	Del.	Sundry
Jan. 1	Established		$40.00				
2	Postage on Sales	1		$ 4.50	$ 4.50		
4	Telegram	2		4.00	4.00		
8	Taxi Fare	3		5.00		$5.00	
10	Coffee for Overtime	4		2.00			$ 2.00
15	Stamps	5		8.00	8.00		
26	Cleaning Windows	6		8.00			8.00
			$40.00	$31.50	$16.50	$5.00	$10.00
	Bal.			8.50			
			$40.00	$40.00			
Feb . 1	Bal.		$ 8.50				
	Replenished Fund		$31.50				

EXAMPLE 4.

The petty cash fund established in Example 2 might yield the following entries for the first month:

Postage Expense	16.50	
Delivery Expense	5.00	
Miscellaneous General Expense	10.00	
Cash		31.50

(3) Proof of petty cash is obtained by counting the currency and adding the amount of all the vouchers in the cash box. The total should agree with the amount in the ledger for the petty cash fund. If it does not, the entry in the cash disbursements journal recording the reimbursement of the petty cash fund will have to include an account known as Cash Short and Over. A cash shortage is debited, a cash overage is credited, to this account. Cash Short and Over is closed out at the end of the year into the expense and income account and is treated as a general expense (if a debit balance) or miscellaneous income (if a credit balance).

Summary

(1) The most liquid asset and also the one most subject to theft and fraud is _____ .

(2) All disbursements, except petty cash payments, should be made by _____ .

(3) A written notice by a depositor instructing his bank to deduct a specific sum from his account and to pay it to the person assigned is known as a _____ .

(4) A check involves three parties: the _____ who writes the check; the _____ , the bank on which it is drawn; and the _____ , the person to whom it is to be paid.

(5) The signature on back of a check showing that the individual accepts responsibility for that amount is known as an _____ .

(6) The _____ endorsement poses the greatest potential loss in the event of a lost or stolen check.

(7) A bank service charge is evidenced by a _____ .

(8) A check which has been deposited but cannot be collected because of insufficient funds is labeled _____ by the bank and is deducted from the _____ balance.

(9) Under the _____ , a fund is established for a fixed petty cash amount which is reimbursed by a single check for amounts expended.

(10) For small differences in the petty cash account a _____ account is generally used.

Answers: (1) cash; (2) prenumbered check; (3) check; (4) drawer, drawee, payee; (5) endorsement; (6) blank; (7) debit memorandum; (8) NSF, book; (9) imprest system; (10) Cash Short and Over

Solved Problems

9.1. Name five sources of cash receipts.

SOLUTION

The following list contains the principal sources (any five sources could be named):

1. Sales of goods and services for cash.
2. Collections of accounts and notes from customers.
3. Renting of property.
4. Loans from individuals.
5. Loans from banks.
6. Customers' notes discounted.
7. New bonds issued.
8. New capital stock issued.
9. Sale of scrap, waste, and by-products.
10. Disposal of equipment.
11. Sale of other assets.

9.2. Name five types of cash disbursements.

SOLUTION

Any five of the following types could be named:

1. Purchase of goods.
2. Purchase of supplies.
3. Payment of wages and salaries.
4. Purchase of equipment.
5. Payment of other operating expenses.
6. Purchase of securities.
7. Retirement of bank loans.
8. Retirement of stocks and bonds.
9. Miscellaneous payments (dividend payments, etc.).

9.3. Answer the following questions about the check shown below. (*a*) Who is the Drawer? (*b*) Who is the Drawee? (*c*) Who is the Payee?

No. 136

January 25, 19 X2

70-4217 / 711

Pay to the Order of *Jason Sloane* $ 75 00/100

Seventy-five and 00/100 — Dollars

WHITESIDE COUNTY BANK
Rock Falls, Illinois   61071

B. Smith

⑈0711⑈4217⑈ 701⑈8702⑈

SOLUTION

(*a*) B. Smith   (*b*) Whiteside County Bank   (*c*) Jason Sloane

9.4. (a) Assume J. Lerner, banking at 1st City Bank, wishes a full endorsement for A. Levy. Prepare a full endorsement.

(b) Prepare a blank endorsement.

(c) Prepare a restrictive endorsement for a deposit.

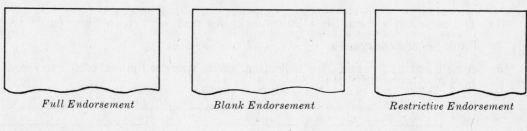

| Full Endorsement | Blank Endorsement | Restrictive Endorsement |

SOLUTION

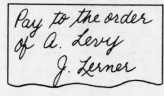 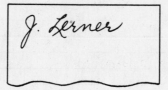 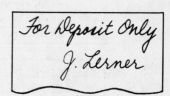

| Full Endorsement | Blank Endorsement | Restrictive Endorsement |

9.5. Indicate for Items 1-8 below, in order to produce equal adjusted balances for Blake Company, whether they should be:

    (a)   added to the bank statement balance

    (b)   deducted from the bank statement balance

    (c)   added to the depositor's balance

    (d)   deducted from the depositor's balance

    (e)   exempted from the bank reconciliation statement.

1. Statement includes a credit memorandum, $402, representing the collection of the proceeds of a note left at the bank.

2. A credit memorandum representing the proceeds of a loan, $4,200, made to Blake Company by the bank.

3. Deposits in transit totaled $3,000.

4. Seven outstanding checks totaling $9,000 were not recorded on the statement.

5. A $150 customer's check that Blake Company had deposited was returned with "not sufficient funds" stamped across the face.

6. The bank erroneously charged someone else's check, $200, against Blake's account.

7. Blake Company was incorrectly credited with the deposit of $240 made by another depositor.

8. A $96 check was erroneously recorded in Blake's check stubs as $69.

SOLUTION

1.	(c)	5.	(d)
2.	(c)	6.	(a)
3.	(a)	7.	(b)
4.	(b)	8.	(d)

9.6. Of the following transactions involving the bank reconciliation statement, which ones necessitate an adjusting entry on the depositor's books?

1. Outstanding checks of $3,000 did not appear on the bank statement.

2. The last two days' deposited receipts, $2,850, did not appear on the bank statement.

3. The depositor's check for $120 for supplies was written in his records as $210.

4. Bank service charge, $4.

5. A note left at the bank for collection, $822, was paid and credited to the depositor's account.

SOLUTION

3.	*Cash*	90	
	Supplies		90
4.	*Bank Service Charge*	4	
	Cash		4
5.	*Cash*	822	
	Notes Receivable		822

9.7. Using the following data, reconcile the bank account of the Kemper Motor Company.

> Bank balance, $7,780.
>
> Depositor's balance, $6,500.
>
> Note collected by bank, $1,000, plus interest of $30;
> a collection charge of $10 was made by the bank.
>
> Outstanding checks, $410.
>
> Deposit in transit, $150.

SOLUTION

Balance per Kemper's books		$6,500	*Balance per bank statement*		$7,780
Add: Note collected by bank			*Add: Deposit in transit*		150
Note	$1,000				$7,930
Interest	30	1,030	*Less:*		
		$7,530	*Outstanding checks*		410
Less: Collection charge		10			
Adjusted balance		$7,520	*Adjusted balance*		$7,520

9.8. Prepare the adjusting entries needed for Problem 9.7.

	Dr.	Cr.

SOLUTION

	Dr.	Cr.
Cash	1,030	
Notes Receivable		1,000
Interest Income		30
Bank Service Charge	10	
Cash		10

9.9. Based on the following information, (*a*) prepare a bank reconciliation and (*b*) journalize the adjusting entries.

1. Bank balance per statement, $7,349.46.
2. Cash account balance, $5,432.76.
3. Check outstanding, $2,131.85.
4. Deposit in transit not recorded by bank, $1,243.15.
5. Note collected by bank, $1,015, including $15 interest.
6. A check for $46 for supplies was erroneously entered as $64.
7. Service charges not entered, $5.

SOLUTION

(*a*)   ***Bank Reconciliation***

Balance per bank statement	$7,349.46	
Add: Deposit in transit	1,243.15	
	$8,592.61	
Less: Outstanding check	2,131.85	
Adjusted balance	$6,460.76	
Balance per depositor's books	$5,432.76	
Add: Note collected by bank		
Note $1,000		
Interest 15	1,015.00	
Error in recording check	18.00	
	$6,465.76	
Less: Service charge	5.00	
	$6,460.76	

(*b*)   **ADJUSTING ENTRIES**

	Dr.	Cr.
Cash	1,033	
Notes Receivable		1,000
Interest Income		15
Supplies		18
Bank Service Charge	5	
Cash		5

9.10. Correct the following incorrect bank reconciliation,

Kaney Company
Bank Reconciliation
December 31, 19X2

Balance per depositor's books	$7,250	
Add:		
Note collected by bank including interest	515	
Deposit in transit	1,200	
Bank error charging Kane's check to Kaney account	860	
Total		$9,825
Deduct:		
Check from customer of Kaney's deposited and returned by bank as NSF	$ 150	
Service charge	5	
Check for $250 written in Kaney's ledger and checkbook stubs as $150	100	
Outstanding checks	1,100	1,355
		$8,470
Less: Unexplained difference		1,920
Balance per bank statement		$6,550

SOLUTION

Kaney Company
Bank Reconciliation
December 31, 19X2

Balance per depositor's books		$7,250	Balance per bank statement		$6,550
Add: Note collected by bank		515	Add: Deposit in transit		1,200
		$7,765	Error		860
Less:					$8,610
NSF check	$150				
Bank service charge	5		Less:		
Error	100	255	Outstanding checks		1,100
Adjusted balance		$7,510	Adjusted balance		$7,510

9.11. Prepare the adjusting entries needed for Problem 9.10.

SOLUTION

Cash	515	
Notes Receivable		515
Service Charge Expense	5	
Accounts Receivable	150	
Supplies	100	
Cash		255

9.12. Based on the following information, prepare a reconciliation of the Armando Company's bank account at December 31, 19X2.

(1)	Balance per bank statement, December 31, 19X2	$88,489.12
(2)	Balance per books, December 31, 19X2	58,983.46
(3)	Outstanding checks, December 31, 19X2	32,108.42
(4)	Receipts of December 31, 19X2, deposited January 2, 19X3	5,317.20
(5)	Service charge for November, 19X2 per bank memorandum of December 15, 19X2	3.85
(6)	Proceeds of bank loan, December 15, 19X2, omitted from company books	9,875.00
(7)	Deposit of December 23, 19X2, omitted from bank statement	2,892.41
(8)	Check of Rome Products Company charged back by bank on December 22, 19X2, for absence of counter-signature. No entry on the books having been made for the charge-back	417.50

(9) Error on bank statement in entering deposit of December 16, 19X2

Current amount	$3,182.40	
Entered in statement	3,181.40	1.00

(10)	Check #3917 of Arandon Manufacturing Company charged by bank in error to company's account	2,690.00

(11) Proceeds of note of J. Somers & Company, collected by bank on December 10, 19X2, not entered in cash book:

Principal	$2,000.00	
Interest	20.00	
	$2,020.00	
Less: collection charge	5.00	2,015.00

(12)	Erroneous debit memorandum of December 23, 19X2, to charge company's account with settlement of bank loan, which was paid by check #8714 on same date	5,000.00

(13) Error on bank statement in entering deposit of
      December 4, 19X2:
                  Entered as $4,817.10
                  Correct amount   4,807.10   10.00

(14) Deposit of Arandon Manufacturing Company of
      December 6, 19X2, credited in error to this com-
      pany   1,819.20

SOLUTION

Bank Statement Balance		$88,489.12
Add:		
Deposit in transit	$ 5,317.20	
Error in deposit	2,892.41	
Dec. 16 deposit error	1.00	
Arandon Manufacturing Co. error	2,690.00	
Debit memorandum of Dec. 23	5,000.00	15,900.61
		$104,389.73
Deduct:		
Outstanding checks	32,108.42	
Dec. 4 error in deposit	10.00	
Arandon Manufacturing Co. deposit in error	1,819.20	33,937.62
Adjusted balance		$70,452.11
		58,983.46
Checkbook balance		
Add:		
Bank loan proceeds	9,875.00	
Loan collection Principal $2,000		
Interest 20	2,020.00	11,895.00
		$70,878.46
Deduct:		
Service charge	3.85	
Collection charge	5.00	
Rome Co. (charge back)	417.50	426.35
Adjusted balance		$70,452.11

9.13. What adjusting entries are needed to record the above data?

SOLUTION

Cash	*11,895.00*	
Notes Payable		*9,875.00*
Notes Receivable, J. Somers & Co.		*2,000.00*
Interest Income		*20.00*
Bank Service Charge	*8.85*	
Accounts Receivable, Rome Products. Co.	*417.50*	
Cash		*426.35*

9.14. Transactions for the Eagan Company for the month of January, pertaining to the establishment of a petty cash fund, were as follows:

January 1: Established an imprest petty cash fund of $50

January 31: Box contained $6 cash and paid vouchers for transportation, $14; freight, $16; charity, $4; office supplies, $6; miscellaneous expense, $4

What are the journal entries necessary to record the petty cash information?

SOLUTION

Petty Cash	50	
Cash		50
Transportation Expense	14	
Freight Expense	16	
Charity Expense	4	
Office Supplies Expense	6	
Miscellaneous Expense	4	
Cash		44

9.15. If in Problem 9.14 the cash on hand was $9, record the January 31 reimbursement.

SOLUTION

Transportation Expense	14	
Freight Expense	16	
Charity Expense	4	
Office Supplies Expense	6	
Miscellaneous Expense	4	
Cash		41
Cash Short and Over		3

9.16. If in Problem 9.14 the cash on hand was only $2, record the January 31 reimburse-
ment.   What will happen to the Cash Short and Over account?

SOLUTION

Transportation Expense	14	
Freight Expense	16	
Charity Expense	4	
Office Supplies Expense	6	
Miscellaneous Expense	4	
Cash Short and Over	4	
Cash		48

At the end of the period the balance of the Cash Short and Over account is closed out to the Expense
and Summary account.

9.17. At the close of the day, the total cash sales as determined by the sales registers were
$1,480.   However, the total cash receipts were only $1,472.   The error cannot be located at the present time.   What entry should be made to record the cash sales for
the day?

SOLUTION

Cash	1,472	
Cash Short and Over	8	
Sales		1,480

Chapter 10

Merchandise Inventory

10.1 INTRODUCTION

In a mercantile business, inventory is merchandise that is held for resale. As such, it will ordinarily be converted into cash in less than a year and is thus a current asset. In a manufacturing business, there will usually be inventories of raw materials and goods in process in addition to an inventory of finished goods.

10.2 PERIODIC AND PERPETUAL METHODS OF INVENTORY

Under the *periodic method,* inventory is physically counted at regular intervals (annually, quarterly, or monthly). When this system is used, credits are made to the inventory account or to Purchases not as each sale is made, but rather in total at the end of the inventory period.

The *perpetual method* is generally used when units are of relatively high value. Running balances by unit and by cost are maintained for units purchased and sold. Individual receipts of goods are debited to the inventory account and individual sales are credited to this account. At the end of the accounting period the cost of goods sold can be determined by adding the costs of the individual items sold.

Of the two methods, the periodic system is the more common in retail businesses such as grocery stores, hardware stores, etc., which sell a wide variety of items of low unit cost. The expense of maintaining records of individual costs for such low-priced items would be prohibitive. The balance of this chapter will be concerned with the periodic system only.

10.3 DETERMINING INVENTORY

When, as is often the case in mercantile businesses, inventory consists of identical articles purchased at different times and at different unit prices, the problem arises as to how to assign a cost to each inventory item. This problem is commonly resolved by use of one or another of five methods, which will be individually described below. In all examples given, the following data will be used:

Date	Type	Units	Unit Cost	Total Amount
Jan. 1	Inventory	100	$ 6.00	$ 600
Feb. 5	Purchases	150	8.00	1,200
April 10	Purchases	200	9.00	1,800
Sept. 25	Purchases	250	10.00	2,500
		700		Available for Sale $6,100

It will also be assumed that a physical inventory on December 31 shows 320 units on hand.

Method 1.   First-In-First-Out (FIFO).   Here the assumption is that the goods are sold in the order in which they were received.

EXAMPLE 1.

Under FIFO, goods on hand are considered to be those most lately received.   Therefore the 320 units on hand at the end of the year would be costed as follows:

Most recent purchase (Sept. 25):	250 units @ $10.00 =	$2,500
Next purchase (April 10):	70 units @ 9.00 =	630
Total units	320 Total cost	$3,130

It should be emphasized that, as a method of assigning *costs,* FIFO may be used regardless of the actual, physical flow of merchandise.   Indeed, we might say that FIFO really stands for First-Price-In-First-Price-Out.

Method 2.   Last-In-First-Out (LIFO).   Under this method, it is assumed that goods are sold in reverse order of receipt.   Hence, it is the most recent costs which are applied against income.

EXAMPLE 2.

Under LIFO, the inventory at the end of the period is considered to be merchandise purchased in the first part of the period.   The cost of the 320 units on hand would be calculated as:

Earliest purchase (Jan.1):	100 units @ $6.00 =	$ 600
Next purchase (Feb. 5):	150 units @ 8.00 =	1,200
Next purchase (April 10):	70 units @ 9.00 =	630
Total units	320 Total cost	$2,430

LIFO has several advantages over FIFO:

1.   LIFO matches the most recent costs against current sales.   In a rising cost market, net income under LIFO would be smaller, thus producing a smaller tax.

2.   LIFO permits a more realistic measurement of realized income because it matches current costs and current revenues.   This method is widely used for tax purposes.

Method 3.   Weighted Average.   In this method a weighted average unit cost is obtained by dividing the total cost of goods available for sale during the inventory period by the total number of units of these goods.   This average unit price is used for both the inventory and cost of goods sold.   An advantage of the weighted average method is that it assigns cost equitably between ending inventory and goods sold.

EXAMPLE 3.

According to the data, the 700 units of available goods cost a total of $6,100.   Therefore:

$$\$6,100 \div 700 = \$8.71$$
(goods)   (units)   (unit cost)

and

$$\$8.71 \times 320 = \$2,787$$
(unit cost)   (on hand)   (ending inventory)

In Example 4 below, we compare the results of the FIFO, LIFO, and weighted average methods, with regard to both ending inventory and cost of goods sold.   Since the two amounts are related through the equation

GOODS AVAILABLE FOR SALE   −   ENDING INVENTORY   =   COST OF GOODS SOLD it is seen that if the ending inventory is *overstated*, the cost of goods sold will be *understated* and net profit *overstated*. On the other hand, if inventory is *understated*, then cost of goods sold will be *overstated* and net profit *understated*. Clearly, the method chosen for inventory computation can have a marked effect on the profit of the firm. There is no *one* method that is the best for all firms, but careful consideration of the following factors will be helpful in making the decision: (1) the effect upon the income statement and balance sheet, (2) the effect upon taxable income, (3) the effect upon the selling price.

EXAMPLE 4.

	First-In-First-Out	Last-In-First-Out	Weighted Average
Goods Available For Sale	$6,100	$6,100	$6,100
Ending Inventory, Dec. 31	3,130	2,430	2,787
Cost of Goods Sold	$2,970	$3,670	$3,313

Method 4. Specific Identification. If the units of inventory can be traced to invoices, the specific identification method may be used to assign to the ending inventory its actual cost. This method is commonly applied where the value of the units is high.

EXAMPLE 5.

Purchase invoice #2146, April 10:	10 units @ $ 90 =	$ 900	
Purchase invoice #2184, Sept. 25:	22 units @ 100 =	2,200	
Total units	32	Total cost	$3,100

Method 5. Lower of Cost or Market. A conservative view is that unrealized profit should not be recorded in accounting. If an asset such as inventory increases in value, there should be no formal record of the fact until the actual gain has been realized through sale. When an asset declines in value, it is important to recognize this as an expense or a loss even though the asset has not yet been sold. One way of keeping the inventory valuation conservatively low is to choose as the effective unit cost the *smaller of* (a) the unit cost as computed by FIFO or by weighted average and (b) the market price (i.e., the current unit replacement cost). This is the so-called "cost or market" method; it need not be used when costs are calculated by LIFO.

EXAMPLE 6.

Assume a market price of $9.00 on December 31. If FIFO is used (see Example 1), the unit cost of the inventory is $3,130 \div 320 = \$9.78$. Since this exceeds the market price, the "cost or market" method would assign $9.00 as the unit cost and would produce a valuation of $320 \times \$9.00 = \$2,880$. However, the weighted average unit cost of $8.71 (see Example 3) is lower than the market price, so that "cost or market" would produce the same valuation obtained in Example 3.

One can also apply "cost or market" when inventory consists of separate lots:

Lot	Quantity	Unit Cost	Unit Market Price	Lower of Cost or Market
A	150 units	$ 6.00	$ 6.50	$ 900 (cost)
B	250 units	7.00	9.00	1,750 (cost)
C	400 units	9.00	8.00	3,200 (market)
D	500 units	10.00	12.00	5,000 (cost)
				Inventory $10,850

Retail Method. An entirely different approach to costing inventory is the *retail method*. This method of periodic inventory costing is used mostly by department stores and is based on the relationship between merchandise available for sale and the retail price of the same merchandise. It is determined by subtracting retail sales from the retail price of goods available for that period. This retail inventory is changed to cost by means of the ratio of cost to selling price.

EXAMPLE 7.

	Cost	Retail
Merchandise Inventory, December 1	$25,000	$35,000
Purchases	42,200	61,000
Goods Available for Sale	$67,200	$96,000
Sales for December		81,000
Merchandise Inventory, December 31, at retail		$15,000
Merchandise Inventory, December 31, at cost	$10,500*	

Ratio:
$$\frac{67,200 \text{ Cost}}{96,000 \text{ Retail}} = 70\%$$

$$* \; \$15,000 \times 70\% = \$10,500$$

Two advantages of this system are apparent, it:

(1) Provides merchandise figures for interim statements.

(2) Aids in disclosing inventory shortages.

10.4 OTHER MERCHANDISING ACCOUNTS

TRANSPORTATION-IN

The cost of transportation-in, such as freight or trucking, is part of the cost of merchandise. Where the purchaser pays the transportation-in, a separate account should be maintained. The entry to record the payment of transportation-in is as follows:

Transportation-In	*1,000*	
Accounts Payable (or Cash)		*1,000*

Transportation-In is combined with Purchases in the income statement as follows:

Partial Income Statement
Year Ended December 31, 19X2

Sales			*$45,000*
Cost of Goods Sold			
Inventory, January 1		*$10,000*	
Purchases	*$25,000*		
Transportation-In	*1,000*	*26,000*	
Goods Available for Sale		*$36,000*	
Inventory, December 31		*12,000*	
Cost of Goods Sold			*24,000*
Gross Profit on Sales			*$21,000*

PURCHASE RETURNS AND ALLOWANCES

Sometimes goods purchased may be found to be unsatisfactory. The entire shipment may be returned to the vendor or the vendor may allow a reduction in price without the return of the goods. A return of $600 of goods to the vendor is shown as follows.

Accounts Payable	*600*	
Purchase Returns and Allowances		*600*

In the income statement, Purchase Returns and Allowances would be shown as follows:

Sales			$45,000
Cost of Goods Sold			
Inventory, January 1		$10,000	
Purchases	$25,000		
Less: Purchase Returns and Allowances	600		
Net Purchases	$24,400		
Transportation-In	1,000	25,400	
Goods Available for Sale		$35,400	
Inventory, December 31		12,000	
Cost of Goods Sold			23,400
Gross Profit on Sales			$21,600

Summary

(1) When inventory is physically counted at the end of an accounting period, we have the _____PERIODIC_____ method.

(2) The inventory method used when units are generally of high value is the PERPETUAL _____ method.

(3) The _____PERIODIC_____ inventory method is most commonly used in retail establishments.

(4) A method of inventory valuation based on the concept that the goods are sold in the order in which received is known as _____FIFO_____ .

(5) The valuation of inventory based upon the concept that the most recent costs incurred should be charged against income is known as _____LIFO_____ .

(6) In a rising market, net income under _____LIFO_____ would be smaller, thus producing a smaller tax.

(7) The inventory method based on the concept that the unit cost of merchandise sold is the average of all expenditures for inventory is known as _____WEIGHTED AVG._____ .

(8) A conservative valuation system which can be used with FIFO or the weighted average method, and is designed to yield the lowest inventory valuation, is known as LOWER OF COST OR MKT .

(9) The cost of transportation-in is considered a part of the cost of _____MERCHANDISE_____ .

(10) The account Transportation-In is combined with _____PURCHASES_____ in the income statement.

Answers:　(1) periodic; (2) perpetual; (3) periodic; (4) First-In-First-Out (FIFO); (5) Last-In-First-Out (LIFO); (6) LIFO; (7) Weighted Average; (8) Lower of Cost or Market; (9) Merchandise; (10) Purchases.

Solved Problems

10.1. The inventory information of product A is given below:

Jan. 1	Inventory	12 units	$15.00
Feb. 16	Purchase	8 units	16.00
Mar. 4	Purchase	15 units	18.00
Oct. 15	Purchase	10 units	20.00

After taking a physical count, we find we have 14 units on hand. Determine the ending inventory cost by the First-In-First-Out method.

SOLUTION

$$
\begin{array}{lrcl}
\text{Most recent purchase (Oct. 15):} & 10 \text{ units @ } \$20 & = & \$200 \\
\text{Next most recent (Mar. 4):} & \underline{4} \text{ units @ } 18 & = & \underline{72} \\
& \text{Total units } \underline{14} & \text{Total Cost} & \underline{\$272}
\end{array}
$$

10.2. Based on the information in Problem 10.1, determine the ending inventory cost by the Last-In-First-Out method.

SOLUTION

$$
\begin{array}{lrcl}
\text{Earliest cost (Inv.):} & 12 \text{ units @ } \$15 & = & \$180 \\
\text{Next earliest (Feb. 16):} & \underline{2} \text{ units @ } 16 & = & \underline{32} \\
& \text{Total units } \underline{14} & \text{Total Cost} & \underline{\$212}
\end{array}
$$

10.3. Based on the information in Problem 10.1, determine the ending inventory cost by the Weighted Average method.

SOLUTION

$$
\begin{array}{lrcl}
\text{Jan. 1:} & 12 \text{ units @ } \$15 & = & \$180 \\
\text{Feb. 16:} & 8 \text{ units @ } 16 & = & 128 \\
\text{Mar. 4:} & 15 \text{ units @ } 18 & = & 270 \\
\text{Oct. 15} & \underline{10} \text{ units @ } 20 & = & \underline{200} \\
& \text{Total units } \underline{45} \quad \text{Total Cost} & & \$778. \\
& \text{Total units } \underline{14} \quad \text{Total Cost} & & \$242.06
\end{array}
$$

The weighted average cost per unit is thus $\$778 \div 45 = \$17.29$, so that the total cost of the 14 units on hand is $\$17.29 \times 14 = \$242.06$.

10.4. Based upon the data below, determine the value of the inventory at the lower of cost or market by completing the table.

Item	Units	Unit Cost	Market Value
A	100	$1.00	$1.50
B	150	4.00	4.50
C	200	6.00	5.00
D	250	8.00	7.00

Item	Units	Basis	Lower of Cost or Market
A	100		
B	150		
C	200		
D	250		

Value of Inventory

SOLUTION

Item	Units	Basis	Lower of Cost or Market
A	100	$1.00	$ 100
B	150	4.00	600
C	200	5.00	1,000
D	250	7.00	1,750

Value of Inventory $3,450

10.5. The beginning inventory and various purchases of product B were as follows:

$$
\begin{array}{llrl}
\text{Jan. 1} & \text{Balance} & 8 \text{ units @ } & \$10.00 \\
\text{Mar. 5} & \text{Purchase} & 12 \text{ units @ } & 11.00 \\
\text{June 9} & \text{Purchase} & 16 \text{ units @ } & 12.00 \\
\text{Aug. 20} & \text{Purchase} & 15 \text{ units @ } & 13.00 \\
\text{Nov. 1} & \text{Purchase} & 18 \text{ units @ } & 14.00
\end{array}
$$

An inventory count under the periodic system disclosed that 30 units of product B were on hand. Determine the ending inventory cost by (a) First-In-First-Out; (b) Last-In-First-Out; (c) Weighted Average.

SOLUTION

(a)

Most recent purchase (Nov. 1)	18 units @ $14 =	$252
Next most recent (Aug. 20)	12 units @ $13 =	156
Total units	30 Total Cost	$408

(b)

Earliest Cost (Jan. 1)	8 units @ $10 =	$ 80
Next earliest (Mar. 5)	12 units @ 11 =	132
Next earliest (June 9)	10 units @ 12 =	120
Total units	30 Total Cost	$332

(c)

	8 units @ $10 =	$ 80
	12 units @ 11 =	132
	16 units @ 12 =	192
	15 units @ 13 =	195
	18 units @ 14 =	252
Total units	69 Total Cost	$851
Total units	30 Total Cost	$369.90

The weighted average cost per unit is $851 ÷ 69 = $12.33. The cost of 30 units on hand is calculated as $12.33 × 30 = $369.90.

10.6. Determine by the retail method the estimated cost of the December 31 inventory.

	Cost	Retail
December 1, Inventory	$280,000	$400,000
Dec. 1 — 31 Purchases	110,000	180,000
Goods Available for Sale	$390,000	$580,000
Sales for December		340,000

SOLUTION

	Cost	Retail
Dec. 1, Inventory	$280,000	$400,000
Dec. 1 – 31 Purchases	110,000	180,000
Goods Available for Sale	$390,000	580,000
Sales for month		340,000
Dec. 31 Inventory at Retail		$240,000
Inventory at estimated cost		
($240,000 × 67%*)	$160,800	

*Cost ratio 67% ($390,000 ÷ $580,000)

10.7. Estimate the cost of inventory of May 31 by the retail method.

	Cost	Retail
May 1 Merchandise	$18,000	$24,000
May Purchases	34,000	41,000
Sales for May		37,000

SOLUTION

	Cost	Retail
May 1 Merchandise	$18,000	$24,000
May Purchases	34,000	41,000
Goods Available for Sale	$52,000	$65,000
$52,000 ÷ 65,000 = 80% ratio		
Sales for May		37,000
May 31 inventory at retail		$28,000
May 31 inventory at estimated cost	$22,400*	

*($28,000 × 80%)

10.8. Prepare an income statement using the following accounts:

Merchandise Inventory Jan. 1, 19X2	$ 21,000
Merchandise Inventory Dec. 31, 19X2	24,000
Purchases	62,000
Sales	103,000
Transportation-In	2,000
Total Selling Expenses	15,500
Total General Expenses	22,400
Sales Returns	3,000

(handwritten income statement — student's work)

Income Statement

Sales		103,000
Less Sales Returns		3,000
Net Sales		100,000
Cost of Goods Sold		
Merchandise Inventory Jan 1	21,000	
Purchases 62,000		
Transportation In 2,000	64,000	
Goods Available for sale	85,000	
Less: Merchandise Inventory Dec 31	24,000	
Cost of Good Sold		61,000
Gross Profit		39,000
Expenses		
Total Selling Expense	15,500	
Total General Expense	22,400	
Total Expenses		37,900
Net Profit		1,100

SOLUTION

Income Statement

Sales		$103,000
Less: Sales Returns		3,000
Net Sales		$100,000
Cost of Goods Sold		
Merchandise Inventory, Jan. 1	$21,000	
Purchases	$62,000	
Add: Transportation-In	2,000	64,000
Goods Available for Sale		$85,000
Less: Merchandise Inventory, Dec. 31		24,000
Cost of Goods Sold		61,000
Gross Profit		$ 39,000
Expenses		
Total Selling Expenses		15,500
Total General Expenses		22,400
Total Expenses		37,900
Net Profit		$ 1,100

10.9. Given the accounts below, prepare the income statement for the Blasberg Company as of December 31, 19X2.

Sales	$86,400
Sales Returns	1,200
Purchases	59,700
Purchase Returns	650
Sales Salaries	14,700
Advertising Expense	2,100
Depreciation Expense, Delivery Equipment	900
Store Supplies Expense	650
Insurance Expense	3,200
Miscellaneous Selling Expense	590
Tax Expense	2,440
Office Supplies Expense	750
Inventory, January 1, 19X2	36,240
Inventory, December 31, 19X2	41,630

Blasberg Company
Income Statement
Year Ended December 31, 19X2

Sales		86,400
Less Sales Returns		1,200
Net Sales		85,200
Cost of Goods Sold		
Inventory, January 1	36,240	
Purchases 59700		
Purchase Returns 650	59,050	
Goods Available for sale	95,290	
Less Inventory, Dec 31	41,630	
Cost of Goods Sold		53,660
Gross Profit		31,540
Operating Expenses		
Selling Expenses		
Sales Salaries 14,700		
Advertising Expense 2100		
Dep. Exp., Delivery Expense 900		
Store Supplies Exp 650		
Insurance Exp. 3200		
Misc. Selling Exp. 590		
Total Selling Exp.	22,140	
General Expenses		
Tax Exp 2440		
Office Supplies Exp 750		
Total Gens Exp.	3,190	
Total Operating Exp		25,330
Net Profit		6,210.00

SOLUTION

Blasberg Company		
Income Statement		
Year Ended December 31, 19X2		
Sales Income	$86,400	
Sales Returns	1,200	
Net Sales		$85,200
Cost of Goods Sold		
Merchandise Inventory, January 1	$36,240	
Purchases	$59,700	
Purchase Returns	650	59,050
Goods Available for Sale		$95,290
Merchandise Inventory, December 31		41,630
Cost of Goods Sold		53,660
Gross Profit		$31,540
Operating Expenses		
Selling Expenses		
Sales Salaries	$14,700	
Advertising Expense	2,100	
Depreciation Expense, Delivery Equipment	900	
Store Supplies Expense	650	
Insurance Expense	3,200	
Miscellaneous Selling Expense	590	
Total Selling Expenses		$22,140
General Expenses		
Tax Expense	$ 2,440	
Office Supplies Expense	750	
Total General Expenses		3,190
Total Operating Expenses		25,330
Net Profit		$ 6,210

10.10. The trial balance of the Altman Sales Company, as of December 31, 19X2 is as follows:

Cash	$14,200	
Accounts Receivable	6,500	
Merchandise Inventory	38,100	
Supplies	4,200	
Prepaid Insurance	8,000	
Equipment	15,100	
Accumulated Deprec.		$ 3,400
Accounts Payable		11,200
J. Altman, Capital		37,200
J. Altman, Drawing	2,400	
Sales		98,200
Purchases	42,100	
Purchase Returns		300
Salaries Expense	11,200	
Transportation-In	4,500	
Misc. Gen. Expense	4,000	

Prepare an eight-column work sheet, using the following additional information for year-end adjustments: (a) merchandise inventory on December 31, $42,500; (b) supplies inventory, December 31, $4,000; (c) insurance expired during this year, $2,000; (d) depreciation for the current year, $800; (e) salaries accrued on December 31, $400.

Account Title	Trial Balance		Adjustments		Income Statement		Balance Sheet	
	Dr.	Cr.	Dr.	Cr.	Dr.	Cr.	Dr.	Cr.
CASH	14,200							
ACCT. REC	6,500							
MERCH. INV.	38,100		42,500	38,100				
SUPPLIES	4,200			200				
PREPAID INS	8,000			2000				
EQUIPMENT	15,100							
ACCUM. DEP.		3,400		800				
ACCT. PAYABLE		14,200						
J. ALT. CAP.		37,200						
J. ALT. DRAWING	2,400							
SALES		98,200						
PURCHASES	42,100							
PURCH RETURNS		300						
SALARIES EXP	11,200		400					
TRANSPORTATION IN	4,500							
MISC. GEN EXP.	400							

SOLUTION

Account Title	Trial Balance		Adjustments		Income Statement		Balance Sheet	
	Dr.	Cr.	Dr.	Cr.	Dr.	Cr.	Dr.	Cr.
Cash	14,200						14,200	
Accounts Receivable	6,500						6,500	
Merchandise Inven.	38,100		(a) 42,500	(a) 38,100			42,500	
Supplies	4,200			(b) 200			4,000	
Prepaid Insurance	8,000			(c) 2,000			6,000	
Equipment	15,100						15,100	
Accumulated Deprec.		3,400		(d) 800				4,200
Accounts Payable		11,200						11,200
J. Altman, Capital		37,200						37,200
J. Altman, Drawing	2,400						2,400	
Sales		98,200				98,200		
Purchases	42,100				42,100			
Purchase Returns		300				300		
Salaries Expense	11,200		(e) 400		11,600			
Transportation-In	4,500				4,500			
Misc. Gen. Expense	4,000				4,000			
	150,300	150,300						
Exp. and Inc. Sum.			(a) 38,100	(a) 42,500	38,100	42,500		
Supplies Expense			(b) 200		200			
Insurance Expense			(c) 2,000		2,000			
Depreciation Exp.			(d) 800		800			
Salaries Payable				(e) 400				400
			84,000	84,000	103,300	141,000	90,700	53,000
Net Income					37,700			37,700
					141,000	141,000	90,700	90,700

10.11. From the information in Problem 10.10, prepare all necessary adjusting and closing entries.

ADJUSTING ENTRIES

(a)			
(b)			
(c)			
(d)			
(e)			

CLOSING ENTRIES

(a)			
(b)			
(c)			
(d)			

SOLUTION

ADJUSTING ENTRIES

(a)	Merchandise Inventory	42,500	
	Expense and Income Summary		42,500
	Expense and Income Summary	38,100	
	Merchandise Inventory		38,100
(b)	Supplies Expense	200	
	Supplies		200
(c)	Insurance Expense	2,000	
	Prepaid Insurance		2,000
(d)	Depreciation Expense	800	
	Accumulated Depreciation		800
(e)	Salaries Expense	400	
	Salaries Payable		400

CLOSING ENTRIES

(a)	Sales	98,200	
	Purchase Returns	300	
	Expense and Income Summary		98,500
(b)	Expense and Income Summary	65,200	
	Purchases		42,100
	Salaries Expense		11,600
	Transportation-In		4,500
	Misc. General Expense		4,000
	Supplies Expense		200
	Insurance Expense		2,000
	Depreciation Expense		800
(c)	Expense and Income Summary	37,700	
	J. Altman, Capital		37,700
(d)	J. Altman, Capital	2,400	
	J. Altman, Drawing		2,400

10.12. From the information in Problem 10.10 prepare all financial statements.

Altman Sales Company		
Income Statement		
Year Ending December 31, 19X2		

Altman Sales Company		
Capital Statement		
Year Ending December 31, 19X2		

Altman Sales Company		
Balance Sheet		
December 31, 19X2		

SOLUTION

Altman Sales Company		
Income Statement		
Year Ending December 31, 19X2		
Sales		$98,200
Cost of Goods Sold		
Merchandise Inventory, Jan. 1	$38,100	
Purchases	$42,100	
Add Transportation-In	4,500	
	$46,600	
Less Purchase Returns	300	46,300
Goods Available for Sale	$84,400	
Less: Merchandise Inventory, Dec. 31	42,500	
Cost of Goods Sold		41,900
Gross Profit		$56,300
Operating Expenses		
Salaries Expense	$11,600	
Insurance Expense	2,000	
Supplies Expense	200	
Depreciation Expense	800	
Misc. General Expense	4,000	
Total Expenses		18,600
Net Income		$37,700

Altman Sales Company		
Capital Statement		
Year Ending December 31, 19X2		
Capital, January 1, 19X2		*$37,200*
Net Income 19X2	*$37,700*	
Less: Drawing 19X2	*2,400*	
Increase in Capital		*35,300*
Capital, December 31, 19X2		*$72,500*

Altman Sales Company		
Balance Sheet		
December 31, 19X2		
ASSETS		
Current Assets		
Cash	*$14,200*	
Accounts Receivable	*6,500*	
Merchandise Inventory	*42,500*	
Supplies	*4,000*	
Prepaid Insurance	*6,000*	
Total Current Assets		*$73,200*
Fixed Assets		
Equipment	*$15,100*	
Less: Accumulated Depreciation	*4,200*	*10,900*
Total Assets		*$84,100*
LIABILITIES AND CAPITAL		
Current Liabilities		
Accounts Payable	*$11,200*	
Salaries Payable	*400*	
Total Current Liabilities		*$11,600*
Capital, December 31, 19X2		*72,500*
Total Liabilities and Capital		*$84,100*

Examination III
Chapters 7-10

1. Prepare an 8-column work sheet for the Honest Taxi Company for the month of September. Balances in the ledger as of August 31 appear below.

Cash	$ 2,230
Supplies	5,100
Prepaid Insurance	600
Equipment	15,000
Accumulated Depreciation	3,000
Honest Taxi Company, Capital	19,600
Honest Taxi Company, Drawing	700
Fares Income	3,950
Salaries Expense	1,400
Maintenance Expense	620
Miscellaneous Expense	900

Adjustment data for September 30, are as follows:

Supplies on hand	$1,800
Expired insurance	200
Depreciation on equipment	350
Salaries payable	190

Honest Taxi Company
Work Sheet
Month Ending September 30, 19X2

Account Title	Trial Balance Dr.	Trial Balance Cr.	Adjustments Dr.	Adjustments Cr.	Income Statement Dr.	Income Statement Cr.	Balance Sheet Dr.	Balance Sheet Cr.
Cash	2,230							
Supplies	5,100							
Prepaid Ins.	600							
Equipment	15,000							
Accum. Deprec.		3,000						
Capital		19,600						
Drawing	700							
Fares Income		3,950						
Salaries Exp.	1,400							
Maint. Exp.	620							
Misc. Exp.	900							
	26,550	26,550						

2. On the basis of Question 1, journalize the closing entries needed.

3. The trial balance of the Harmin Company, before adjustments of December 31, 19X2,
    includes the following selected accounts:

Merchandise Inventory	$160,000
Sales	840,000
Sales Returns	40,000
Purchases	620,000
Transportation-in	2,000

Merchandise Inventory on December 31 totals $135,000.

(a) Present the income statement, through Gross Profit on Sales, for the Harmin Company. (b) Present the journal entries necessary to adjust the merchandise inventory
at December 31.

4. The accounts and the balances appearing in the ledger of the Capo Company, as of
    December 31, 19X2, are listed below.

Cash	$73,200
Accounts Receivable	11,000
Merchandise Inventory	33,000
Supplies	3,600
Prepaid Insurance	1,400
Equipment	10,000
Accumulated Depreciation	2,000
Accounts Payable	8,200
Notes Payable	6,000
J. Capo, Capital	22,500
J. Capo, Drawing	$ 3,000
Sales	244,000
Sales Returns	1,200
Purchases	115,000
Transportation-in	2,000
Salaries Expense	18,000
Rent Expense	4,000
Advertising Expense	2,600
Maintenance and Repairs	3,000
Miscellaneous Expense	1,700

The data for the year-end adjustments are as follows:

Merchandise inventory on December 31	$28,600
Supplies inventory on December 31	1,100
Insurance expired during the year	950
Depreciation for the current year	750
Salaries accrued at December 31	350

Prepare an eight-column work sheet.

Account Title	Trial Balance		Adjustments		Income Statement		Balance Sheet	
	Dr.	Cr.	Dr.	Cr.	Dr.	Cr.	Dr.	Cr.
Cash	73,200							
Acct. Rec.	11,000							
Merch. Inv.	33,000							
Supplies	3,600							
Prepaid Ins.	1,400							
Equipment	10,000							
Accum. Deprec.		2,000						
Acct. Pay.		8,200						
Notes Pay.		6,000						
Capo, Capital		22,500						
Capo, Drawing	3,000							
Sales		244,000						
Sales Returns	1,200							
Purchases	115,000							
Transportation	2,000							
Salaries Exp.	18,000							
Rent Exp.	4,000							
Adv. Exp.	2,600							
Maint. Exp.	3,000							
Misc. Exp.	1,700							
	282,700	282,700						

5. The beginning inventory and purchases of product X for the year are given below:

> Beginning Inventory   7 units @ $41 each
> Purchase, March 10   8 units @ $43 each
> Purchase, July 22   5 units @ $45 each
> Purchase, October 9   5 units @ $46 each

At the end of the year there were 8 units on hand. Determine the inventory cost by (a) First-In-First-Out method; (b) Last-In-First-Out; (c) weighted average.

6. Based on the above problem, determine the Cost of Goods Sold under the First-In-First-Out, Last-In-First-Out, and the weighted average methods.

7. Based on the data below, determine the inventory cost at March 31 by the retail method.

	Cost	Retail
Inventory, March 1	$39,700	$63,000
Purchases in March (net)	24,000	31,600
Sales for March		56,000

8. Transactions for the Blaky Company for the month of January, pertaining to the establishment of a petty cash fund, were as follows.

January 1: Established an imprest petty cash fund for $75

January 31: Examination of the petty cash box showed: Office Supplies, $10; Transportation, $20; Freight, $15; Charity, $6; Miscellaneous Expense, $15

What are the journal entries necessary to record the petty cash information?

Answers to Examination III

1.
Honest Taxi Company
Work Sheet
Month Ending September 30, 19X2

Account Title	Trial Balance Dr.	Cr.	Adjustments Dr.	Cr.	Income Statement Dr.	Cr.	Balance Sheet Dr.	Cr.
Cash	2,230						2,230	
Supplies	5,100			(a) 3,300			1,800	
Prepaid Ins.	600			(b) 200			400	
Equipment	15,000						15,000	
Accum. Deprec.		3,000		(c) 350				3,350
Capital		19,600						19,600
Drawing	700						700	
Fares Income		3,950				3,950		
Salaries Exp.	1,400		(d) 190		1,590			
Maint. Exp.	620				620			
Misc. Exp.	900				900			
	26,550	26,550						
Supp. Exp.			(a) 3,300		3,300			
Ins. Exp.			(b) 200		200			
Deprec. Exp.			(c) 350		350			
Salaries Pay.				(d) 190				190
			4,040	4,040	6,960	3,950	20,130	23,140
Net Loss						3,010	3,010	
					6,960	6,960	23,140	23,140

2.
Fares Income	3,950	
Expense and Income Summary		3,950
Expense and Income Summary	6,960	
Salaries Expense		1,590
Maintenance Expense		620
Miscellaneous Expense		900
Supplies Expense		3,300
Insurance Expense		200
Depreciation Expense		350
Capital	3,010	
Expense and Income Summary		3,010
Capital	700	
Drawing		700

3.   (a)

Harmin Company
Income Statement
Period Ending December 31, 19X2

Sales	$840,000	
Less: Sales Returns	40,000	$800,000
Cost of Goods Sold		
Merchandise Inv. (beg.)	160,000	
Purchases $620,000		
Transportation 2,000	622,000	
Goods Available for Sale	782,000	
Less: Merchandise Inv. (end)	135,000	
Cost of Goods Sold		647,000
Gross Profit on Sales		$153,000

(b)

Expense and Income Summary	160,000	
Merchandise Inventory		160,000
Merchandise Inventory	135,000	
Expense and Income Summary		135,000

4.

Capo Company
Work Sheet
Year Ending December 31, 19X2

Account Title	Trial Balance Dr.	Trial Balance Cr.	Adjustments Dr.	Adjustments Cr.	Income Statement Dr.	Income Statement Cr.	Balance Sheet Dr.	Balance Sheet Cr.
Cash	73,200						73,200	
Acct. Rec.	11,000						11,000	
Merch. Inv.	33,000		(a) 28,600	(a) 33,000			28,600	
Supplies	3,600			(b) 2,500			1,100	
Prepaid Ins.	1,400			(c) 950			450	
Equipment	10,000						10,000	
Accum. Deprec.		2,000		(d) 750				2,750
Acct. Pay.		8,200						8,200
Notes Pay.		6,000						6,000
Capo, Capital		22,500						22,500
Capo, Drawing	3,000						3,000	
Sales		244,000				244,000		
Sales Returns	1,200				1,200			
Purchases	115,000				115,000			
Transportation	2,000				2,000			
Salaries Exp.	18,000		(e) 350		18,350			
Rent Exp.	4,000				4,000			
Adv. Exp.	2,600				2,600			
Maint. Exp.	3,000				3,000			
Misc. Exp.	1,700				1,700			
	282,700	282,700						
Exp. & Inc. Sum.			(a) 33,000	(a) 28,600	33,000	28,600		
Supp. Exp.			(b) 2,500		2,500			
Ins. Exp.			(c) 950		950			
Deprec. Exp.			(d) 750		750			
Salaries Pay.				(e) 350				350
			66,150	66,150	185,050	272,600	127,350	39,800
Net Income					87,550			87,550
					272,600	272,600	127,350	127,350

5. (a)   Most recent cost   5 units @ $46 = $ 230
                 Next most recent cost   3 units @ 45 =   135
                 Inventory 12/31   Total units 8   Total Cost $ 365

    (b)   Earliest cost   7 units @ $41 = $ 287
                 Next earliest cost   1 units @ 43 =   43
                 Inventory 12/31   Total units 8   Total Cost $ 330

    (c)   Beginning   7 units @ $41 = $ 287
                 First purchase   8 units @ 43 =   344
                 Second purchase   5 units @ 45 =   225
                 Third purchase   5 units @ 46 =   230
                             Total units 25   Total Cost $1,086 *

                 Inventory 12/31   Total units 8   Total Cost $ 347.52

             * Average cost per unit $43.44 ($1,086 ÷ 25)

6.   First-In-First-Out   Last-In-First-Out   Weighted Average
    Merchandise Available for Sale $1,086 $1,086 $1,086
    Merchandise Inventory 12/31   365   330   348
    Cost of Goods Sold $ 721 $ 756 $ 738

7.   Cost   Retail
    Inventory $39,700 $63,000
    Purchases in March   24,000   31,600
    Merchandise Available for Sale $63,700 $94,600
    Cost ratio ($63,700 ÷ $94,600)   67%

    Less: Sales   56,000
    Inventory March 31, at retail $38,600
    Inventory March 31, at cost $25,862*

    *(38,600 × 67%)

8.   Petty Cash   75
                 Cash   75

            Transportation Expense   20
            Freight Expense   15
            Charity Expense   6
            Office Supplies Expense   10
            Miscellaneous Expense   15
                 Cash   66

Chapter 11

Payroll

11.1 GROSS PAY

The pay rate at which employees are paid is generally arrived at through negotiations between the employer and the employees. The employer, however, must conform with all applicable federal and state laws (minimum wage, and so on). One law requires that certain workers be compensated at one and one-half times their regular pay for hours worked over forty (40).

Gross pay for wage earners is generally computed by using an individual time card.

EXAMPLE 1.

Based on the time card, the computation of Ms. Horesnick's gross pay appears below. Note that one hour is allowed for lunch each day.

TIME CARD

Name	Dotty Horesnick	Pay Rate/Hour	$5.00

Week Ended _____ 3/6/81 _____

	Time In	Time Out	Working Hours
Monday	8:00 A.M.	5:00 P.M.	8
Tuesday	8:00 A.M.	7:00 P.M.	10
Wednesday	8:00 A.M.	8:00 P.M.	11
Thursday	8:00 A.M.	5:00 P.M.	8
Friday	8:00 A.M.	6:00 P.M.	9
Approved _____		Total Hours for Week	46

Regular Pay: 40 hrs × $5.00 $200.00
Overtime Pay: 6 hrs × $1\frac{1}{2}$ × $5.00   45.00
Gross Pay: $245.00

11.2. DEDUCTIONS FROM GROSS PAY

A. *Federal Withholding Taxes.* Under the Federal Withholding Tax System (commonly known as "pay as you go"), federal income tax is collected in the year in which the income is received, rather than in the following year. Thus, employers must withhold funds for the payment of federal income taxes of their employees. The amount to be withheld depends upon the number of exemptions the employee is allowed (Form W-4), the amount of the employee's earnings, and the employee's marital status. An employee is entitled to one personal exemption and one for his or her spouse, each dependent, an extra exemption if either the employee or spouse is blind or over 65.

B. *Social Security Taxes (Federal Insurance Contributions Act – FICA).* The FICA tax helps pay for Federal programs for old age and disability benefits, Medicare,

Form **W-4**	**Employee's Withholding Allowance Certificate**
(Rev. December 1978) Department of the Treasury Internal Revenue Service	(Use for Wages Paid After December 31, 1978) This certificate is for income tax withholding purposes only. It will remain in effect until you change it. If you claim exemption from withholding, you will have to file a new certificate on or before April 30 of next year.

Type or print your full name | Your social security number

Home address (number and street or rural route)

City or town, State, and ZIP code

Marital Status
☐ Single ☐ Married
☐ Married, but withhold at higher Single rate
Note: *If married, but legally separated, or spouse is a nonresident alien, check the single block.*

1 Total number of allowances you are claiming . . . .
2 Additional amount, if any, you want deducted from each pay (if your employer agrees) . . . . | $
3 I claim exemption from withholding (see instructions). Enter "Exempt" . . . .

Under the penalties of perjury, I certify that the number of withholding allowances claimed on this certificate does not exceed the number to which I am entitled. If claiming exemption from withholding, I certify that I incurred no liability for Federal income tax for last year and I anticipate that I will incur no liability for Federal income tax for this year.

Signature ▶..   Date ▶......................................, 19..........

and insurance benefits to survivors. During the working years of an employee, funds will be set aside from his or her earnings (Social Security taxes). When the employee's earnings cease because of disability, retirement, or death, the funds are made available to his or her dependents or survivors. Under the act, both employees and employers are required to contribute based on the earnings of the employee.

Currently (1979) the amount to be withheld from an employee's pay is 6.13% of the first $22,900 of earnings.

EXAMPLE 2.

If, in a given payroll period, a total of $85 was withheld from employees' wages for Social Security taxes, the employer must remit $170 to the Government, representing the $85 contribution by his employees plus the employer's matching share.

Wages in excess of $22,900 paid to a worker in one calendar year by one employer are not subject to FICA taxes.

EXAMPLE 3.

B's earnings prior to this week were $21,000. This week his salary is $200. His FICA deduction is $12.26 ($200 × 6.13%). If B had earned $22,850 prior to this pay period, only $50 would be taxed and the FICA tax would be only $3.06 ($50 × 6.13%).

If an individual works for more than one employer during a year, each employer must withhold and pay taxes on the first $22,900. The employee would be granted a refund from the Government if he or she exceeds the $22,900 base.

Notice that the withholding of any wages represents, from the employer's viewpoint, a liability, because the employer must pay to the Government the amount withheld from the employee.

In addition to taxes, or involuntary deductions, there may be a number of voluntary deductions made for the convenience of the employee, such as group insurance premiums, hospitalization programs, savings plans, retirement payments, union dues, and charitable contributions.

EXAMPLE 4.

Harold Eccleston earned $300 for the week. Deductions from his pay were: Federal Withholding, $50, FICA, $18.39, Insurance, $6, Union Dues, $10. What is his Net Pay?

$$\text{Net Pay} = \$300 - (\$50 + \$18.39 + \$6 + \$10)$$
$$= \$300 - \$84.39$$
$$= \$215.61$$

11.3   THE PAYROLL SYSTEM

The payroll system generally consists of Input Data (Individual Time Cards), Payroll Register (to compute the payroll each payroll period), Individual Earnings Cards (a detached record for each employee), and a procedure for recording the payroll and the related employer taxes with appropriate liabilities.

INDIVIDUAL TIME CARD

Although the overall payroll is recorded periodically in a Payroll Register, it is also necessary to accumulate the earnings and the deductions for *each* employee separately. These individual records facilitate the preparation of required governmental reports and assist the employer in maintaining control over payroll expenditures. They also act as convenient references to basic employee information such as earnings to date, exemptions, filing status, and employee classification. Information from the Payroll Register is posted to the Individual Earnings Cards after recording the payroll.

INDIVIDUAL EARNINGS CARD

Name_____   Filing Status _____

Address_____   Exemptions Claimed _____

_____   Position _____

S.S. #_____   Pay Rate _____ Per _____

First Quarter

Payroll Period	Gross			Deductions					Net	
	Reg.	Ot.	Total	FICA	Fed. With.	State With.	Oth. Ded.	Total Ded.	Net Pay	Ck. #
First Quarter										

PAYROLL REGISTER

A payroll register is a specially designed form used at the close of each payroll period (weekly, biweekly, and so on) to summarize and compute the payroll for the period. Although the design of this form may vary slightly depending on desired information and the degree of automation, most contain the same basic information.

Refer to the Payroll Register (Table 11-1) and note that it is broken into five sections:

Section 1.   Gross earnings (regular, overtime, total).

Section 2.   Taxable earnings (information only) used as a reference to compute FICA tax withheld or paid by the employer and unemployment tax payable by the employer.

Section 3.   Deductions from gross pay — a place is provided for each tax withheld and for total deductions.

Section 4.   Net Pay. This is the employee's take home pay. This may be checked by adding the total of deductions to the net pay. The result should be the gross pay.

Section 5.   Gross salaries charged to specific accounts.

EXAMPLE 5.

Complete Table 11-1 using the payroll data in Table 11-2. Table 11-3 shows the completed Payroll Register for the Atlas Company as of June 15.

PAYROLL REGISTER

Date	Name	(1) Gross Pay			(2) Taxable			(3) Deductions						(4) Net		(5) Distribution	
		Reg.	Ot.	Total	FICA	Unemp.	Total	FICA	State With.	Fed. With.	Code	Oth. Ded.	Total Ded.	Net Pay	Ck. #	Office Salaries	Factory Salaries

Table 11-1

PAYROLL DATA

Name	(Prior to Payroll) Earnings to Date	Gross Pay			Classification	Fed. With.	FICA	State With.	Other Deductions
		Reg.	Ot.	Total					
P. Smith	2,500	100	20	120	Office	18.00	7.35	2.40	Union A $7
S. Jones	7,000	240	—	240	Office	30.00	14.70	4.80	—
R. Campbell	5,900	150	30	180	Factory	20.10	11.03	3.60	Union A $5

Table 11-2

PAYROLL REGISTER

Date	Name	Gross Pay			Taxable			Deductions						Net		Distribution	
		Reg.	Ot.	Total	FICA	Unemp.	Total	FICA	State With.	Fed. With.	Code	Oth. Ded.	Total Ded.	Net Pay	Ck. #	Office Salaries	Factory Salaries
6/15	P. Smith	100	20	120	120	120	120	7.35	2.40	18.00	A	7.00	34.75	85.25	44	120.00	
6/15	S. Jones	240	—	240	240	-0-*	240	14.70	4.80	30.00		-0-	49.50	190.50	45	240.00	
6/15	R. Campbell	150	30	180	180	100 *	180	11.03	3.60	20.10	A	5.00	39.73	140.27	46		180.00
	Total	490	50	540	540	220	540	33.08	10.80	68.10		12.00	123.98	416.02		360.00	180.00

Table 11-3

* Only first $6,000 is subject to Unemployment Tax.

11.4   RECORDING THE PAYROLL

The payroll entry is generally recorded in the General Ledger. Since the Payroll Register is the input for the entry, it is generally totaled for the payroll period and proved before any entry is made.

EXAMPLE 6.

From the summarized data in Table 11-3, record the payroll in General Journal form.

GENERAL JOURNAL

Date	Description	P.R.	Debit	Credit
June 15	Office Salary Expense		360.00	
	Factory Salary Expense		180.00	
	FICA Taxes Payable			33.08
	Federal Taxes Payable			68.10
	State Withholding Tax Payable			10.80
	Union Dues Payable			12.00
	Cash			416.02
	To record the payroll for the week ended June 15			

PAYROLL TAXES IMPOSED ON THE EMPLOYER

A. *Social Security (Federal Insurance Contributions Act).* Not only is Social Security (FICA) withheld from the employee's pay, but a matching amount is paid in by the employer. The employer's contribution is generally computed by multiplying the total *taxable* payroll for the current period by 6.13%. The two 6.13% contributions (6.13% from the employee; 6.13% from the employer) are reported quarterly by the employer on the Federal Form 941.

B. *Unemployment Taxes.* Employers are required to pay unemployment taxes to both the Federal and the State Governments. Under current legislation, the tax is imposed only on the first $6,000 of each employee's earnings. Although the typical state unemployment tax rate is 2.7%, rates vary from 0 to 5% depending on the state, the nature of the business, and the employer's experience with unemployment. For the current year (1979) the official federal unemployment tax rate is 3.4%. However, as long as the employer is up to date on the State Tax, the employer is allowed an automatic credit of 2.7% no matter what rate the employer actually pays. The effective Federal Unemployment Tax rate is therefore 0.7%.

Table 11-4. Payroll Taxes

Tax	Paid by		Rate
	Employee	Employer	
FICA	Yes	Yes	6.13% on first $22,900 of employee's wages each year*
Fed. Income	Yes	No	Varies with exemptions; based upon table
Fed. Unemp.	No	Yes	0.7% of first $6,000
State Unemp.	No	Yes	Up to 2.7% of first $6,000

*Subject to statutory change.

RECORDING THE EMPLOYER'S TAXES

When the payroll entry is recorded, the employer's contribution will also be recorded.

EXAMPLE 7.

From the data summarized in the Payroll Register (Table 11-3), record the employer's taxes for the payroll period. (Assume a 2% State Unemployment Tax rate and a 0.7% Federal rate.)

GENERAL JOURNAL

Date	Description	P.R.	Debit	Credit
June 15	Payroll Tax Expense		39.02	
	FICA Taxes Payable*			33.08
	State Unem. Ins. Payable**			4.40
	Federal Unem. Ins. Payable**			1.54
	To record the employer's taxes for the			
	week ended June 15			

* Must match employees' contribution.
** Note that by reference to the Payroll Register (Taxable Unemployment) only $220 is subject to the tax.

Summary

(1) Compensation is paid at the rate of time and one-half when an employee works more than _____ hours.

(2) The amount of federal income tax withheld from an employee is based upon the individual's _____ and _____ .

(3) Form _____ will show information as to the number of exemptions an employee is claiming.

(4) The rate of FICA tax is _____ percent.

(5) FICA is reported _____ by the employer on Form _____ .

(6) The payroll _____ is the input for the payroll entry.

(7) Generally, all payroll entries are recorded in the _____ journal.

(8) The two types of payroll taxes imposed on the employer are _____ and _____ .

(9) The payroll tax expense entry is recorded in the _____ journal.

(10) The one tax usually paid by the employee and matched by the employer is _____ .

Answers: (1) 40; (2) filing status, number of exemptions; (3) W-4; (4) 6.13; (5) quarterly, 941; (6) register; (7) general; (8) FICA, Unemployment; (9) general; (10) FICA.

Solved Problems

11.1. Below is a time card for Betty Walters. Complete the hours section of her time card and compute her gross pay. Allow one hour for lunch each day.

TIME CARD

Name	Betty Walters		Pay Rate/Hour	$4.00
Week Ended	9/20/81			
	Time In		Time Out	Hours
Monday	8:00 A.M.		5:00 P.M.	
Tuesday	8:00 A.M.		5:00 P.M.	
Wednesday	8:00 A.M.		7:00 P.M.	
Thursday	8:00 A.M.		8:30 P.M.	
Friday	8:00 A.M.		7:30 P.M.	
Approved			Total Hours for Week	

SOLUTION

TIME CARD

Name	Betty Walters		Pay Rate/Hour	$4.00
Week Ended	9/20/81			
	Time In		Time Out	Hours
Monday	8:00 A.M.		5:00 P.M.	8
Tuesday	8:00 A.M.		5:00 P.M.	8
Wednesday	8:00 A.M.		7:00 P.M.	10
Thursday	8:00 A.M.		8:30 P.M.	11½
Friday	8:00 A.M.		7:30 P.M.	10½
Approved			Total Hours for Week	48

Regular Pay: 40 hours × $4.00 = $160.00
Overtime Pay: 8 hours × $6.00* =   48.00
Total Gross Pay $208.00

* Time and one-half rate.

11.2. How many exemptions are permitted to be claimed on Form W-4 in the following cases:

    (*a*) Taxpayer and spouse (nonworking)

    (*b*) Taxpayer, spouse, and two children

    (*c*) Taxpayer, age 67, spouse, aged 61

    (*d*) Taxpayer age 68, blind, spouse age 66, blind

SOLUTION

    (*a*) 2, (*b*) 4, (*c*) 3 (taxpayer 2, spouse 1), (*d*) 6 (each get 3 exemptions)

11.3. Based on the assumption of an FICA rate of 6.13% on the first $22,900, how much will be withheld from the following employees:

	Employee	Amount Earned Prior to Current Payroll	Amount Earned This Week	Amount Withheld for FICA
(a)	I. Blanton	$15,000	$250	?
(b)	P. Burday	22,700	$250	?
(c)	M. Fleming	25,000	$250	?

SOLUTION

(a) $15.32 ($250 × 6.13%)

(b) $12.26 ($200 balance × 6.13%)

(c)　0　Maximum of $22,900 has been reached.

11.4. Complete the table below based upon the employer's payroll obligation. Assume a state rate of 2.5% and a federal rate of 0.7%.

	Employee	Amount Earned This Week	Prior Earnings	FICA	Federal Unemployment	State Unemployment
(a)	B. Orzech	$200	$3,600	$12.26	?	?
(b)	M. Felson	$250	$5,950	$15.32	?	?
(c)	H. Hendricks	$275	$6,200	$16.85	?	?

SOLUTION

	Federal Unemployment	State Unemployment
(a)	$1.40	$5.00
(b)	$0.35*	1.25†
(c)	None	None

* Federal rate is 0.7% on first $6,000. Balance subject to tax $50.
† State rate is 2.5% on first $6,000. Balance subject to tax $50.

11.5. Judy Bagon worked 44 hours during the first week in February of the current year. The pay rate is $3.50 per hour. Withheld from her wages were FICA (6.13%), federal income tax ($21.00), hospitalization ($6.00). Determine the necessary payroll entry.

SOLUTION

Salary Expense	161.00*	
FICA Taxes Payable		9.87
Federal Income Tax Payable		21.00
Hospitalization Payable		6.00
Cash		124.13
* 40 hours × $3.50 = $140.00 (regular)		
4 hours × 5.25 = 21.00 (overtime)		
Total $161.00		

11.6. Based on the information in Problem 11.5, what is the entry to record the employer's payroll tax if it is assumed the state tax rate is 2% and the federal unemployment rate is 0.7%?

SOLUTION

Payroll Tax Expense	14.22	
FICA Taxes Payable		9.87
Federal Unemployment Insurance Payable		1.13
State Unemployment Insurance Payable		3.22

11.7. The total payroll for the Berchid Realty Company for the week ending May 30 was $26,000. Of the total amount, $19,000 was subject to FICA tax, $3,800 withheld for federal income tax, $1,500 deducted for pensions, and the balance paid in cash. Present the journal entry necessary to record the payroll for this week, assuming that the FICA tax rate is 6.13%.

SOLUTION

Salaries Expense	26,000	
FICA Taxes Payable		1,164.70
Federal Income Taxes Payable		3,800.00
Pension Contributions Payable		1,500.00
Cash		19,535.30

11.8. Based on Problem 11.7, present the employer's payroll tax entry, assuming a state unemployment tax rate of 2.7% and federal unemployment tax rate of 0.7%, and that of the total payroll $7,000 was subject to federal and state unemployment.

SOLUTION

Payroll Tax Expense	1,402.70	
FICA Taxes Payable		1,164.70*
State Unemployment Insurance Payable		189.00
Federal Unemployment Insurance Payable		49.00

* Matched

11.9. For the week ending June 30, the Benezran Company had a gross payroll of $20,000. Of that amount, earnings subject to FICA were $12,000 and the amount subject to unemployment compensation tax was $8,000. Present the journal entry to record the employer's payroll tax for the week, assuming the following rates: FICA 6.13%, state unemployment 2%, federal unemployment 0.7%.

SOLUTION

Payroll Tax Expense	951.60	
FICA Taxes Payable		735.60
State Unemployment Insurance Payable		160.00
Federal Unemployment Insurance Payable		56.00

11.10. Below is the payroll information for three of the employees of the S. Board Company.

Employee	Amount Earned to Date	Gross Pay for Week
L. Benjamin	$3,800	$300
R. Hochian	$5,900	$300
C. Murphy	$6,400	$300

The company is located in a state that imposes an unemployment insurance tax of 2.6% on the first $6,000. Federal unemployment tax is 0.7%; FICA tax is 6.13%. Present the entry necessary to record the employer's payroll tax expense.

SOLUTION

	FICA	State	Federal
Benjamin	$18.39 (6.13% × $300)	$ 7.80 (2.6% × $300)	$2.10 (0.7% × $300)
Hochian	18.39 (6.13% × $300)	2.60 (2.6% × $100)	0.70 (0.7% × $100)
Murphy	18.39 (6.13% × $300)	None	None
Total	$55.17	$10.40	$2.80

Payroll Tax Expense	68.37	
FICA Taxes Payable		55.17
State Unemployment Insurance Payable		10.40
Federal Unemployment Insurance Payable		2.80

11.11. Based on the information below, complete the March 28 payroll register for the J. Rakosi Medical Center.

Name	Earnings to Date	Gross Pay Reg.	Gross Pay Ot.	Total	Federal Withholding	Other Deductions
J. Erin	$3,800	100	30	130	$12.00	Union $6.—
M. Ribble	$5,950	150	20	170	$ 8.50	Union $7.—
W. Mondstein	$6,200	200	—	200	$14.60	—
M. Yamura	$8,000	250	—	250	$29.50	—

PAYROLL REGISTER

| Date | Name | Gross Pay | | | Taxable | | Deductions | | | Net |
		Reg.	Ot.	Total	FICA	Unemp.	FICA	Fed. With.	Other Ded.	Net Pay

SOLUTION

PAYROLL REGISTER

| Date | Name | Gross Pay | | | Taxable | | Deductions | | | Net |
		Reg.	Ot.	Total	FICA	Unemp.	FICA	Fed. With.	Other Ded.	Net Pay
3/28	J. Erin	100	30	130	130	130	7.97	12.00	U-6.00	104.03
	M. Ribble	150	20	170	170	50	10.42	8.50	U-7.00	144.08
	W. Mondstein	200	—	200	200	—	12.26	14.60	—	173.14
	M. Yamura	250	—	250	250	—	15.33	29.50	—	205.17
	Totals:	700	50	750	750	180	45.98	64.60	13.00	626.42

11.12. Based on the information in Problem 11.11, present the payroll journal entry needed.

SOLUTION

Salaries Expense	750.00	
FICA Taxes Payable		45.98
Federal Income Taxes Payable		64.60
Union Dues Payable		13.00
Cash		626.42

11.13. Based on the information presented in the payroll register of Problem 11.11, present the necessary payroll tax expense entry for the employer. Assume a state tax rate of 2% and a federal rate of 0.7%.

SOLUTION

Payroll Tax Expense	50.84	
FICA Taxes Payable		45.98
State Unemployment Insurance Payable		3.60*
Federal Unemployment Insurance Payable		1.26*

* The total amount of the payroll subject to the $6,000 maximum earned limitation for unemployment insurance is $180. (Erin $130 and Ribble $50.)

Chapter 12

Receivables and Payables

12.1 INTRODUCTION

A large proportion of all business transactions are credit transactions. One way of extending credit is by the acceptance of a *promissory note*, a contract in which one person (the maker) promises to pay another person (the payee) a specific sum of money at a specific time, with or without interest. A promissory note is used for the following reasons:

1. The holder of a note can usually obtain money by taking the note to the bank and selling it (*discounting* the note).

2. The note is a written acknowledgment of a debt and is better evidence than an open account. It takes precedence over open accounts in the event that the debtor becomes bankrupt.

3. It facilitates the sale of merchandise on long-term or installment plans.

For a note to be negotiable, it must meet the requirements of the Uniform Commercial Code (UCC). The requirements are that the note must:

1. Be in writing and signed by the maker.

2. Contain an order to pay a definite sum of money.

3. Be payable to order on demand or at a fixed future time.

12.2 METHODS OF COMPUTING INTEREST

For the sake of simplicity, interest is commonly computed on the basis of a 360-day year divided into 12 months of 30 days each. Two widely used methods are (1) the cancellation method and (2) the 6%-60 days method.

EXAMPLE 1. The Cancellation Method.

The basic formula is:

$$\text{INTEREST} = \text{PRINCIPAL} \times \text{RATE} \times \text{TIME}$$

Consider a note for $400 at 6% for 90 days. The *principal* is the face amount of the note ($400). The *rate of interest* is written as a fraction: $6\%/100\% = 6/100$. The *time*, if less than a year, is expressed as a fraction by placing the number of days the note runs over the number of days in a year: 90/360. Thus,

$$\text{INTEREST} = \$400 \times \frac{6}{100} \times \frac{90}{360} = \$6$$

EXAMPLE 2. The 6%-60 Days Method.

This is a variation of the cancellation method, based on the fact that 60 days, or $\frac{1}{6}$ year, at 6% is equivalent to 1%, so that the interest is obtained simply by shifting the decimal point of the principal two places to the left. The method also applies to other time periods or other interest rates. For instance:

$400 Note	30 Days	6%

(a)	Determine the interest for 60 days	$4.00
(b)	Divide the result by 2 (30 days is one-half of 60 days)	*Ans.* $2.00

$400 Note	45 Days	6%

(a)	Determine the interest for 30 days	$2.00
(b)	Determine the interest for 15 days	$1.00
(c)	Add the interest for 30 days and 15 days	*Ans.* $3.00

$400 Note	60 Days	5%

(a)	Determine the interest at 6%	$4.00
(b)	Determine the interest at 1% by taking one-sixth of the above amount	.67
(c)	Multiply the interest at 1% by the rate desired, .67 × 5	*Ans.* $3.35

DETERMINING MATURITY DATE

The maturity date is the number of specified days after the note has been issued and may be determined by:

1. Subtracting the date of the note from the number of days in the month in which it was written.

2. Adding the succeeding full months (in terms of days), stopping with the last full month before the number of days in the note are exceeded.

3. Subtracting the total days of the result of steps 1 and 2 above from the time of the note. The resulting number is the due date in the upcoming month.

EXAMPLE 3.

The maturity date of a 90-day note dated April 4 would be computed as follows:

Period of Note			90
April	30		
Date of Note	4	26	
May		31	
June		30	
TOTAL			87
Maturity Date	July		3

If the due date of a note is expressed in months, the maturity date can be determined by counting that number of expressed months from the date of writing:

EXAMPLE 4.

A five-month note dated March 17 would be due for payment on August 17. A one-month note dated March 31 would mature on April 30.

12.3   ACCOUNTING FOR NOTES RECEIVABLE AND NOTES PAYABLE

A promissory note is a note payable from the standpoint of the maker, while it is a note receivable from the standpoint of the payee.

12.3A   NOTES PAYABLE

A note payable is a written promise to pay a creditor an amount of money in the future. Notes are used by a business to

1.   Make purchases.

2.   Settle an open account.

3.   Borrow money from a bank.

1.   *Make Purchases.*

EXAMPLE 5.

Assume that you, as the owner, bought Office Equipment costing $2,000 by giving a note.

Office Equipment	2,000	
Notes Payable		2,000

2.   *Settle an Open Account.*

EXAMPLE 6.

There are times when a note is issued in settlement of an account payable. Assume that the Harmin Agency bought merchandise from Laska Corporation for $500, terms 2/10, n/30. The entry would be recorded in the purchases journal and would appear in the general ledger as:

Purchases	Accounts Payable
500 |	| 500

However, 30 days later, the agency is unable to pay and gives to the Laska Company a 60-day, 6% note for $500 to replace its open account. When the Harmin Agency issues the note payable, an entry is made in the general journal that will decrease the accounts payable and increase the notes payable.

Accounts Payable	500	
Notes Payable		500

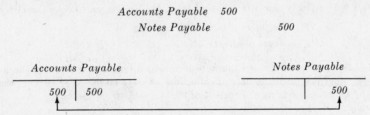

Note that the Harmin Agency still owes the debt to the Laska Company. However, it now becomes a different form of an obligation as it is a written, signed promise in the form of a note payable.

When the maker pays the note in 60 days at 6%, the amount of his payment will be the total of the principal and interest and will be recorded in the cash disbursements journal.

EXAMPLE 7.

Notes Payable	500	
Interest Expense	5	
Cash		505

3.   ***Borrow Money from a Bank.*** On occasions, businesses find that it may be necessary to borrow money by giving a note payable to the bank. Frequently, banks require the interest to be paid in advance. This is accomplished by deducting the amount of the interest from the principal when the loan is made and is known as "discounting a note payable." The proceeds will be the amount of money that the maker of the note receives after the discount has been taken from the principal.

EXAMPLE 8.

Assume that the Rhulen Agency seeks to borrow $3,000 for 60 days at 6% from the Commercial National Bank. The bank will deduct the interest ($30.00) from the $3,000 principal and will give the difference of $2,970 (proceeds) to the Rhulen Agency.

The entry recorded in the Cash Receipts journal would be

Cash	*2,970*	
Interest Expense	*30*	
Notes Payable		*3,000*

Sixty days after the issuance of the instrument, the note becomes due, and the Rhulen Agency sends a check for the face of the note ($3,000). Because the interest was deducted immediately when the loan was made, no further interest will be paid at that time. The entry to record the payment of the note will be made in the Cash Payments journal.

Notes Payable	*3,000*	
Cash		*3,000*

Note: When a business issues many notes payable, a special subsidiary book, known as the notes payable register, may be used. This register will give the complete data for all notes issued and paid by the business. It must be noted, however, that this is merely a source of information and not a journal, as no postings to the ledger are made from it.

12.3B   NOTES RECEIVABLE

A note received from a customer is an asset because it becomes a claim against the buyer for the amount due.

EXAMPLE 9.

Assume that James Allen owes A. Bagon $400 and gives him a 90-day, 6% note in settlement. Mr. Allen still owes the debt, but his obligation is now of a different type. On Mr. Bagon's books the entry is:

Notes Receivable	*400*	
Accounts Receivable		*400*

Only the principal ($400) is recorded when the note is received, since it represents the amount of the unpaid account. The interest is not due until the date of collection, 90 days later. At that time, the interest earned (income) will be part of the entry recognizing the receipt of the proceeds from the note:

Cash	*406*	
Notes Receivable		*400*
Interest Income		*6*

12.4   DISCOUNTING

The negotiability of a note receivable enables the holder to receive cash from the bank before the due date. This is known as "discounting."

Once the interest to be paid has been determined, the procedure for discounting a note is quite simple. The *maturity value* of a note is:

(1)   **MATURITY VALUE = FACE OF NOTE + INTEREST INCOME**

where the *face* is the principal and the interest income is computed as in Sec. 12.2. The holder of a note may discount it at the bank *prior to its due date*. He will receive the maturity value, less the *discount*, or interest charge imposed by the bank for holding the note for the unexpired portion of its term. In other words,

(2)   **DISCOUNT = MATURITY VALUE × DISCOUNT RATE × UNEXPIRED TIME**

and

$$\text{(3)} \quad \textbf{NET PROCEEDS} \ = \ \textbf{MATURITY VALUE} \ - \ \textbf{DISCOUNT}$$

EXAMPLE 10.

Mr. Bagon holds a $400, 90-day, 6% note written on April 10 (see Example 9). It is discounted at 6% on May 10. The interest on the note, as found in Example 2, amounts to $6. Hence,

$$\text{(1)} \qquad \text{MATURITY VALUE} \ = \ \$400 + \$6 \ = \ \$406$$

Since, at the time of discounting, Mr. Bagon has held the note for only 30 days, the bank will have to wait $90 - 30 = 60$ days until it can receive the maturity value. The discount charge is then:

$$\text{(2)} \qquad \text{DISCOUNT} \ = \ \$406 \times \frac{6}{100} \times \frac{60}{360} \ = \ \$4.06$$

and Mr. Bagon receives

$$\text{(3)} \qquad \text{NET PROCEEDS} \ = \ \$406 - \$4.06 \ = \ \$401.94$$

In this example the bank's discount rate happened to be equal to the interest rate of the note; this need not always be the case (see Problem 12.9).

12.5 DISHONORED NOTES RECEIVABLE

If the issuer of a note does not make payment on the due date, the note is said to be *dishonored*. It is no longer negotiable and the amount is charged back to Accounts Receivable. The reasons for transferring the dishonored notes receivable to the accounts receivable account are: (1) the notes receivable account is then limited to current notes that have not yet matured, and (2) the accounts receivable account will then show the dishonoring of the note, giving a better picture of the transaction.

EXAMPLE 11.

A $500, 60-day, 6% note written by A. Black was dishonored on the date of maturity. The entry runs:

Accounts Receivable, A. Black	505	
Notes Receivable		500
Interest Income		5

Observe that the interest income is recorded and is charged to the customer's account.

When a payee discounts a note receivable, he creates a *contingent* (potential) *liability*. This occurs because there is a possibility that the maker may dishonor the note. Bear in mind that the payee has already received payment from the bank in advance of the maturity date. He is, therefore, contingently liable to the bank to make good on the amount (maturity value) in the event of default by the maker. Any *protest fee* arising from the default of the note is charged to the maker of the note and is added to the amount to be charged against his account.

EXAMPLE 12.

An $800, 90-day, 6% note, dated May 1, is discounted on May 31 at 6%. Upon presentation on the due date, the note is dishonored. The entry will be:

Accounts Receivable	812*	
Cash		812

* $800 (Face)

<u> 12 </u> (Interest)

$812 (Maturity value)

Had the bank issued a protest fee of $3, the amount charged to the customer would be $815.

12.6   DRAFTS

Sometimes drafts rather than promissory notes are used in settlement of a business obligation.

A draft is an order by the seller (drawer) to the buyer (drawee) stating that the buyer must pay a certain amount of money to a third party (payee).

EXAMPLE 13.

If the seller is not acquainted with the buyer, he or she may draw a draft on the buyer and attach to it a bill of lading for the purchase. (A bill of lading is prepared by the transportation company.) The draft and bill of lading are sent to the bank at which time the bank presents the documents to the buyer. When the buyer pays the amount of the draft to the bank, he or she receives the bill of lading and obtains the purchase from the transportation company. The bank forwards the amount collected to the seller, deducting from it a service charge.

12.7   RECORDING OF UNCOLLECTIBLE ACCOUNTS

Businesses must expect to sustain some losses from uncollectible accounts and should therefore show on the balance sheet the *net amount of accounts receivable,* the amount expected to be collected, rather than the gross amount. The difference between the gross and net amounts represents the estimated uncollectible accounts, or bad debts. These expenses are attributed to the year in which the sale is made, though they may be realized at a later date.

There are two methods of recording uncollectible accounts.

1. ***Direct write-off method.*** In small businesses losses that arise from uncollectible accounts are recognized in the accounts *in the period in which they become uncollectible.* Under this method, when an account is deemed uncollectible, it is written off the books by a debit to the expense account, Uncollectible Accounts Expense, and a credit to the individual customer's account and to the controlling account.

EXAMPLE 14.

If William Anderson's $300 account receivable, dated May 15, 19X1, was deemed uncollectible in January of 19X2, the entry in 19X2 would be:

Uncollectible Accounts Expense	*300*	
Accounts Receivable, William Anderson		*300*

2. ***Allowance method.*** As has been stated before, one of the fundamentals of accounting is that revenue be matched with expenses in the same year. Under the direct write-off method, in Example 14, the loss was not recorded until a year after the revenue had been recognized. The allowance method does not permit this. The income statement for each period must include all losses and expenses related to the income earned *in that period.* Therefore, losses from uncollectible accounts should be deducted in the year the sale was made. Since it is impossible to predict which particular accounts will not be collected, an adjusting entry is made, usually at the end of the year.

EXAMPLE 15.

Assume that in the first year of operation a firm has estimated that $2,000 of accounts receivable will be uncollectible. The adjusting entry would be:

Uncollectible Accounts Expense	*2,000*	
Allowance for Uncollectible Accounts		*2,000*

The credit balance of Allowance for Uncollectible Accounts appears on the balance sheet as a deduction from the total amount of Accounts Receivable:

Accounts Receivable	$29,920	
Less: Allowance for Uncollectible Accounts	2,000	$27,920

The $27,920 will become the estimated realizable value of the accounts receivable at that date. The uncollectible accounts expense will appear as an operating expense in the income statement.

12.8   COMPUTATION OF UNCOLLECTIBLE ACCOUNTS

There are two generally accepted methods of calculating the amount of uncollectible accounts. One method is to use a flat percentage of the net sales for the year. The other method takes into consideration the ages of the individual accounts at the end of the fiscal year.

1. *Percentage of sales method.* Under this method, a fixed percentage of the total sales on account is taken. For example, if charge sales were $200,000 and experience has shown that approximately 1% of such sales will become uncollectible at a future date, the adjusting entry for the uncollectible accounts would be:

Uncollectible Accounts Expense	2,000
Allowance for Uncollectible Accounts	2,000

The same amount is used whether or not there is a balance in Allowance for Uncollectible Accounts. However, if any substantial balance should accumulate in the allowance account, a change in the percentage figure would become appropriate.

2. *Balance sheet method.* Under this method, every account is "aged"; that is, each item in its balance is related to the sale date. The further past due the account, the more probable it is that the customer is unwilling or unable to pay. A typical analysis is shown in Example 16.

EXAMPLE 16.

Age of Account	Accounts Receivable Balance	Estimated % Uncollectible	Amount
1–30 days	$ 8,000	1%	$ 80
31–60 days	12,000	3%	360
61–90 days	6,000	5%	300
91–180 days	3,000	20%	600
Over 180 days	920	50%	460
	$29,920		$1,800

The calculated allowance for uncollectible accounts ($1,800 in Example 16) is reconciled at the end of the year with the actual balance in the allowance account, and an adjusting entry is made. The amount of the adjusting entry must take into consideration the balance of the Allowance for Uncollectible Accounts.

EXAMPLE 17.

The analysis showed that $1,800 would be required in the Allowance for Uncollectible Accounts at the end of the period. The Allowance for Uncollectible Accounts has a credit balance of $200. The adjusting entry at the end of the year would be:

Uncollectible Accounts Expense	1,600*	
Allowance for Uncollectible Accounts		1,600

* ($1,800-$200)

If, however, there had been a debit balance of $200, a credit to Allowance for Uncollectible Accounts of $2,000 would be necessary to bring the closing balance to $1,800.

When it becomes evident that a customer's account is uncollectible, it is written off the books. This is done by crediting Accounts Receivable and the individual customer's account in the subsidiary ledger for the amount deemed uncollectible and by debiting Allowance for Uncollectible Accounts.

EXAMPLE 18.

John Andrews' account (a) was deemed uncollectible.

Allowance for Uncollectible Accounts	600	
Accounts Receivable, J. Andrews		600

GENERAL LEDGER	ACCOUNTS RECEIVABLE LEDGER

Allowance for Uncollectible Accounts

(a) 600	Bal. 1,800

John Andrews

Bal. 600	(a) 600

Accounts Receivable

Bal. 29,920	(a) 600

12.9   RECOVERY OF BAD DEBTS

If a written-off account is later collected in full or in part (a *recovery of bad debts*), the write-off will be reversed for the amount received.

EXAMPLE 19.

At a later date, Mr. Andrews (see Example 18) pays his account in full. The reversing entry (b) to restore his account will be:

Accounts Receivable, John Andrews	600	
Allowance for Uncollectible Accounts		600

A separate entry, (c), will then be made in the cash receipts journal to record the collection, debiting Cash $600 and crediting Accounts Receivable, John Andrews. If a partial collection was made, the reversing entry should be made for the amount recovered.

GENERAL LEDGER	ACCOUNTS RECEIVABLE LEDGER

Cash

(c) 600	

John Andrews

Bal. 600	(a) 600
(b) 600	(c) 600

Accounts Receivable

29,200	(a) 600
(b) 600	(c) 600

Allowance for Uncollectible Accounts

(a) 600	Bal. 1,800
	(b) 600

Summary

(1)   The practice of transferring a customer's note to the bank is called _____.

(2)   The face of a note plus the interest due is known as _____.

(3) Under the _____ method, uncollectible accounts are charged to expense when they become uncollectible.

(4) Uncollectible Accounts Expense appears in the _____ statement, while Allowance for Uncollectible Accounts appears in the _____.

(5) The method based on the age of the accounts receivable is known as the _____ _____ approach.

(6) Ascertaining the amount and time outstanding for each account is known as _____.

(7) If Bill Henderson issues to Sam Borach a $400 note, Bill Henderson is called the _____ and Sam Borach the _____.

(8) The interest on a $800, 90-day, 6% note would be _____.

(9) Normally, banks will base their discount on the _____ of the note.

(10) What effect does the acceptance of a note receivable have on the total assets of a firm? _____.

Answers: (1) discounting; (2) maturity value; (3) direct write-off; (4) income, balance sheet; (5) balance sheet; (6) aging; (7) maker, payee; (8) $12; (9) maturity value; (10) no effect

Solved Problems

12.1. The Hudson Corp. borrowed $5,000 for 90 days at 6% from the Sullivan National Bank. What entries are needed to (a) record the loan, and (b) record the payment? Assume that the interest payment must be made in advance.

(a)

CASH	4,925	
INTEREST EXPENSE	75	
NOTES PAYABLE		5000

(b)

NOTES PAYABLE	5,000	
CASH		5,000

SOLUTION

(a)

Cash	4,925	
Interest Expense	75*	
Notes Payable		5,000

* Interest for 90 days at 6% deducted in advance.

(b)

Notes Payable	5,000	
Cash		5,000

12.2. Based on the information in Problem 12.1, what entry would be necessary if after 90 days, M. Erin was unable to repay the loan and was granted another 90-day renewal.

INTEREST EXPENSE	75	
CASH		75

SOLUTION

Interest Expense	75*	
Cash		75

  * Only the interest has to be paid since the note is renewed.

12.3. Assume in Problem 12.1 that Mr. Hudson's note required the interest payment upon the maturity of the note. What entries are needed to (a) record the loan and (b) record the payment?

(a)

(b)

SOLUTION

(a)	Cash	5,000	
	Notes Payable		5,000
(b)	Notes Payable	5,000	
	Interest Expense	75	
	Cash		5,075

12.4. Below is an example of a note receivable.

> Date: July 1, 19X2
>
> "I, Charles Nelson, promise to pay Acme Stores $800, 60 days from date, at 6% interest."
>
>   Charles Nelson

(a) Who is the maker of the note? (b) Who is the payee of the note? (c) What is the maturity date of the note? (d) What is the maturity value of the note?

SOLUTION

 (a) Charles Nelson
 (b) Acme Stores
 (c) August 30
 (d) $808

12.5. A note written on August 1 and due on November 15 was discounted on October 15. (a) For how many days was the note written? (b) For how many days did the bank charge in discounting the note?

SOLUTION

(a)	August 1–31	30 days	(b)	October 15–31	16 days
	September	30 days		November 1–15	15 days
	October	31 days			31 days *Ans.*
	November	15 days			
		106 days *Ans.*			

12.6. Determine the interest on the following notes: (a) $750 principal, 6% interest, 96 days; (b) $800 principal, 4% interest, 90 days.

SOLUTION

(a)	$750	6%	60 days	$ 7.50	(b)	$800	6%	60 days	$ 8.00
		6%	30 days	3.75			6%	30 days	4.00
		6%	6 days	.75			6%	90 days	$12.00
		6%	96 days	$12.00 *Ans.*					

The interest at 4% is then

$$\frac{4\%}{6\%} \times \$12.00 = \$8.00 \ Ans.$$

12.7. A 90-day, 6%, $4,000 note receivable in settlement of an account, dated June 1, is discounted at 6% on July 1. Compute the proceeds of the note.

SOLUTION

$4,000.00	Principal
60.00	Interest income (90 days, 6%)
$4,060.00	Maturity value
40.60	Discount (60 days, 6% of maturity value)
$4,019.40	Proceeds, July 1–August 30 (due date)

12.8. What are the entries needed to record the information in Problem 12.7 (a) on June 1? (b) on July 1?

(a)		
(b)		

SOLUTION

(a)	Notes Receivable	4,000.00	
	Accounts Receivable		4,000.00
(b)	Cash	4,019.40	
	Interest Income		19.40
	Notes Receivable		4,000.00

12.9. Record the following transactions in the books of Robert Ryan Company.

    (a) May 1:   Received a $6,000, 90-day, 6% note in settlement of the Happy Valley account

    (b) May 31:   Discounted the note at 7% at the bank

    (c) July 30:   Happy Valley paid the note in full

(a)

(b)

(c)

SOLUTION

(a)	Notes Receivable	6,000.00	
	Accounts Receivable, Happy Valley		6,000.00
(b)	Cash	6,018.95*	
	Interest Income		18.95
	Notes Receivable		6,000.00

* $6,000.00	Principal	
90.00	Interest income	
6,090.00	Maturity value	
71.05	Discount $(6{,}090 \times \frac{7}{100} \times \frac{60}{360})$	
$6,018.95	Proceeds	

(c)   No entry

12.10. If in Problem 12.9 Happy Valley dishonored their obligation on July 30 and a $5 protest fee was imposed by the bank, what entry would be required to record this information?

SOLUTION

Accounts Receivable, Happy Valley	6,095*	
Cash		6,095

* $6,090 (maturity value) + $5 (protest fee)

12.11. Record the following transactions in the books of Carl Bresky.

    (a) September 5:   Received an $8,000, 90-day, 6% note in settlement of the M. Ribble account and immediately discounted it at 6% at the bank

    (b) December 4:   M. Ribble dishonored the note, and a protest fee of $2 was imposed

    (c) December 31:   M. Ribble paid her obligation including the protest fee

(a)

(b)

(c)

SOLUTION

(a)

Notes Receivable	8,000.00	
Accounts Receivable, M. Ribble		8,000.00
Cash	7,998.20*	
Interest Expense	1.80	
Notes Receivable		8,000.00

*$8,000.00	Principal
120.00	Interest Income
$8,120.00	Maturity Value
121.80	Discount
$7,998.20	Proceeds

(b)

Accounts Receivable, M. Ribble	8,122.00*	
Cash		8,122.00
* (Maturity value + protest fee)		

(c)

Cash	8,122.00	
Accounts Receivable, M. Ribble		8,122.00

12.12. Shown are balances for Prurient Press:

Accounts Receivable	Sales	Allowance for Uncollectible Accounts
120,000	350,000	400

What is the adjusting entry needed to record the provision for uncollectible accounts if the uncollectible expense is estimated: (a) as 1% of net sales? (b) by aging the accounts receivable, the allowance balance being estimated as $3,600?

(a)

(b)

SOLUTION

(a)

Uncollectible Accounts Expense	3,500*	
Allowance for Uncollectible Accounts		3,500
*1% of $350,000		

(b)

Uncollectible Accounts Expense	3,200**	
Allowance for Uncollectible Accounts		3,200
** $3,600 − $400. Balance of $400 in allowance must be taken into consideration.		

12.13. Using the aging schedule below, prepare the adjusting entry providing for the uncollectible accounts expense.

Amount	Age	Estimated % Uncollectible
$24,000	1-30 days	1%
$18,000	31-60 days	3%
$10,000	61-180 days	25%
$6,000	181 days and over	60%

SOLUTION

Uncollectible Accounts Expense	6,880*	
Allowance for Uncollectible Accounts		6,880
* $240 1-30 days (24,000 × 1%)		
$540 31-60 days (18,000 × 3%)		
$2,500 61-180 days (10,000 × 25%)		
$3,600 181 days and over (6,000 × 60%)		

12.14. Below are some accounts of the Jay Balding Company, as of January 19X2.

GENERAL LEDGER	ACCOUNTS RECEIVABLE LEDGER
Accounts Receivable	*D. Grego*
210,000	1,400
Allowance for Uncollectible Accounts	*J. Philips*
2,600	1,200

Prepare entries needed to record the following information:

(*a*) March 5: D. Grego account was determined to be uncollectible

(*b*) April 14: Wrote off J. Philips account as uncollectible

(*a*)

(*b*)

SOLUTION

(*a*)	Allowance for Uncollectible Accounts	1,400	
	Accounts Receivable, D. Grego		1,400
(*b*)	Allowance for Uncollectible Accounts	1,200	
	Accounts Receivable, J. Philips		1,200

12.15. If, in Problem 12.14, J. Philips later paid his account in full, what entries would be necessary?

SOLUTION

Accounts Receivable, J. Philips	1,200	
Allowance for Uncollectible Accounts		1,200
Cash	1,200	
Accounts Receivable, J. Philips		1,200

Chapter 13

Property, Plant, and Equipment

13.1 FIXED ASSETS

Tangible assets that are relatively permanent and are needed for the production or sale of goods or services are termed *property, plant, and equipment,* or *fixed assets*. These assets are not held for sale in the ordinary course of business. The broad group is usually separated into classes according to the physical characteristics of the items (e.g. land, buildings, machinery and equipment, furniture and fixtures).

The cost of property, plant, and equipment includes all expenditures necessary to put the asset into position and ready for use.

EXAMPLE 1.

For a lathe purchased by AB Optical Company, the data were: invoice price, $11,000; cash discount, $220; freight-in, $300; trucking, $200; electrical connections and installation, $720. The total cost is $11,000 − 220 + 300 + 200 + 720 = $12,000. Therefore, the entry is:

Machinery and Equipment	12,000	
Cash		12,000

13.2 DEPRECIATION AND SCRAP VALUE

Though it may be long, the useful life of a fixed asset is limited. Eventually the asset will lose all productive worth and will possess only salvage value (scrap value). The accrual basis of accounting demands a period-by-period matching of costs against derived revenues. Hence, the cost of a fixed asset (over and above its scrap value) is distributed over its entire estimated lifetime. This spreading of the cost over the periods which receive benefits is known as *depreciation*.

Depreciation decreases the fixed asset's book value and also decreases capital. Depreciation is considered an operating expense of the business. It may be recorded by an entry at the end of each month or at the end of the year, usually depending on the frequency of preparing financial statements. Fixed assets are recorded at cost and remain at that figure as long as they are held. The depreciation taken to date is shown as a credit in the offset account Accumulated Depreciation (Sec. 6.2), and is deducted from the asset account on the balance sheet, as shown in Example 2 below.

EXAMPLE 2.

Equipment	10,000	
Less: Accumulated Depreciation	4,000	6,000

The book value of the equipment has gone from $10,000 to $6,000.

There is one exception to the above considerations: land. This fixed asset is non-depreciable; it is usually carried on the books permanently at cost.

13.3 METHODS OF DEPRECIATION

The depreciable amount of a fixed asset — that is, cost minus scrap value — may be written off in different ways. For example, the amount may be spread evenly over the years affected, as in the straight-line method. Two accelerated methods, the double declining balance method and the sum-of-the-years'-digits method, provide for larger amounts of depreciation in the earlier years. Repairs, on the other hand, are generally lower in the earlier years so that the total cost of depreciation and repairs should be about the same each year. The units of output method bases depreciation each period on the amount of output.

STRAIGHT-LINE METHOD

This is the simplest and most widely used depreciation method. Under this method an equal portion of the cost of the asset is allocated to each period of use. The periodic charge is expressed as:

$$\frac{\text{COST} - \text{SCRAP VALUE}}{\text{USEFUL LIFE (IN YEARS)}} = \text{ANNUAL DEPRECIATION CHARGE}$$

EXAMPLE 3.

Cost of machine, $17,000; scrap value, $2,000; estimated life, 5 years.

$$\frac{\$17,000 - \$2,000}{5} = \$3,000 \text{ per year}$$

The entry to record the depreciation would be:

Depreciation Expense, Machinery	*3,000*	
Accumulated Depreciation, Machinery		*3,000*

SUM-OF-THE-YEARS'-DIGITS METHOD

The years of the asset's lifetime are labeled 1, 2, 3, etc., and the depreciation amounts are based on a series of fractions having the sum of the years' digits as the common denominator. The largest digit is used as the numerator for the first year, the next largest digit for the second year, and so forth.

EXAMPLE 4.

Cost of machine, $17,000; scrap value, $2,000; estimated life, 5 years.

The depreciable amount is $17,000 - 2,000 = $15,000. To find the fraction of this amount to be written off each year, proceed as follows:

(1) Label the years 1, 2, 3, 4, and 5.

(2) Calculate the sum of the years' digits: $S = 1 + 2 + 3 + 4 + 5 = 15$.

(3) Convert the sum to a series of fractions: $\frac{1}{15} + \frac{2}{15} + \frac{3}{15} + \frac{4}{15} + \frac{5}{15} = 1$.

(4) Take the above series of fractions *in reverse order* as the depreciation rates. Thus:

Year	Fraction		Amount		Depreciation
1	5/15	×	$15,000	=	$ 5,000
2	4/15	×	$15,000	=	$ 4,000
3	3/15	×	$15,000	=	$ 3,000
4	2/15	×	$15,000	=	$ 2,000
5	1/15	×	$15,000	=	$ 1,000
			Total depreciation		$15,000

If the life expectancy of a machine were five years as stated above, you could follow step 2 by adding $1 + 2 + 3 + 4 + 5 = 15$. However, for a machine that has a long life expectancy, it is simpler to use the formula:

$$S = \frac{N(N + 1)}{2}$$

In the above equation:

$$S = \frac{5(5 + 1)}{2} = 15$$

EXAMPLE 5.

The life of a piece of equipment is calculated to be 30 years. The sum of the years' digits would be:

$$S = \frac{30(30 + 1)}{2} = 465$$

DOUBLE DECLINING BALANCE METHOD

The double declining balance method produces the highest amount of depreciation in the earlier years. *It does not recognize scrap value.* Instead, the book value of the asset remaining at the end of the depreciation period becomes the scrap value. Under this method, the straight-line rate is doubled and applied to the declining book balance each year. Many companies prefer the double declining balance method because of the faster write-off in the earlier years when the asset contributes most to the business and when the expenditure was actually made. The procedure is to apply a *fixed rate* to the declining book value of the asset each year. As the book value declines, the depreciation becomes smaller.

EXAMPLE 6.

A $17,000 asset is to be depreciated over five years, the double declining balance rate is thus 40% per year.

Year	Book Value at Beginning of Year	Rate	Depreciation for Year	Book Value at End of Year
1	$17,000	40%	$6,800	$10,200
2	10,200	40%	4,080	6,120
3	6,120	40%	2,448	3,672
4	3,672	40%	1,469	2,203
5	2,203	40%	881	1,322

The $1,322 book value at the end of the fifth year becomes the scrap value. If, however, a scrap value had been estimated at $2,000, the depreciation for the fifth year would be $203 ($2,203 − $2,000) instead of $881.

The date of purchase should also be considered. In Example 6, it was assumed that the equipment was purchased at the beginning of the year, which is usually not a common occurrence. Therefore a change in the computation for the first partial year of service is needed.

EXAMPLE 7.

If in Example 6, the equipment had been purchased and placed into use at the end of the ninth month of the fiscal year, the pro-rata portion of the first full year's depreciation would be:

$$\frac{3}{12} (40\% \times 17,000) \text{ or } \$1,700$$

The method of computation for the remaining years would not be affected. Thus in the second year:

$$40\%(\$17,000 - \$1,700) \text{ or } \$6,120$$

would be the depreciation for the second year and $9,180 ($17,000 − $7,820) its book value.

UNITS OF OUTPUT METHOD

Where the use of equipment varies substantially from year to year, the units of output method is appropriate. For example, in some years logging operations can be carried on for 200 days, in other years for 230 days, in still other years only for 160 days, depending on weather conditions. Under this method depreciation is computed for the appropriate unit of output or production (such as hours, miles, or pounds) by the following formula:

$$\frac{\text{COST} - \text{SCRAP VALUE}}{\text{ESTIMATED UNITS OF OUTPUT DURING LIFETIME}} = \text{UNIT DEPRECIATION}$$

The total number of units for each year is then multiplied by the unit depreciation to arrive at the depreciation amount for that year.

This method has the advantage of relating more directly the depreciation cost to revenue.

EXAMPLE 8.

Cost of a machine, $17,000; scrap value, $2,000; estimated life, 8,000 hours.

$$\frac{\$17,000 - \$2,000}{8,000} = \$1.875 \text{ depreciation per hour}$$

If during the year in question the machine was operated for 1,800 hours, the depreciation would be:

$$1,800 \text{ hours} \times \$1.875 \text{ per hour} = \$3,375$$

The four principal methods of depreciation are compared in Table 13-1 below. It is assumed that over a five-year lifetime the asset was in operation for the following numbers of hours: 1,800, 1,200, 2,000, 1,400, 1,600. Cost of asset, $17,000; scrap value, $2,000.

Table 13-1. Annual Depreciation Charge

Year	Straight-Line	Sum of the Years' Digits	Double Declining Balance	Units of Production
1	$3,000	$5,000	$6,800	$3,375
2	3,000	4,000	4,080	2,250
3	3,000	3,000	2,448	3,750
4	3,000	2,000	1,468	2,625
5	3,000	1,000	204	3,000
Total	$15,000	$15,000	$15,000	$15,000

13.4   DISPOSAL OF FIXED ASSETS

BY DISCARDING OF THE ASSET

When plant assets are no longer needed (and usually are fully depreciated), they may be sold for scrap.

EXAMPLE 9.

An item of equipment bought for $15,000 is fully depreciated at the close of the preceding year and is now deemed to be worthless. The entry to record the disposal of the asset is:

Accumulated Depreciation	15,000	
Equipment		15,000

If the asset has book value (has not been fully depreciated), entries are made (1) to bring the depreciation up to the date of disposal, (2) to record the loss on disposal. posal.

EXAMPLE 10.

A $15,000 asset with accumulated depreciation of $12,600 had been depreciated at the annual rate of 10%. If we decide to discard the asset on April 30, an adjusting entry is needed to record the depreciation for the period January 1–April 30 (4 months), since no entry to record the expense has been made. Therefore, one-third of the annual depreciation of $1,500 ($15,000 × 10%) must be recorded.

Entry 1	Depreciation Expense	500	
	Accumulated Depreciation		500

This entry is necessary to bring the accumulated depreciation up to date of disposal. The entry to record the disposal of the asset would be:

Entry 2	Accumulated Depreciation	13,100	
	Loss on Disposal of Fixed Asset	1,900	
	Equipment		15,000

The $1,900 loss ($15,000 − $13,100) would appear as nonoperating expense under the heading "Other Expense" in the income statement.

BY SALE OF THE ASSET

Assets that are no longer useful to a business may be sold. The sale requires entries (1) to bring the depreciation (and hence the book value) up to date, (2) to record the sale at either a gain (if the selling price exceeds the updated book value) or a loss (if the selling price is below the updated book value).

EXAMPLE 11. Gain on Sale.

A $15,000 asset with accumulated depreciation of $12,600 as of December 31, and an estimated straight-line life of 10 years, is sold on the following April 30 for $2,300.

Entry 1	Depreciation Expense	500*	
	Accumulated Depreciation		500
	*1/3 × $1,500		

Entry 2	Cash	2,300	
	Accumulated Depreciation	13,100	
	Equipment		15,000
	Gain on Disposal of Fixed Asset		400

Proof of Gain	Sale of Equipment	$2,300	
	Book Value	1,900	(15,000 − 13,100)
	Gain on Disposal of Fixed Assets	$ 400	

Gain on disposal of fixed assets would be treated as nonoperating income in the income statement, under the heading "Other Income."

EXAMPLE 12. Loss on Sale.

Assume the same information as in Example 11 except that the equipment is sold for $1,600.

Entry 1	Depreciation Expense	500	
	Accumulated Depreciation		500

Entry 2	Cash	1,600	
	Accumulated Depreciation	13,100	
	Loss on Disposal of Fixed Assets	300	
	Equipment		15,000

Proof of Loss

	Sale of Equipment	$1,600
	Book Value	1,900
	Loss on Disposal of Fixed Assets	$ (300)

Loss on Disposal of fixed assets would be treated as nonoperating expense in the income statement, under the heading "Other Expense."

BY TRADE-IN OF THE ASSET

Old equipment may be traded in for new equipment. The trade-in allowance is deducted from the price of the new equipment and the balance, known as the *boot*, is paid in accordance with the agreement. If the allowance is greater than the carrying value of the asset, a gain results. However, the gain is not recorded but is subtracted from the cost of the new equipment. An alternative method of computation of the new asset would be to add the book value of the old asset and the amount of boot.

Again entries are required (1) to bring the depreciation up to date and (2) to record the trade-in.

NON-RECOGNITION OF GAIN

EXAMPLE 13.

	Old Equipment		New Equipment	
DATA:	Cost of equipment	$15,000	Price of new	
	Accumulated depreciation		equipment	$20,000
	as of December 31,		Trade-in allowance	2,500
	previous year	12,600	Cash to be paid	$17,500
	Depreciation for the			
	current year	500		
	Book value at date of			
	exchange	1,900		

Entry 1	Depreciation Expense	500		
	Accumulated Depreciation		500	
Entry 2	Accumulated Depreciation	13,100 *		
	Equipment (new)	19,400 **		
	Equipment (old)		15,000	
	Cash		17,500	

* $12,600 + $500

** Cost	$20,000		Cost of New Equipment	
Less: Gain	−600		Old Equipment (Book Value)	$ 1,900
New Equipment	$19,400	or	Cash Paid	17,500
			Cost of New Equipment	$19,400

Proof of Gain:	Trade-In	$2,500
	Book Value	1,900
	Gain	$ 600

RECOGNITION OF LOSS

A loss on trade-in is recognized when the trade-in is less than the book value. The new asset is recorded at its cost.

EXAMPLE 14.

Using the information in Example 13, assume that the trade-in allowance had been $1,000 instead of $2,500. The entries that are required would be (1) to bring the depreciation up to date and (2) to record the trade.

Entry 1	Depreciation Expense	500	
	Accumulated Depreciation		500
Entry 2	Accumulated Depreciation	13,100	
	Equipment (new)	20,000	
	Loss on Disposal of Fixed Asset	900 *	
	Equipment (old)		15,000
	Cash		19,000

* Equipment (old)	$15,000
Accumulated Depreciation	13,100
Book Value	$ 1,900
Trade-In	−1,000
Loss on Trade-In	$ 900

Generally accepted accounting principles, as expressed in APB Opinion 29, do not recognize a gain on a trade-in but do recognize a loss on a trade-in. The Internal Revenue Code does not permit either a gain or loss to be recognized for income tax purposes. Where a trade-in involves only a small loss, many companies, for practical purposes, follow the income tax rule.

Summary

(1) The main reason for depreciation is _____.

(2) Accumulated Depreciation is an example of an _____ account, since the fixed asset remains at cost while the offset builds up.

(3) The market value of a fixed asset at the end of its service is known as _____.

(4) The uniform distribution of depreciation over the life of the asset is known as the _____ method.

(5) The _____ method is used to write off the asset based upon a series of fractions.

(6) The method that produces the largest amount of depreciation in the earlier years, then rapidly declines, is known as the _____ method.

(7) Loss on disposal of fixed assets is _____ in a journal entry.

(8) A new machine costing $24,000, with a gain on trade-in of $2,000, will be recorded at $_____ .

(9) The amount paid for an item, after a trade-in has been deducted, is known as the _____ .

Answers: (1) aging; (2) offset or valuation; (3) scrap value; (4) straight-line; (5) sum of the years' digits; (6) double declining balance; (7) debited; (8) $22,000; (9) boot

Solved Problems

13.1. Hacol Company acquired an asset on January 1, 19X2, at a cost of $38,000, with an estimated useful life of 8 years and a salvage value of $2,000. What is the annual depreciation based upon the straight-line method?

SOLUTION

Cost	$38,000
Scrap value	2,000
Amount to be depreciated	$36,000

$36,000 ÷ 8 years = $4,500 depreciation per year

13.2. For the asset of Problem 13.1, compute the depreciation for the first two years by the sum-of-the-years'-digits method.

SOLUTION

$$S = 8\left(\frac{8+1}{2}\right) = 36$$

Year 1: $\frac{8}{36} \times \$36,000 = \$8,000$

Year 2: $\frac{7}{36} \times \$36,000 = \$7,000$

13.3. Repeat Problem 13.2, but using the double declining balance method.

SOLUTION

For the depreciation rate we take twice the straight-line rate; i.e.,

$$2 \times \frac{100\%}{8 \text{ years}} = 25\% \text{ per year}$$

Therefore,

Year 1: $38,000 × 25% = $9,500

Year 2:   ($38,000 − $9,500) × 25% = $7,125

13.4. A truck was purchased on January 1, 19X2, for $8,500, with an estimated scrap value of $500. It will be depreciated for 8 years using the straight-line method. Show how the truck account and the related accumulated depreciation account would appear on the balance sheet on (a) December 31, 19X2; (b) December 31, 19X3.

(a)

(b)

SOLUTION

(a)	Truck	$8,500		
	Less: Accumulated Depreciation	1,000*	$7,500	
(b)	Truck	$8,500		
	Less: Accumulated Depreciation	2,000**	$6,500	

* $\dfrac{\$8,500 - \$500}{8 \text{ years}} = \$1,000$ per year

** $1,000 per year × 2

13.5. Based on Problem 13.4, what amount will appear in the income statement for Depreciation Expense, Truck (*a*) For the year 19X2? (*b*) For the year 19X3?

SOLUTION

(*a*) $1,000   (1 year's depreciation)

(*b*) $1,000   (1 year's depreciation)

13.6. Equipment costing $9,600, with an estimated scrap value of $1,600, was bought on July 1, 19X2. The equipment is to be depreciated by the straight-line method for a period of 10 years. The company's fiscal year is January through December. Show how the equipment account and the related accumulated depreciation account would appear in the balance sheet on (*a*) December 31, 19X2; (*b*) December 31, 19X3.

(*a*)

(*b*)

SOLUTION

(*a*)

Equipment		$9,600		
Less: Accumulated Depreciation	400*	$9,200		

$$* \frac{\$9,600 - \$1,600}{10 \ years} = \$800 \ depreciation \ per \ year$$

$\frac{1}{2}$ year (July 1 to Dec. 31) × $800 per year = $400

(*b*)

Equipment		$9,600		
Less: Accumulated Depreciation	1,200*	$8,400		

* $1\frac{1}{2}$ years × $800 per year = $1,200

13.7. What amount will appear in the income statement for Depreciation Expense, Equipment (Problem 13.6) (*a*) For the year 19X2? (*b*) For the year 19X3?

SOLUTION

(*a*) $400 ($\frac{1}{2}$ year's depreciation)   (*b*) $800 (1 year's depreciation)

13.8. As of December 31, 19X2, accumulated depreciation of $9,000 has been recorded on equipment which originally cost $14,000. What is the entry to record the disposal of the asset if the equipment was discarded with no salvage value?

SOLUTION

Accumulated Depreciation, Equipment	9,000	
Loss on Disposal of Fixed Assets	5,000	
Equipment		14,000

The book value of $5,000 is considered a loss because there is no salvage value.

13.9. For Problem 13.8, what entry would be recorded if the equipment were sold for $6,000?

SOLUTION

Accumulated Depreciation, Equipment	9,000	
Cash	6,000	
Equipment		14,000
Gain on Disposal of Fixed Assets		1,000*

* Cost	$14,000	Cash Sale	$6,000
Accumulated Depreciation	9,000	Book Value	5,000
Book Value	$ 5,000	Gain	$1,000

13.10. Based on Problem 13.9, what entry would be recorded if the equipment were sold for $4,000?

SOLUTION

Accumulated Depreciation, Equipment	9,000	
Cash	4,000	
Loss on Disposal of Fixed Assets	1,000	
Equipment		14,000

13.11. S. Altman Company traded in a cutting machine for a new one priced at $2,600, receiving a trade-in allowance of $600 and paying the balance in cash. The old machine cost $1,800 and had an accumulated depreciation of $1,400. What is the entry to record the acquisition of the new machine?

SOLUTION

Accumulated Depreciation, Machine	1,400	
Machine (new)	2,400*	
Machine (old)		1,800
Cash		2,000

* Price of New Machine	$2,600		Equipment (old) Book Value	$ 400
Less: Unrecognized Gain	200	or	Cash paid	2,000
Cost of New Machine	$2,400		Cost of New Equipment	$2,400

13.12. Based on the information above, assume that the trade-in allowance had been $100 instead of $600. What is the entry to record the acquisition of the new machine?

SOLUTION

Accumulated Depreciation, Machine	1,400	
Machine (new)	2,600	
Loss on Disposal of Fixed Assets	300	
Cash		2,500
Machine (old)		1,800

13.13. Equipment which was acquired at a cost of $5,000 has an accumulated depreciation of $3,800. It is traded in for similar equipment costing $8,400, and a trade-in allowance of $1,500 is received. Present the entry to record the acquisition of the new equipment.

SOLUTION

Accumulated Depreciation	3,800	
Equipment (new)	8,100*	
Equipment (old)		5,000
Cash		6,900

* Trade-in Allowance	$1,500	Price of New Equipment	$8,400
Book Value	1,200	Less: Unrecognized Gain	300
Gain	$ 300	Cost of New Equipment	$8,100

13.14. A fixed asset costing $60,000, with an estimated salvage value of $5,000, has a life expectancy of 10 years. Compare the results of the various depreciation methods by filling in the tables below. Take twice the straight-line rate as the rate in the double declining balance method.

STRAIGHT-LINE METHOD

Year	Depreciation Expense	Accumulated Depreciation	Book Value at End of Year
1			
2			
3			
4			

SUM-OF-THE-YEARS'-DIGITS METHOD

Year	Depreciation Expense	Accumulated Depreciation	Book Value at End of Year
1			
2			
3			
4			

DOUBLE DECLINING BALANCE METHOD

Year	Depreciation Expense	Accumulated Depreciation	Book Value at End of Year
1			
2			
3			
4			

SOLUTION

STRAIGHT-LINE METHOD

Year	Depreciation Expense	Accumulated Depreciation	Book Value at End of Year
1	$5,500*	$ 5,500	$54,500**
2	5,500	11,000	49,000
3	5,500	16,500	43,500
4	5,500	22,000	38,000

$* (60,000 - 5,000) \div 10 = 5,500$ $** 60,000 - 5,500 = 54,500$

SUM-OF-THE-YEARS'-DIGITS METHOD

Year	Depreciation Expense	Accumulated Depreciation	Book Value at End of Year
1	$10,000*	$10,000	$50,000
2	9,000	19,000	41,000
3	8,000	27,000	33,000
4	7,000	34,000	26,000

$* S = \dfrac{10(10 + 1)}{2} = 55$ $\dfrac{10}{55} \times 55,000 = 10,000$

DOUBLE DECLINING BALANCE METHOD

Year	Depreciation Expense	Accumulated Depreciation	Book Value at End of Year
1	$12,000*	$12,000	$48,000
2	9,600**	21,600	38,400
3	7,680	29,280	30,720
4	6,144	35,424	24,576

$* (2 \times 10\%) \times 60,000 = 12,000$ $** 20\% \times (60,000 - 12,000) = 9,600$

13.15. The four transactions below were selected from the ledger of J. B. Adam regarding the disposal of some of his fixed assets. Depreciation is considered to be recorded only at the end of the prior year. Present journal entries for each transaction. (*Note*: If an item is disposed of before the 15th, do not count the month.)

(*a*)   March 3: Discarded four typewriters, realizing no scrap value. Total cost, $3,000; accumulated depreciation as of Dec. 31, $2,000; annual depreciation, $360.

(*b*)   March 29: Sold office furniture for cash, $1,600. Total cost, $8,000; accumulated depreciation through Dec. 31, $6,800; annual depreciation, $600.

(*c*)   May 2: Traded in an old automobile for a new one priced at $4,000, receiving a trade-in allowance of $1,400 and paying the balance in cash. Data on the old automobile: Cost, $3,900; Accumulated Depreciation, $2,700; Annual Depreciation, $960

(*d*)   May 5: Traded in dictating equipment costing $1,000, with $800 accumulated depreciation as of Dec. 31. The annual depreciation is $240. Received a trade-in allowance of $100, paying the balance in cash for a new dictating unit at $1,400.

(a) **(1)** _____ | | |
     _____ | | |
     (2) _____ | | |
     _____ | | |
     _____ | | |

(b) **(1)** _____ | | |
     _____ | | |
     (2) _____ | | |
     _____ | | |
     _____ | | |

(c) **(1)** _____ | | |
     _____ | | |
     (2) _____ | | |
     _____ | | |
     _____ | | |

(d) **(1)** _____ | | |
     _____ | | |
     (2) _____ | | |
     _____ | | |
     _____ | | |
     _____ | | |

SOLUTION

(a)	**(1)**	_Depreciation Expense_	60	
		Accumulated Depreciation		60
		[2 months × $30 per month = $60]		
	(2)	_Accumulated Depreciation_	2,060	
		Loss on Disposal of Fixed Assets	940	
		Typewriters		3,000
(b)	**(1)**	_Depreciation Expense_	150	
		Accumulated Depreciation		150
		[3 months × $50 per month = $150]		
	(2)	_Accumulated Depreciation_	6,950	
		Cash	1,600	
		Office Equipment		8,000
		Gain on Disposal of Fixed Assets		550
(c)	**(1)**	_Depreciation Expense_	320	
		Accumulated Depreciation		320
		[4 months × $80 per month = $320]		

(2) Accumulated Depreciation			3,020	
Automobile (new)			3,480 *	
Cash				2,600
Automobile (old)				3,900

* Price of Auto (new)	$4,000	Trade-in	$1,400
Less: Unrecognized Gain	520	Book Value	880
Auto to be recorded at	$3,480	Gain	$ 520

(d)	(1) Depreciation Expense		80	
	Accumulated Depreciation			80
	[4 months × $20 per month = $80]			
	(2) Equipment (new)		1,400	
	Accumulated Depreciation		880	
	Loss on Disposal of Fixed Assets*		20	
	Equipment (old)			1,000
	Cash			1,300

* Book Value	$120
Trade-In	100
Loss	$ 20

13.16. The transactions below were selected from the records of the S. Harris Restaurant regarding the disposal of some of her fixed assets. Depreciation is considered to be recorded only at the end of the year, December 31. Record the entries for each transaction.

(a) April 2:   Sold refrigerators for cash, $600. Total cost, $4,000; accumulated depreciation, $3,600; annual depreciation, $600.

(b) April 18:   Discarded mixer realizing no scrap value. Total cost, $10,500; accumulated depreciation, $9,360; annual depreciation, $720.

(c) May 4:   Traded in a freezer case costing $13,000 with accumulated depreciation of $10,000, receiving $2,500 trade-in allowance. The annual depreciation was $600. The cost of the new freezer was $16,500, and the balance was paid in cash.

(d) August 8:   Traded in a delivery van costing $6,000 with accumulated depreciation of $4,200. The annual depreciation was $1,800. Received a trade-in allowance of $1,900. The price of the new van was $9,800 and the balance was paid by a note.

(a)

(b)

(c)

(d)		

SOLUTION

(a)	**(1)**	Depreciation Expense	150	
		Accumulated Depreciation		150
		[3 months × $50 per month = $150]		
	(2)	Accumulated Depreciation	3,750	
		Cash	600	
		Equipment		4,000
		Gain on Disposal of Fixed Assets		350
(b)	**(1)**	Depreciation Expense	240	
		Accumulated Depreciation		240
		[4 months × $60 per month = $240]		
	(2)	Accumulated Depreciation	9,600	
		Loss on Disposal of Fixed Assets	900	
		Equipment		10,500
(c)	**(1)**	Depreciation Expense	200	
		Accumulated Depreciation		200
		[4 months × $50 per month = $200]		
	(2)	Accumulated Depreciation	10,200	
		Equipment (new)	16,500	
		Loss on Disposal of Fixed Assets	300	
		Equipment (old)		13,000
		Cash		14,000
(d)	**(1)**	Depreciation Expense	1,050	
		Accumulated Depreciation		1,050
		[7 months × $150 per month = $1,050]		
	(2)	Equipment (new)	8,650*	
		Accumulated Depreciation	5,250	
		Equipment (old)		6,000
		Notes Payable		7,900

* Trade-In	$1,900	Price of Equipment (new)	$9,800
Book Value (6,000 − 5,250)	750	Less Gain	1,150
Gain (to be deducted	$1,150	Equipment (new)	$8,650
from price of new equip.)			

or

Proof: Paid for by:

Book Value of Old Equipment	$ 750	(6,000 − 5,250)
Notes Payable	7,900	
Cost of New Equipment	$8,650	

Examination IV

Chapters 11-13

1. The total amount of earnings shown on the Jamison Company payroll on April 15 was $26,000. Of that amount $20,000 was subject to FICA (6.13%). Total payroll deductions included: hospitalization, $1,000, and pension, $2,500. Present the general journal entry needed to record this payroll.

2. Below is the payroll information for three of the employees of the Ernst Company.

Employee	Amount Earned to Date	Gross Pay for Week
A	$4,000	$100
B	$5,800	$250
C	$7,000	$200

The company is located in a state that imposes an unemployment insurance tax of 2% on the first $6,000. Federal unemployment tax is 0.7%; FICA tax, 6.13%. Present the journal entry necessary to record the employer's payroll tax expenses.

3. A 60-day, 6%, $3,000 note received in settlement of an account, dated June 1, is discounted at 6% on July 1. What are the entries needed to record the information (a) on June 1? (b) on July 1?

4.

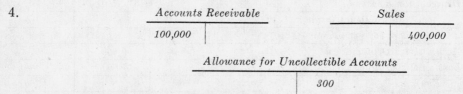

For the balances given above, what is the adjusting entry to record the provision for uncollectible accounts, if the uncollectible expense is estimated as:

    (a) 1% of sales?

    (b) $3,600, by the balance sheet method?

5. The Washington Company acquired an asset on January 1, 19X2, at a cost of $28,000, with an estimated useful life of 10 years and a salvage value of $500. Find the annual depreciation for the first two years, using the (a) straight-line method, (b) sum-of-the-years'-digits method, (c) double declining balance method.

6. As of December 31, 19X2, accumulated depreciation of $10,000 has been recorded on equipment which originally cost $15,000. What is the entry to record the disposal of the assets (a) if the equipment was discarded and no funds received for it? (b) if it was sold for $8,000?

7. Saltman Company traded in an electric motor for a new one priced at $5,200, receiving a trade-in allowance of $600 and paying the balance in cash. For the old motor the cost and accumulated depreciation were $3,800 and $3,400 respectively. What is the entry need to record the acquisition?

8. Equipment purchased on July 1, 19X2 for $5,500 has an estimated scrap value of $1,000. The equipment will be depreciated by the straight line method for a period of five years. The company's fiscal year begins January 1. Show how the equipment and the related accumulated depreciation would appear in the balance sheet on (a) December 31, 19X2 and (b) December 31, 19X3.

9. Based on the data above, what amount would appear in the income statement for Depreciation Expense — Equipment on (*a*) For the year 19X2 and (*b*) For the year 19X3.

Answers to Examination IV

1.

Salary Expense	26,000	
FICA Taxes Payable		1,226
Hospitalization Payable		1,000
Pension Contributions Payable		2,500
Cash		21,274

2.

Employee	FICA	State	Federal
A	$ 6.13 (6.13% × $100)	$2.00 (2% × $100)	$0.70 (.007 × $100)
B	$15.33 (6.13% × $250)	$4.00 (2% × $200)	1.40 (.007 × $200)
C	$12.26 (6.13% × $200)	– –	– –
	$33.72	$6.00	$2.10

Payroll Tax Expense	41.82	
FICA Taxes Payable		33.72
State Unemployment Insurance Payable		6.00
Federal Unemployment Insurance Payable		2.10

3.

$3,000.00	Principal
30.00	Interest income
$3,030.00	Maturity value
15.15	Discount
$3,014.85	Net proceeds

(*a*)

Notes Receivable	3,000.00	
Accounts Receivable		3,000.00

(*b*)

Cash	3,014.85	
Interest Income		14.85
Notes Receivable		3,000.00

4. (*a*)

Uncollectible Accounts Expense	4,000	
Allowance for Uncollectible Accounts		4,000

(*b*)

Uncollectible Accounts Expense	3,300*	
Allowance for Uncollectible Accounts		3,300

* 3,600 − 300 = 3,300; the balance in the allowance account must be taken into consideration

5.

	First Year	Second Year
(*a*)	$2,750	$2,750
(*b*)	5,000	4,500
(*c*)	5,600	4,480

6. (*a*)

Accumulated Depreciation, Equipment	10,000	
Loss on Disposal of Fixed Asset	5,000	
Equipment		15,000

(b)   Accumulated Depreciation, Equipment   10,000
                 Cash   8,000
                      Equipment   15,000
                      Gain on Disposal of Fixed Asset   3,000

7.   Accumulated Depreciation   3,400
          Equipment (new)   5,000*
                 Equipment (old)   3,800
                 Cash   4,600

      * Price of New Machine $5,200
         Less: Unrecognized Gain   200   ($600 Trade-In — $400 Value)
         New Machine $5,000

8.   (a)   Equipment $5,500
            Less: Accumulated Depreciation   450* $5,050
            $$\frac{*\$5,500 - \$1,000}{5 \text{ years}} = \$900 \text{ depreciation per year}$$

            1/2 year (July 1-December 31) × $900 per year = $450

      (b)   Equipment $5,500
            Less: Accumulated Depreciation   1,350* $4,150

            *1.5 years × $900 per year = $1,350

9.   (a) $450 (1/2 year's depreciation)
      (b) $900 (1 year's depreciation)

Chapter 14

Revenue, Expenses, and Net Income

14.1 WHAT IS REVENUE?

Revenue is the inflow of resources resulting from the delivery of goods or services in the effort to produce a profit. The revenue which derives from the principal business of the firm is called *operating revenue,* the term *other revenue* is used for any incidental gains, such as sales of noncurrent assets or retirement of noncurrent liabilities.

14.2 RECOGNITION OF REVENUE

Revenue should be recognized at the earliest point at which it is secured, measurable, and earned. There are three general bases for deciding when that point has been reached.

Sales basis. Recognition occurs at the time the company's products or services are *delivered* to the customer. This is the most frequently used basis.

Production basis. Revenue may be recognized at the completion of production and before a sale is made if there is a guaranteed market. For example, gold and certain other products have assured sales prices and thus revenue can be recognized when the product is ready. Revenue is sometimes recognized *before* production is complete or an exchange has taken place. For example, in the case of long-term construction projects, which may extend two or three years or more, revenue is recognized according to the percentage of completion. If the job is 50% complete, then 50% of the expected earnings is recognized in the current period.

Collection basis. Revenue is recognized only when cash is actually collected from customers. Also called the *cash basis,* it is used by doctors, lawyers, etc., and by small businesses with little or no amount of inventory. Retail stores that sell goods on the installment plan and recognize revenue as collections are made call this the *installment basis.*

14.3 REVENUE REDUCTIONS

Closely related to the earning of revenue are the reductions and adjustments which must be made in order to arrive at the proper revenue amount. There are three principal types.

Sales returns and allowances. If the customer returns goods or if the goods or services are faulty, an allowance is made to the customer. The result is a decrease in sales. The debit is made to a separate account in order that records can be maintained and control exerted over such returns and allowances.

EXAMPLE 1.

If cash is given, the entry is as follows:

Sales Returns and Allowances	100	
Cash		100

If the customer's account is credited, the entry is:

Sales Returns and Allowances	100	
Accounts Receivable		100

Cash discounts. Often a discount is offered to customers to encourage payment before the normal due date. Generally it is 2 percent for payment within 10 days, or the full amount is due in 30 days. These terms are abbreviated to "2/10, n/30." A discount is an expense of the business and is now generally shown as a reduction of sales. Less desirably, the discount may be considered a payment of interest for receiving cash early, and shown as sales expense.

EXAMPLE 2.

The entry to record the cash discount when a customer pays his bill of $400 within the discount period is:

Cash	392	
Cash Discount	8	
Accounts Receivable		400

Credit losses. Experience shows that a small percentage of credit sales will never be collected. This amount can be closely estimated and provided for in the accounts.

EXAMPLE 3.

Assume that 1% of the sales on account during the period will be uncollectible. Then, if the sales on account were $100,000 and the accounts receivable balance at the year end was $25,000 the entry will be as follows:

Uncollectible Accounts Expense	1,000	
Allowance for Uncollectible Accounts		1,000

The debit is an operating expense. The allowance is a valuation account (see Sec. 12.7) to be deducted from Accounts Receivable.

Balance Sheet

Accounts Receivable	$25,000	
Less: Allowance for Uncollectible Accounts	1,000	$24,000

14.4 SALES TAXES

Sales taxes are not revenue and should be separately recorded and paid. Thus if a sale of $100 is made and the state, city, or other retail tax is 6%, then the entry is as follows:

Cash	106	
Sales		100
Sales Taxes Payable		6

14.5 WHAT IS AN EXPENSE?

The consumption of resources in the effort to produce revenue is expense. It is important that an expense be matched with the revenue to which it relates. There are two forms of expenses: *consumption of goods* (cost of goods sold, supplies, depreciation of property, etc.) and *consumption of services* (salaries, wages, rent, interest, taxes, etc.).

It is useful to distinguish an expense, as just defined, from a cost and from an expenditure. A *cost* — say, the cost of merchandise — does not expire in the usual sense. The merchandise is sold rather than consumed, and one speaks of "cost of goods sold," not of an expense. An *expenditure* is merely the payment for an item, which may be either an expense item, such as salaries, or a capital item, such as equipment.

14.6 PREPAID, UNEARNED, DEFERRED, AND ACCRUED ITEMS

There are a number of revenue and expense items which have all or a part of their balance recognized as income or expense in succeeding periods. In fact, the accrual method of accounting rests on recognizing income or expense only in the specific period in which income is *earned* or expense *incurred*.

Prepaid and Unearned items. These are commodities or services purchased but unconsumed at the end of the accounting period (prepaid expenses) or revenue received but not earned (unearned revenue). The portion used or earned during the period is expense or income, the remainder will be an expense or income normally in the next period. Prepaid expenses are ordinarily included as current assets. Unearned revenue will be included as a current liability unless the income will apply to more than one year.

EXAMPLE 4.　Prepaid Expense.

An advance rent payment of $900 was made on November 1, 19X2. The monthly rate is $300. The entry to record this information is:

Prepaid Rent	900	
Cash		900

On December 31, 19X2, an adjusting entry must be made to recognize the expense for the year 19X2.

Rent Expense	600	
Prepaid Rent		600

EXAMPLE 5. Unearned Income.

Unearned rent of $600 is entered as:

Cash	600
Unearned Rent Income	600

If the advance is only for a month or a quarter and will be earned before the year end, it may be recorded as earned upon receipt:

Cash	600
Rent Income	600

Deferred items. These result from the postponement of the recognition of an expense already paid or of a revenue already received, if the deferment will extend more than one year. They would ordinarily be shown on the balance sheet as noncurrent assets, under a caption such as Deferred Charges or Other Assets or Deferred Credits.

EXAMPLE 6.

The company has a substantial investment in patterns and molds used in producing machine parts. The patterns and molds are amortized over a four-year period. On January 1, $5,000 worth of patterns and molds were purchased for cash.

Patterns and Molds	5,000	
Cash		5,000

By December 31 of the same year, one-fourth ($1,250) of the asset had been used up.

Patterns and Molds Expense	*1,250*	
Patterns and Molds		*1,250*

Accrued items. *Expenses or revenues that have gradually accumulated but have not yet been recognized in the accounts.* An accrued expense may be shown on the balance sheet without the word "accrued" occurring; for instance, "salaries payable." Similarly, accrued revenue may appear as "interest receivable," etc. Since these items relate to a short period, they are classified respectively as current liabilities and current assets.

EXAMPLE 7. Accrued Liability.

The payroll for salaries is $1,250 weekly, or $250 per day, and is paid the week after it is earned. The month of December ended on Tuesday and thus two days' pay, or $500, had acrrued and was unpaid on December 31. The entry on December 31 is:

Salaries Expense	*500*	
Salaries Payable		*500*

EXAMPLE 8. Accrued Asset.

A company holds a $5,000, 9%, 90-day note receivable dated December 1. The accrued interest receivable entry to reflect the interest earned (December 1-31) is:

Interest Receivable	*37.50*	
Interest Income		*37.50*
($5,000 × 9% × 30 days)		

14.7   WHAT IS NET INCOME?

Net income is the excess of the earned inflow of resources over the consumption of resources used in earning that inflow. Thus, it is gross sales, less sales reductions and all costs and expenses incurred in earning the sales.

14.8   FORMS OF THE INCOME STATEMENT

The definition of net income given in Sec. 14.7, together with the division of revenue and expenses into operating and nonoperating groups, implies the following general categories for the income statement.

    REVENUE (SALES) *(Inflow of resources)*

− **COSTS AND EXPENSES** *(Consumption of resources, such as merchandise, wages, salaries, rent)*

    NET INCOME FROM OPERATIONS *(Excess of revenue over operating expenses)*

+ **OTHER INCOME** *(Incidental, nonoperating income, such as interest income)*

− **OTHER EXPENSES** *(Incidental, nonoperating expense, such as loss on sale of assets)*

    NET INCOME *(Excess of revenue over all expenses; an increase in capital)*

This basic plan can be adapted to the needs of a particular concern through the inclusion of various intermediary captions and subtotals. Differing treatments of extraordinary items are also possible. Examples 9 through 12 display the forms of income statement most commonly found.

EXAMPLE 9. Classified Multiple-Step Form.

(a)	*Sales Revenue*		
	Gross Sales		*$700,000*
	Less: Sales Returns and Allowances	*$ 15,300*	
	Cash Discounts on Sales	*12,400*	*27,700*
	Net Sales		*$672,300*

Net sales (repeated from previous page)			$672,300

(b) Cost of Goods Sold

Beginning Inventory		$ 58,700	
Purchases	$400,000		
Less: Purchase Returns and Allowances	12,100		
Net Purchases	$387,900		
Transportation-In	43,200	431,100	
Goods Available for Sale		489,800	
Less: Ending Inventory		45,600	
Cost of Goods Sold			444,200

(c) Gross Profit on Sales $228,100

(d) Operating Expenses

Selling Expenses

Sales Salaries and Commissions	$ 30,000		
Sales Travel	15,000		
Advertising and Promotion	28,000		
Delivery Expense	7,000		
Other Selling Expenses	5,000	85,000	

General and Administrative Expenses

Administrative Salaries	$ 32,000		
Insurance	8,000		
Depreciation of Office Equipment	3,000		
Other Administrative Expenses	12,000	55,000	
Total Operating Expenses			140,000

(e) Operating Income $ 88,100

(f) Other Revenues

Interest	$ 7,000		
Dividends	3,000	$ 10,000	

(g) Other Expenses

Interest Expense		2,100	
Other Revenues (net)			7,900
Net Income Before Taxes			$ 96,000
Federal and State Income Taxes			50,000

(h) Net Income $ 46,000

In this form of income statement a number of subcategories of cost and expense are used. The key items are labeled with letters and we will describe them briefly.

(a) This is the total of all charges to customers for merchandise sold, both for cash and on account.

(b) This is one of the most important sections of the income statement. It shows the cost of the goods delivered to customers during the period and the relationship to sales. This relationship can be conveniently compared with the figures for other periods.

(c) The amount of gross profit (gross margin) must be sufficient to pay all expenses (other than those in Cost of Goods Sold) and to yield a reasonable return or profit. The gross profit ratio, is a key control figure in managing a business. The selling price must be kept in such relationship to cost as to yield a desired gross profit. To improve the gross profit ratio, sales prices may be increased or costs decreased. Favorable or unfavorable trends can be easily seen by comparing the gross profit ratio with the ratios for other periods.

(d) These are the expenses necessary in carrying on the operations of the business. They do not include unusual expenses or financial expenses not of an operating nature, which are classed separately.

(e)   This is the amount by which the gross profit exceeds total operating expenses. It measures the degree of profitability from operations, before nonoperating items are considered.

(f)   Another example is Gain on Disposal of Plant Assets.

(g)   Another example is Loss on Disposal of Plant Assets. Like Other Revenues, this non-operating item is offset and the net amount is shown in the summary column of the income statement.

(h)   This represents the net increase in capital for the period. (Had capital decreased, the figure would have been called *net loss*.)

EXAMPLE 10.   Classified, Single-Step Form.

Revenues		
Net Sales		$672,300
Interest		7,000
Dividends		3,000
Total Revenues		$682,300
Expenses		
Wages, Salaries, and Employee Benefits	$ 90,200	
Merchandise and Supplies	424,600	
Payments for Services	42,400	
Depreciation	6,500	
Rent	8,000	
Property Taxes	12,500	
Interest	2,100	
Federal and State Income Taxes	50,000	
Total Expenses		636,300
Net Income		$ 46,000

Proponents of the single-step form maintain that only the final figure, net income, is significant. Often the expenses are grouped according to type of expense (e.g., selling) rather than by their nature. (e.g., depreciation). Notice that in this form all revenue — operating and other — appears at the top of the statement. The categories in the following forms could be condensed, as shown, or detailed as in the forms above.

EXAMPLE 11.   All-Inclusive Form.

Sales Revenue		$672,300
Cost of Goods Sold		444,200
Gross Margin		$228,100
Operating Expenses		140,000
Operating Income		$ 88,100
Other Income (net)		7,900
Net Income Before Taxes		$ 96,000
Income Taxes		50,000
Income Before Extraordinary Loss		$ 46,000
Flood Loss	$40,000	
Less: Applicable Taxes	16,000	24,000
Net Income		$ 22,000

This form, unlike those of Examples 9 and 10, reflects all *extraordinary gains and losses*; that is, those arising from such unusual events as earthquakes, riots, embezzlements, etc. Note that the income tax relating to the extraordinary item is shown separately and the net amount after tax is deducted.

EXAMPLE 12.   Current Operating Performance Form.

Sales Revenues	$672,300
Cost of Goods Sold	444,200
Gross Margin	$228,100
Operating Expenses	140,000
Operating Income	$ 88,100
Other Income (net)	7,900
Net Income Before Taxes	$ 96,000
Income Taxes	50,000
Net Income	$ 46,000

This form excludes all extraordinary items. It does not comply with generally accepted accounting principles and is generally used only for internal purposes.

Summary

(1) At the time goods are produced, in most firms it is not known exactly how much will be received for them or even if they will be sold. Therefore, revenue is recognized only when goods are _____.

(2) Where there is a guaranteed market for the product, revenue is recognized when the _____ is completed.

(3) For long-term construction projects, revenue is recognized on the basis of the _____ of completion.

(4) On the collection basis of accounting, revenue is recognized only when _____ is collected.

(5) The principal types of revenue reductions and adjustments are _____ _____, _____, and _____.

(6) Resources consumed in the effort to produce revenue are termed _____.

(7) Commodities or services purchased but unconsumed at the end of the period represent _____ expenses.

(8) An expense that has gradually accumulated but has not yet been recognized in the accounts is called an _____ expense.

(9) Gross sales, less sales reductions, costs, and expenses, is called _____.

(10) The _____ form of income statement shows various categories of cost and expense.

Answers: (1) delivered; (2) production; (3) percentage; (4) cash; (5) sales returns and allowances, cash discounts, credit losses; (6) expenses; (7) prepaid; (8) accrued; (9) net income; (10) multiple-step

Solved Problems

14.1. The C-L Company produces parts which are sold to auto manufacturers. During 19X2 the company collected $200,000 in cash. Of this amount $35,000 represented collections of accounts receivable balances at the end of the previous year. Accounts receivable balances at the end of the current year are $45,000. How much revenue should be recognized for the current year (a) on the accrual basis? (b) on the cash basis?

SOLUTION

(a) The revenue or sales for the period would be $210,000.

Total Collections	$200,000
Less: Sales for Previous Year	35,000
Sales Made and Collected	165,000
Sales Made but Not Yet Collected	45,000
Sales for Current Year	$210,000

(b) Sales for the year would be $200,000, representing the amount of cash collected during the year.

14.2. The Jack McLaurin Company leased a store to a tenant in December 19X1 for $6,000 for the following calendar year, receivable upon signing of the lease. How much revenue should be reported for 19X1 and for 19X2 (a) on the accrual basis? (b) on the cash basis?

SOLUTION

	19X1	19X2
Accrual basis	0	$6,000
Cash basis	$6,000	0

14.3. The Gary Charles Mining Company produces lead, silver, and gold. The price of lead fluctuates widely, but the prices for silver and gold are fixed by the government. In 19X2 the costs of production for the year were: lead, $600,000; silver, $500,000; and gold, $400,000. The following percentages of production were sold: lead, 75% for $550,000; silver, 80% for $600,000; and gold, 50% for $300,000. The sales prices of the production unsold were: lead, $200,000; silver, $150,000; and gold, $160,000. What is the revenue for 19X2?

	Sales	On Hand	Total Revenue
Lead			
Silver			
Gold			

SOLUTION

	Sales	On Hand	Total Revenue
Lead	$ 550,000	– –	$ 550,000
Silver	600,000	$150,000	750,000
Gold	300,000	160,000	460,000
	$1,450,000	$310,000	$1,760,000

14.4. The Henry Hogg Company has a $1,000,000 construction contract which was 25% complete at the end of the first year (with $250,000 revenue recognized) and 75% complete at the end of the second year. How much revenue should be reported for the second year?

SOLUTION

The total revenue to be reported on the contract to date is $750,000. This amount, less that previously reported, or $500,000, is the amount to be reported for the second year.

14.5. The Harold Dalton Company had sales of $150,000 for 19X2. The sales returns and allowances were $5,000 for the year, including the December 15 allowance of $500 to Kenneth Connolly. Prepare (a) the journal entry to record the Connolly transaction and (b) the revenue section of the income statement for the year.

(a)

(b)

SOLUTION

(a)	Sales Returns and Allowances		500	
	Accounts Receivable			500
(b)	Revenue			
	Sales		$150,000	
	Less: Sales Returns and Allowances		5,000	
	Net Sales			$145,000

14.6. The Harold Dalton Company also had sales discounts of $2,000 for the year. Prepare the revenue section of the income statement based on the data in Problem 14.5.

SOLUTION

Revenue			
Sales		$150,000	
Less:			
Sales Returns and Allowances	$5,000		
Sales Discounts	2,000	7,000	
Net Sales			$143,000

14.7. The Alan Friedman Company paid $300 rent on November 30 for the following three months. Prepare the journal entry for Friedman's books at the end of the year, if the rent had been recorded as (a) Rent Expense and (b) Prepaid Rent.

(a)

(b)

SOLUTION

(a)	Prepaid Rent	200	
	Rent Expense		200
(b)	Rent Expense	100	
	Prepaid Rent		100

14.8. On December 1, 19X2, Debbie Realty received $1,800 in advance rent representing a three month prepayment. (*a*) Record the entry on December 1, 19X2; (*b*) What adjusting entry will be needed as of December 31, 19X2

(a)			
(b)			

SOLUTION

(a)	Cash	1,800	
	Unearned Rent Income		1,800
(b)	Unearned Rent Income	600	
	Rent Income		600

14.9. Based on the information in Problem 14.8, how are the accounts Unearned Rent Income and Rent Income treated?

SOLUTION

   Unearned Rent Income is a liability and will appear on the Balance Sheet under "Current Liabilities."

   Rent Income is current revenue and appears in the Income section of the Income Statement. Note that only the current portion of the income ($600 representing one month in 19X2) is recognized as revenue.

14.10. A special pattern purchased for $6,000 on July 6, 19X2, is to be amortized over a period of 3 years. Record the entries on (*a*) July 6, 19X2; (*b*) December 31, 19X2; (*c*) December 31, 19X3.

(a)			
(b)			
(c)			

SOLUTION

(a)	Patterns	6,000	
	Cash		6,000
(b)	Patterns Expense	1,000	
	Patterns (½ year)		1,000
(c)	Patterns Expense	2,000	
	Patterns		2,000

14.11. A $4,000, 90-day, 9% note receivable dated December 1, 19X2 was paid in full at maturity. Record the entry needed for the accrual as of December 31, 19X2.

SOLUTION

Interest Receivable	30	
Interest Income		30
$(\$4,000 \times \dfrac{9}{100} \times \dfrac{30}{360} \ days)$		

14.12. The Ross Dixon Company offers premiums to its customers upon receipt of coupons from its product Happybird. A bird food tray which costs the company 30¢ is given for every 10 coupons redeemed. During the current year there were 150,000 packages of Happybird sold, for which it is estimated that 10% of the coupons will be redeemed. What is the additional amount to be accrued for this year, if 10,000 coupons from this year's sales have already been redeemed?

SOLUTION

Estimated annual cost (150,000 × 10% × 3¢): $450

Redeemed this year to date (10,000 × 3¢): 300

Amount to accrue at year end: $150

14.13. From the information given below, compute the gross purchases for the year.

Cost of Goods Sold $115,000

Beginning Inventory 38,500

Transportation-In 1,600

Ending Inventory 32,600

Purchase Returns 1,850

SOLUTION

The gross purchases are $109,350, computed as follows:

Total Goods Available		Gross Purchases	
Cost of Goods Sold	$115,000	Total Goods Available	$147,600
Add: Ending Inventory	32,600	Less: Beginning Inventory	38,500
	$147,600		$109,100
		Add: Purchase Returns	1,850
			$110,950
		Less: Transportation-In	1,600
			$109,350

14.14. Prepare journal entries for the following transactions of the Wilson Company for the month of June.

June 1: Purchased merchandise on account from H. Brown, $500, at terms of 2/10, n/30

1: Sold merchandise to A. Pesnow, $1,000, receiving a 30-day, 6% note in exchange

1: Purchased delivery equipment from W. Green, $3,500, paying $500 and issuing a series of five 6% notes of $600 each, maturing at 30-day intervals

5: Paid invoice of H. Brown

15: Sold merchandise, $400, to S. Meyer, at terms of 2/10, n/30

17: Mr. Meyer returned $100 worth of goods purchased

24: Received check from S. Meyer settling his account

30: The electric bill for June is estimated to be $200

30: Interest accrual for the Pesnow note

30: Interest accrual for the Green notes

1.			
1.			
1.			
5.			
15.			
17.			
24.			
30.			
30.			
30.			

SOLUTION

1.	Purchases	500	
	Accounts Payable, H. Brown		500
1.	Notes Receivable, A. Pesnow	1,000	
	Sales		1,000
1.	Delivery Equipment	3,500	
	Notes Payable		3,000
	Cash		500
5.	Accounts Payable, H. Brown	500	
	Cash		490
	Purchase Discount		10
15.	Accounts Receivable, S. Meyer	400	
	Sales		400
17.	Sales Returns and Allowances	100	
	Accounts Receivable, S. Meyer		100
24.	Cash	294	
	Sales Discount	6	
	Accounts Receivable, S. Meyer		300
30.	Electricity Expense	200	
	Accrued Expense, Electricity		200
30.	Interest Receivable	5	
	Accrued Interest Income		5
30.	Interest Expense	15	
	Accrued Interest Payable		15

Chapter 15

Investments, Intangibles, Deferred, and Other Assets

15.1 INTRODUCTION

The past six chapters, those following the eight chapters on theory, recording and accounting procedures, have dealt with topics that were clearly balance sheet or income statement items. There remain a number of asset items that do not wholly fit into one category or the other. These items, which may or may not be of sufficient dollar value to warrant separate captions on the balance sheet, are described below.

15.2 INVESTMENTS

By *investments* we mean funds which a company does not put into working capital or tangible assets, but applies in various other ways. The purpose of the investment, rather than the type of security involved, determines whether the investment is short-term, and therefore a current asset, or long-term, and thus a noncurrent asset.

SHORT-TERM INVESTMENTS

Many companies, particularly those in seasonal businesses, have idle cash during certain times of the year, which they can profitably invest in corporate stocks, bonds, or notes, or in government securities. The important thing is that the asset be readily convertible to cash.

LONG-TERM INVESTMENTS

These generally serve one of the following purposes: (1) to achieve control of another company, (2) to diversify products, (3) to meet contractual requirements. In the case of (1), it is not essential to acquire 50% of the voting stock; a considerable influence over the other company can be presumed if 20% or more of its stock is owned. The motive in (2) is to enable a supplier or subsidiary to bring out additional products, or to diversify the investor's own product line. As regards (3), the terms of an issue of bonds may require that funds be set aside in a special account called a *sinking fund* to pay off the principal or interest. Often these funds may be invested in bonds or stocks of other companies to earn income for the fund. Likewise there are thousands of pension funds, many over a million dollars, which must be maintained in accordance with the terms of the pension plan.

In view of the above purposes, the following assets constitute long-term investments:

- marketable securities which are to be held for long periods
- stocks of, and advances to, subsidiaries or affiliates
- bonds, notes, mortgages, etc., not traded in open markets
- cash surrender value of life insurance
- nonoperating real estate
- bond sinking funds
- other interests held for income or appreciation in value

15.3 ACCOUNTING FOR INVESTMENTS

Investments in stocks, whether short-term or long-term, are recorded at total cost; that is, the cost of the stock plus commissions.

EXAMPLE 1.

On July 1, 1,000 shares of Whyte Metal Company common stock were purchased as an investment at $15\frac{1}{2}$, plus $200 broker's commission.   The entry is as follows:

July 1	Whyte Metal Company Stock	15,700	
	Cash		15,700

On October 1, dividends of $1 per share were received and recorded as follows:

October 1	Cash	1,000	
	Dividend Income		1,000

On December 15, the 1,000 shares of Whyte Metal Company stock were sold at $17\frac{1}{2}$, less commission and taxes of $300.   The transaction is recorded as follows:

December 15	Cash	17,200	
	Whyte Metal Company Stock		15,700
	Gain on Sale of Investment		1,500

Investments in bonds, like those in stocks, are recorded at total cost.   Bonds, however, pay interest, and this interest accrues; whereas dividends on capital stock are earned only as they are declared.

EXAMPLE 2.

On July 1, ten Blacke Metal Company 6%, $1,000 bonds were purchased at $93\frac{1}{2}$, plus commissions of $100 and accrued interest of $150, 10 years before maturity.   Interest is payable April 1 and October 1. The entry is as follows:

July 1	Investment in Bonds	9,450	
	Bond Interest Receivable	150	
	Cash		9,600

On October 1, interest of $300 was received and recorded:

October 1	Cash	300	
	Bond Interest Receivable		150
	Bond Interest Income		150

As of December 31, the close of the fiscal year, the interest earned since the last interest received should be recorded.   The amount would be $150 for the 3 months ($10,000 \times 6\%$ per year $\times 3/12$ year).

December 31	Accrued Bond Interest	150	
	Bond Interest Income		150

Another feature of accounting for bond investments is amortization.   When bonds are bought as a long-term investment (and, usually, only then), any discount or premium is treated as an interest adjustment and amortized over the remaining life of the bonds.

EXAMPLE 3.

In Example 2, assume that the ten $1,000 face value, 6%, 10-year bonds were purchased for $9,450, a discount of $550. During each year, then, a portion of the $550 is to be recorded as additional interest. On the straight-line method the additional interest would be $55 per year. Since the bonds were purchased July 1, the prepaid interest would be $27.50.

Investment in Bonds	*27.50*
Bond Interest Income	*27.50*

Stocks, bonds, etc., when held as short-term investments, appear on the balance sheet under "Current Assets." When held as long-term investments, they appear below the current asset section—either in a classification of their own, "Investments," or under a heading such as "Other Assets."

EXAMPLE 4.

Current Assets	
Cash	*$15,000*
Marketable Securities (market value $13,000)	*12,500*
Accounts Receivable	*3,000*
Investments	
Securities	*$20,000*
Real Estate Not Used in Business	*25,000*
Other Assets	
Bond Sinking Fund	*$100,000*
Deposit on Lease	*10,000*
Securities Held	*5,000*

15.4 INTANGIBLES

Intangible assets are those which benefit the business through special rights and privileges, as distinguished from the physical characteristics of tangible assets. Intangible assets may be either acquired or developed internally. The following are the principal types:

Patents

Copyrights

Franchises

Leaseholds

Trademarks

Leasehold Improvements

Organization Costs

Goodwill

EXAMPLE 5.

The Stroble Company has net assets of $1,200,000, which includes intangibles of $200,000. Another firm has agreed to buy the business, paying book value for the net assets and for goodwill to be capitalized at 20%. Goodwill is to be based on excess earnings over 10%. The earnings per year have averaged 13% of net tangible assets. What is the amount of goodwill?

Average annual earnings ($1,000,000 × 13%)	$130,000
Normal earnings ($1,000,000 × 10%)	100,000
Excess earnings per year	$ 30,000
Goodwill, capitalized at 20% (30,000 ÷ .20)	$150,000

15.5 ACCOUNTING FOR INTANGIBLES

Significant changes in accounting for intangible assets were specified in APB Opinion 17, the main directives of which are given in the following paragraphs.

Acquired intangibles should be recorded as assets at cost. This includes goodwill acquired in a business combination. If an intangible is acquired for consideration other than cash, then cost is determined by either the market value of the consideration or by the fair market value of the right acquired, whichever is the more evident. It is seen that arbitrary write-offs of intangibles, once the practice, are not allowed under this directive.

Internally developed intangibles which are identifiable should be recorded as assets, those which are not specifically identifiable should be recorded as expenses.

Identifiable intangibles, whether acquired or developed internally, should be recorded at cost, except those not covered by APB Opinion 17. Examples of intangibles which may be identified are patents, franchises, and trademarks. *Unidentifiable intangibles,* where acquired, should be recorded at cost and shown as assets; where such items are internally developed, they should be recorded as expenses when incurred. The most common unidentifiable intangible is goodwill, representing the excess of cost of an acquired company over the sum of identifiable intangibles. Such intangibles cannot be acquired singly but must be part of a group of assets or an entire enterprise.

All intangible assets should have their cost amortized over a limited service life of at most 40 years. Previous to this directive it was held that certain intangibles had unlimited life and were thus not subject to amortization. Intangibles should be amortized by systematic charges against income over the estimated periods of useful life. They are normally amortized by a debit to expense and a credit directly to the asset account.

Depending on their characteristics, the various intangibles may be shown in the accounts and classified on the balance sheet as current assets, investments, fixed assets, deferred charges, or other assets. The latter two categories will be discussed in the two sections to follow.

15.6 DEFERRED CHARGES

Prepaid expenses and deferred charges are similar in that they are to be charged to expense in a subsequent period. *However, prepaid expenses are recurring expenses, of short duration, and limited to one or two future periods. Deferred charges are seldom recurring, of longer duration, and are allocated to a number of future periods.* Typical deferred charges are: (1) bond issue costs, (2) organization and reorganization costs, (3) plant rearrangements.

Deferred charges are classified as noncurrent assets on the balance sheet. They usually do not have significant dollar value in relation to total assets and are ordinarily shown as the last asset classification. Sometimes they may be shown as a separate item under Other Assets. Unamortized bond discount is sometimes shown as a deferred charge, but it is preferable to show it as a contra item to the bond liability.

15.7 OTHER ASSETS

This classification includes noncurrent items which cannot reasonably be included under any of the classifications discussed above. The conditions will vary by kind of item and by amount. If the dollar amounts are not large, there may be only one amount for the caption. Generally it is desirable to try to put items in other classifications before including them in Other Assets.

EXAMPLE 6.

Other Assets

Fixed Assets Held for Resale	*$2,100*
Miscellaneous Other Assets	*120*

Summary

(1) The Whitecavage Company has excess cash and buys 5,000 shares of the readily marketable stock of the Petersen Company. The Compton Company obtains most of its raw material from the Petersen Company and buys stock in the latter company to guarantee its source of supply. The securities would be shown on the Whitecavage Company's balance sheet under_____and on the Petersen Company's balance sheet under _____.

(2) The Oken Company purchases, as a marketable security, $10,000 in bonds of the Barclay Company at 104, plus accrued interest of $200 and brokerage commission of $50. The investment amount should be recorded as $_____.

(3) Assets which are long-term and useful in the operation of a business but are not held for sale and have no physical attributes are termed _____.

(4) A patent which has 12 years of legal life remaining was purchased for $15,000. Because of possible obsolescence the economic life was estimated at 10 years. The amount of the annual amortization is $_____.

(5) In the course of forming a corporation there are legal fees, accounting fees, incorporation fees, expenses for meetings, etc. These expenditures are considered to be _____under the account title _____.

(6) Among (*a*) marketable securities held temporarily, (*b*) savings accounts, (*c*) cash surrender value of life insurance, (*d*) bond sinking funds, (*e*) franchises, (*f*) goodwill, _____ are current assets, whereas _____ are noncurrent assets.

Answers: (1) Current Assets, Other Assets (or a separate caption); (2) 10,450; (3) intangible assets; (4) 1,500; (5) assets, Organization Costs; (6) (*a*) and (*b*), (*c*) through (*f*)

Solved Problems

15.1. The John Shavelson Company has products which are highly seasonal and consequently at certain times of the year excess funds are available for investment. Heretofore such investments have been made in short-term Government securities, but management has decided to purchase AT&T common stock. How should these latter securities be reported on the balance sheet?

SOLUTION

Since AT&T securities are readily marketable, they should be shown as current assets. Ordinarily they would be shown at cost, with the current market value cited parenthetically.

15.2. The E. R. Serotta Company management has decided to purchase stock of the Richmond Corporation, a small manufacturer, in order to provide a guaranteed source of raw materials. How should these securities be reported on the balance sheet?

SOLUTION

Since the purpose of the investment is to influence or exert control over another company, it would not be an investment primarily of idle funds but one of longer duration. The stock would ordinarily not be readily marketable and would thus be a noncurrent asset. The stock would be valued at cost.

15.3. The Brown Company on January 1 purchased, with idle funds, 100 shares of the Green Company at $101, plus commission of $100. On July 1, a dividend of $5 per share was received. The stock was sold on October 1 for $105, less commission of $125. Prepare the necessary journal entries.

SOLUTION

January 1	Marketable Securities	10,200	
	Cash		10,200
July 1	Cash	500	
	Dividend Income		500
October 1	Cash	10,375	
	Marketable Securities		10,200
	Gain on Sale of Securities		175

15.4. The Murray Company purchased $100,000 of 6% bonds of the Enright Corporation at 94. The bonds are due 10 years from date of purchase. Assuming that the bonds are temporary investments, compute (1) the annual income, (2) the gain or loss if the bonds are sold at 97 two years from date of purchase.

SOLUTION

   (1) $6,000   (2) $3,000 gain

15.5. The Folk Company has net assets of $400,000 and average net earnings of 5% on sales of $600,000 per year. An investor offers to pay for the net assets and to compute goodwill based on excess earnings over 6% of net assets, capitalized at 10%. What is the amount of goodwill?

SOLUTION

Average annual earnings ($600,000 × 5%)	$30,000
Normal earnings ($400,000 × 6%)	24,000
Excess earnings per year	$ 6,000
Goodwill, capitalized at 10% (6,000 ÷ .10)	$60,000

15.6. The Weag Company purchased a patent from the inventor for $24,000 after 5 years of the 17-year legal life had expired. The company estimates that the useful life will be 15 years. Prepare the journal entries to record (a) the original purchase and (b) the annual amortization.

(a)

(b)

SOLUTION

(a)	Patents	24,000	
	Cash (or Accounts Payable)		24,000
(b)	Amortization Expense, Patents	2,000*	
	Patents		2,000

* $24,000 \div 12$ unexpired years $= $2,000$ per year

15.7. The Kelso Company has been informed by the local chapter of the Ecology Council that a complaint is being issued against its disposal of waste material. Equipment needed to meet antipollution standards will cost $100,000. Ordinarily, that general classification of fixed assets would be depreciated over a 15-year period. However, to encourage the installation of such equipment the Internal Revenue Service has allowed the cost to be amortized over a 5-year period. Write (a) the journal entry for the cost of the equipment, (b) the journal entry for the annual write-off, and (c) the presentation on the balance sheet after one year's amortization.

(a)

(b)

(c)

SOLUTION

(a)	Antipollution Equipment	100,000	
	Cash (or Accounts Payable)		100,000
(b)	Amortization, Antipollution Equipment	20,000	
	Antipollution Equipment		20,000
(c)	Deferred Charges:		
	Antipollution Equipment		$ 80,000

15.8. The Krautwurst Company has decided to purchase an insurance policy for $50,000 on the life of its president. The company will pay the insurance cost, which will be offset by the cash surrender value of the policy, which increases each year. The annual premium is $2,000, and the cash surrender value is: at the end of year 2, $850; at the end of year 3, $1,350. Prepare the journal entries for (a) the first year, (b) the second year, and (c) the third year; and (d) give the balance sheet presentation at the end of the third year.

(a)

(b)

(c)

(d)

SOLUTION

Each year the company's insurance expense is the annual premium, less the appreciation of the policy's cash surrender value during that year.   Therefore:

(a)	Insurance Expense	2,000	
	Cash		2,000
(b)	Insurance Expense	1,150	
	Cash Surrender Value, Life Insurance	850	
	Cash		2,000
(c)	Insurance Expense	1,500	
	Cash Surrender Value, Life Insurance	500	
	Cash		2,000
(d)	Other Assets:		
	Cash Surrender Value, Life Insurance		$1,350

Chapter 16

Liabilities and Equity

LIABILITIES

16.1 GENERAL DESCRIPTION

Liabilities are claims which require the payment or consumption of business resources. Most liabilities of a business are based on *commitments* or *contracts* and are legally enforceable by the creditor. Examples are accounts payable, notes payable, salaries, and interest. Some liabilities are due to provisions of law, such as various taxes imposed on the company which are legally enforceable.

The complexities of business operations and tax regulations in recent years have caused the recognition of liabilities based on economic considerations rather than strictly on legal enforcement. Examples are various kinds of performance obligations, such as product warranties and guarantees, and deferred income taxes, which arise when deductions are taken on tax returns earlier than on company books.

Liabilities are classified into two general groups: current liabilities and long-term liabilities.

16.2 CURRENT LIABILITIES

These are liabilities that are due for payment within the operating cycle or one year, whichever is longer. The settlement of a current liability usually requires the use of current assets. The ratio of current assets to current liabilities, or *current ratio*, is a useful index of a company's debt-paying capacity. It tells how many times current liabilities could be paid with current assets.

EXAMPLE 1.

Current Assets $70,000
Current Liabilities   32,000

$$\text{CURRENT RATIO} = \frac{\text{CURRENT ASSETS}}{\text{CURRENT LIABILITIES}} = \frac{70,000}{32,000} = 2.19:1$$

Thus, $2.19 of current assets is available for every $1 of current liabilities.

Following are the seven principal types of current liabilities.

(1) *Notes payable.* Liabilities evidenced by a written promise to pay at a later date.

(2) *Accounts payable.* Liabilities for goods or services purchased on account, trade payables, and also nontrade obligations.

(3) *Accrued liabilities.* Liabilities that have accumulated but are not yet due, as payment does not coincide with the end of the period. These are *expenses* and are shown on the income statement under:

Salaries and Wages	Payroll Taxes
Commissions	Sales Taxes
Insurance	Income Taxes
Interest	Pensions
Property Taxes	Royalties

(4) **Withholdings.** Amounts which have been withheld from employees' pay and are to be turned over to governmental agencies, insurance companies, etc. These are *not* expenses of the company but must be properly safeguarded until transmitted to the specified agency. These include:

- income taxes
- Social Security taxes
- unemployment taxes
- hospitalization
- group insurance
- pension

(5) **Dividends payable.** Dividends become payable only as declared by the Board of Directors of the company. They do not accrue, or accumulate, as does interest on bonds.

(6) **Unearned revenues.** Sometimes revenue is received in advance, such as magazine subscriptions or rent. These are liabilities, as they represent claims against the enterprise. Generally they are settled by delivery of goods or services in the next accounting period. Where these are long-term advances extending well beyond the next period, they should be classed on the balance sheet as noncurrent.

(7) **Portion of long-term debt.** The portion of long-term debt payable in the next twelve months should be included in the current liabilities category. This includes such amounts due on bonds, mortgages, or long-term notes.

16.3 ACCOUNTING FOR CURRENT LIABILITIES

Entries to current liabilities very often result from accrual entries made at the end of the month. Many others, especially the tax withholding entries, accompany payrolls.

Accrued expenses. For expenses which have accrued or accumulated, but have not been recorded at the end of the month, adjusting entries have to be made.

EXAMPLE 2.

At the end of February it was found that there were accrued salaries and wages of $500. The adjusting entry would be:

Salaries and Wages Expense	500	
Salaries and Wages Payable		500

Payroll deductions. As explained in Sec. 16.2, these represent amounts owed to others, and thus are current liabilities rather than current expenses.

EXAMPLE 3.

The payroll totals for the pay period ending February 15 were: salaries, $2,000; withholdings for income taxes, $300; social security, $100; state unemployment, $75; hospitalization insurance, $50; and a net amount payable of $1,475.

Salaries and Wages	2,000	
Income Taxes Payable		300
Social Security Taxes Payable		100
State Unemployment Taxes Payable		75
Hospitalization Insurance Payable		50
Accrued Payroll		1,475

When employees' checks for the net amounts are issued in a few days, the entry is:

Accrued Payroll	1,475	
Cash		1,475

16.4 LONG-TERM LIABILITIES

Where funds are needed for a long-term purpose such as construction of a building, a long-term liability account would be used. Presumably, increased earnings will be used to retire the debt. Almost always, long-term liabilities are interest-bearing and have a fixed due date. Following are the principal types:

(1) **Long-term notes payable.** The company may be able to obtain the needed amount from one lender rather than by issuing bonds for sale to the public. Sometimes notes may be issued to await better terms for issuing bonds.

(2) **Mortgages payable.** The terms of a mortgage generally pledge the property of the company as security. The mortgage involves a lien on the property, not a transfer of title.

(3) **Bonds payable.** If the amount of funds needed is larger than a single lender can supply, bonds may be sold to the investing public, splitting the loan into thousands of units. A bond is a written promise to pay the face amount, generally $1,000, at a future date and to make interest payments semiannually at a stipulated rate of interest. Interest payments on bonds are deductible as expense for income tax purposes, but dividends paid on preferred or common stock are not. This is an important consideration in deciding whether to use stocks or bonds for long-term financing.

16.5 CONTINGENT LIABILITIES

These are potential liabilities arising from past events. When, for example, a note receivable is endorsed and transferred to another person, no liability is created. However, there is a possibility that a liability in the future could exist, because the maker of the note might not honor it. In that event, the business which endorsed the note would be required to make payment. Some other examples of contingent liabilities are: additional tax assessments, product guarantees, pending lawsuits, and litigation.

It is not necessary to prepare an entry before the potential liability becomes an actuality. However, it cannot be ignored. Therefore, a contingent liability should be reflected in the balance sheet as a footnote describing the possibility of the loss. This will give the reader a more accurate picture of the financial position of the firm.

EQUITY

16.6 SOLE PROPRIETORSHIP

A sole proprietorship is a business owned by one individual. It is a separate business entity but it is not a separate *legal entity*. The proprietor owns the assets and owes the creditors personally, not as a business, as in the case of a corporation.

The equity of the sole proprietor consists of three accounts: a capital account, a drawing account, and an expense and income summary account. These accounts are described and illustrated below.

Capital account. The proprietor's capital account reflects the changes in his equity during the year. Examples 4 through 6 follow the sequence of events in the business of Aaron Baker.

EXAMPLE 4.

On January 1, Aaron Baker invested $20,000 in his business. The entry is as follows:

Jan. 1   Cash   20,000

    Aaron Baker, Capital   20,000

Drawing account. Before earnings are made, the proprietor usually has to draw compensation for his living expenses. He is not an employee; therefore, he does not earn a salary; his earnings result from profits of the company. Such drawings reduce his equity and reduce cash.

EXAMPLE 5.

Aaron Baker decided that he would withdraw $500 a month for personal expenses. He expects this equity reduction to be more than offset by earnings which will be determined at the end of the year. The entry to be made each month is:

Aaron Baker, Drawing	*500*	
Cash		*500*

The account Aaron Baker, Drawing is used to accumulate the details of the drawings so that only one figure, the total, is transferred to the capital account at the end of the year.

When the drawings of $6,000 for the year are transferred, the entry is as follows:

Dec. 31	*Aaron Baker, Capital*	*6,000*	
	Aaron Baker, Drawing		*6,000*

Expense and income summary account. When the accounts are summarized and closed, the various expenses are debited in total to Expense and Income Summary and the individual expense accounts are credited. The income is credited in total to Expense and Income Summary and debited to the individual income accounts. The net difference, a profit or a loss, is transferred to the capital account. This process was treated in Chapter 6 (see, in particular, Sec. 6.4).

EXAMPLE 6.

The business of Aaron Baker had income from fees of $20,000 and expenses for: rent, $5,000; salary, $2,000; and supplies, $2,000.

The income of $20,000, less total expenses of $9,000, results in net income of $11,000. The account is closed out and the balance transferred to the capital account with the following entry:

Dec. 31	*Expense and Income Summary*	*11,000*	
	Aaron Baker, Capital		*11,000*

The account Aaron Baker, Capital will now reflect the proprietor's investment, drawings, and income:

Aaron Baker, Capital, 19X2

Dec. 31	Drawings	6,000	Jan. 1, 19X2	Investment	20,000
31	Balance	25,000		Net Income	11,000
		31,000			31,000
			Jan. 1, 19X3	Balance	25,000

Instead of showing a single capital item on the closing balance sheet it is preferable to present: the opening balance, the increase and decrease for the period, and the closing balance, as shown below.

OWNER'S EQUITY

Aaron Baker, Capital		
Balance, January 1, 19X2		$20,000
Net Income for Year	$11,000	
Drawings for Year	6,000	5,000
Balance, December 31, 19X2		$25,000

16.7 PARTNERSHIP

A partnership according to the Uniform Partnership Act, is "an association of two or more persons to carry on as co-owners of a business for profit." Such an association should preferably be expressed in a partnership agreement. Profits may be shared equally, according to invested capital, or on any other basis. A partner's share is called his *interest* in the business.

The partnership capital accounts consist of a capital account for each partner, a drawing account for each partner, and an expense and income summary account. These accounts are described and illustrated below.

Capital accounts. Like the sole proprietor's account (Example 4), each partner's account reflects the changes in his equity during the year.

EXAMPLE 7.

On January 1, Joseph Kelso invested $15,000 and James Murray invested $10,000 to begin a retail hardware business.   The entry is as follows:

Jan. 1	Cash	25,000	
	Joseph Kelso, Capital		15,000
	James Murray, Capital		10,000

Drawing accounts. The individual drawing accounts will also be similar to the sole proprietor's drawing account.

EXAMPLE 8.

It was agreed that Joseph Kelso would draw $400 a month and James Murray $300 a month. The entry each month will be as follows:

Joseph Kelso, Drawing	400	
James Murray, Drawing	300	
Cash		700

The monthly amounts will be accumulated in each partner's drawing accounts as in Example 5. At the end of the year, the totals for the year will be transferred to the partners' accounts as follows:

Dec. 31	Joseph Kelso, Capital	4,800	
	James Murray, Capital	3,600	
	Joseph Kelso, Drawing		4,800
	James Murray, Drawing		3,600

Expense and income summary account.   The expense and income accounts are closed into Expense and Income Summary as described for a single proprietor (Example 6). However, the profit or loss will be transferred to two or more accounts rather than a single account. The Expense and Income Summary, like the drawing accounts, will be closed out for the period.

EXAMPLE 9.

At the end of the year the partnership showed net income of $15,000. Profits are shared as follows: Kelso, 60%; Murray, 40%.   The closing entry would be:

Dec. 31	Expense and Income Summary	15,000	
	Joseph Kelso, Capital		9,000
	James Murray, Capital		6,000

Each partnership account will show the partner's investment, drawings, and net income as follows:

Joseph Kelso, Capital

Dec. 31	Drawings	4,800	Jan. 1	Investment	15,000
Dec. 31	Balance	19,200	Dec. 31	Net Income	9,000
		24,000			24,000
			Jan. 1	Balance	19,200

James Murray, Capital

Dec. 31	Drawings	3,600	Jan. 1	Investment	10,000
Dec. 31	Balance	12,400	Dec. 31	Net Income	6,000
		16,000			16,000
			Jan. 1	Balance	12,400

The partners' equities would be shown on the balance sheet as follows:

Partners' Equities

Kelso, Capital	$19,200	
Murray, Capital	12,400	$31,600

While the amounts for net income and drawings may be shown on the balance sheet for a sole proprietorship, such detail is cumbersome where two or more partners are involved. It is preferable to have a separate statement, called Statement of Partners' Capital or simply Capital Statement. A form is shown below.

Kelso and Murray
Statement of Partners' Capital
Year Ended December 31, 19X3

	Total	Kelso	Murray
Investment, Jan. 1, 19X3	$25,000	$15,000	$10,000
Net Income for the Year	15,000	9,000	6,000
	$40,000	$24,000	$16,000
Less: Drawings for the Year	8,400	4,800	3,600
Balance, December 31, 19X3	$31,600	$19,200	$12,400

Further details on the nature of partnerships and their formation and dissolution are discussed in the sequel to this volume, *Accounting II*.

16.8 CORPORATION

A corporation is a separate legal entity organized in accordance with state or federal laws, with ownership represented by shares of stock. The applicable laws require that a distinction be made between the amount invested in a corporation by its owners (stockholders) and the subsequent changes due to profits or losses. Because of these requirements, the stockholders' equity is shown in at least two parts. If there is more than one class of stock, such as preferred and common, there may be more parts in the Stockholders' Equity section.

STOCKHOLDERS' EQUITY

Capital Stock	$100,000	
Retained Earnings	25,000	$125,000

The principal corporation equity accounts are those for capital stock, dividends, and retained earnings.

Capital stock. Corporate capital stock is evidenced by stock certificates. There are a specified number of shares of stock authorized by the state, generally at a specified par value. No-par stock also can be issued in most states. When stock is issued at a price above par, the amount above par is termed a *premium*. If stock is issued below par, the difference is termed a *discount*. If only one type of stock is issued, it may be termed *capital stock* or, specifically, *common stock*. Capital stock that has been issued, fully paid, and reacquired by the company, but not canceled, is called *treasury stock*.

EXAMPLE 10.

The ABC Corporation issued on January 1, 19X2, 5,000 shares of capital stock at $100 par value. The entry is as follows:

Cash	500,000	
Capital Stock		500,000

Dividends. A dividend is a distribution to stockholders. It is on a pro rata basis and generally represents a distribution from retained earnings (see below). Most commonly, dividends are paid in cash. Less frequently, dividends may be paid in stock, scrip, or in property (particularly, liquidating dividends).

EXAMPLE 11.

On December 1, 19X2, the board of directors declares a quarterly cash dividend of $1 per share on the 5,000 shares of capital stock outstanding. The dividend is payable to stockholders of record as of December 10, and will be paid January 15, 19X3. The dividend becomes a current liability when declared and would be included as a current liability on the balance sheet of December 31.

Dec. 1	Retained Earnings	5,000	
	Dividends Payable		5,000

Retained earnings. Retained earnings represent stockholders' equity that has accumulated from profitable operation of the business. Generally they represent total net income less dividends declared. Retained earnings result only from operations of the business, and no entries from transactions in company stock are to be made to the account. The account is to be debited for dividends declared and credited for net income for the period. At the end of the year, Expense and Income Summary is debited and Retained Earnings credited for net income.

EXAMPLE 12.

The net income for the year ended December 31, 19X2, was determined to be $20,000. The entry is:

Expense and Income Summary	20,000	
Retained Earnings		20,000

The stockholders' equity section for most companies would appear as follows:

STOCKHOLDERS' EQUITY

Capital stock, $100 par value, 500 shares	$500,000
Retained Earnings	15,000*
Total Stockholders' Equity	$515,000

* Net income	$ 20,000
Less: Dividend declared	5,000
	$ 15,000

Summary

(1) Liabilities are classified into _____ liabilities and _____ liabilities.

(2) Current liabilities are those due for payment within the operating cycle or _____ , whichever is longer.

(3) Liabilities that have accumulated but are not yet due are known as _____ liabilities.

(4) When the amount of funds needed is larger than a single lender can supply, then _____ are offered for sale to the investing public.

(5) The face amount of bonds is generally $ _____, and interest is paid _____ at a fixed rate.

(6) If the current assets of a firm are $80,000 and the current liabilities are $20,000, the current ratio is _____.

(7) Contingent liabilities are defined as _____ liabilities arising from past events.

(8) A contingent liability should be reflected in the balance sheet as a _____ describing the possibility of the loss.

(9) If there is a credit balance in the Expense and Income Summary after closing the accounts, then a _____ has been made for the period.

(10) When the proprietor invests $10,000 cash in the business, the debit is to Cash and the credit is to _____ .

(11) A business operated for profit by two or more co-owners is called a _____ .

(12) When capital stock has been issued and later reacquired, it is called _____ .

(13) The price at which the stock of a corporation is selling on the stock exchange is the _____ of the stock.

(14) The two principal sections of the stockholders' equity section are _____ and _____ .

Answers: (1) current, long-term; (2) one year; (3) accrued; (4) bonds; (5) 1,000, semiannually; (6) 4:1; (7) potential; (8) footnote; (9) profit; (10) Capital; (11) partnership; (12) treasury stock; (13) market value; (14) paid-in capital, retained earnings

Solved Problems

16.1. A summary of the balance sheet of the Alden Company appears below.

ASSETS

Current	$40,000
Fixed	26,000
Total Assets	$66,000

LIABILITIES AND CAPITAL

Current Liabilities	$15,000
Long-Term Liabilities	28,000
Total Liabilities	$43,000
Capital	23,000
Total Liabilities and Capital	$66,000

Determine the current ratio.

SOLUTION

$$\frac{\text{CURRENT ASSETS}}{\text{CURRENT LIABILITIES}} = \frac{40,000}{15,000} = 2.67:1$$

Therefore $2.67 of current assets is available for every $1 of current liabilities.

16.2. Match the item in Column I with the appropriate description in Column II. (Use the letter adjacent to the description.)

COLUMN I	COLUMN II
1. Notes receivable	(a) Liabilities for goods or services purchased on account
2. Accounts payable	
3. Accrued liabilities	(b) Income received but not yet earned
4. Withholding	(c) A lien on property
5. Dividends payable	(d) Written promise to pay at future date
6. Unearned revenue	(e) Written promise to pay face amount at future date and to make interest payments semiannually
7. Mortgage payable	
8. Bonds payable	
	(f) Amount withheld from employees' salaries
	(g) Amount payable arising from distribution of earnings
	(h) Liabilities accumulated but not yet due for payment

SOLUTION

1. (d)   2. (a)   3. (h)   4. (f)   5. (g)   6. (b)   7. (c)   8. (e)

16.3. Salary expense of $1,000 represents $200 a day for a 5-day week. If the last day of the calendar year (December 31) falls on a Wednesday, what is the entry to record the accrued liability for the year?

SOLUTION

Salary Expense	600*	
Salary Payable		600
* 3 days × $200 per day = $600		

16.4. A note payable written on November 1, 19X2 for $10,000 with interest at 12% is due February 2, 19X3. What adjusting entry is needed to record this accrued liability at December 31, 19X2?

SOLUTION

Interest Expense	200*	
Interest Payable		200
*$10,000 × 12% × 60 days		

16.5. Wages paid for the week total $12,400, from which the following items were withheld: Income taxes, $1,400; Social Security, $650; Hospitalization, $450; Union dues, $560. Present the entry necessary to record (a) the accrued payroll, (b) the payment of the payroll.

(a)

(b)

SOLUTION

(a)	Wages Expense	12,400	
	Withholding Taxes Payable		1,400
	Social Security Taxes Payable		650
	Hospitalization Payable		450
	Union Dues Payable		560
	Accrued Wages Payable		9,340
(b)	Accrued Wages Payable	9,340	
	Cash		9,340

16.6. (a) The rent income account has a credit balance of $14,400 which includes $1,200 of rental income that will not be earned until the new calendar year. What entry is necessary to record this unearned revenue?

(b) What classification is given to Unearned Rent Income?

SOLUTION

(a)	Rent Income	1,200	
	Unearned Rent Income		1,200

(b)   It is a current liability.

16.7. The Penthome Publishing Company, by the end of its first year of operations had received $800,000 for subscriptions. Of that amount $500,000 is applicable to succeeding periods. Present the entry needed to adjust the above data.

Unearned Subscriptions Income

	800,000

SOLUTION

Unearned Subscriptions Income	300,000	
Subscriptions Income		300,000

16.8. (a) Jan. 6:   Joan Rivera opened a business investing $25,000 cash.

(b) Jan. 20: Ms. Rivera invested an additional $5,000 in the business.

(c) Jan. 30: The owner withdrew $1,000 as a personal withdrawal.

Record the above information in the following accounts.

Cash	Rivera Drawing	Rivera Capital

SOLUTION

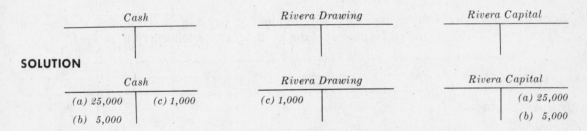

Cash		Rivera Drawing	Rivera Capital
(a) 25,000	(c) 1,000	(c) 1,000	(a) 25,000
(b) 5,000			(b) 5,000

16.9. Assume a profit of $8,000 was made during the first month of business. Prepare the equity section of Joan Rivera Company (see Problem 16.8).

SOLUTION

Capital, January 6		$25,000
Add: Additional Investment		5,000
		$30,000
Net Income for period	8,000	
Less: Drawing	1,000	
Increase in Capital		7,000
Capital, January 31		$37,000

16.10. What entry is needed to record the issuance of 10,000 shares of capital stock at $40 par value? In what section of the balance sheet would this information be placed?

SOLUTION

Cash		400,000	
Capital Stock			400,000

Cash is a current asset while Capital Stock would appear in the stockholders' equity section.

16.11. On December 10, 19X2, the directors of the Costa Corporation declared an annual dividend of $2 per share on the 6,000 shares of capital stock outstanding. What entry is needed to record the above information? How is Dividends Payable treated on the balance sheet?

SOLUTION

Dec. 10 Retained Earnings		12,000	
Dividends Payable			12,000

The dividend becomes a current liability when declared and appears as such on the balance sheet.

16.12. In the above problem, assume that the dividend is payable to stockholders of record December 20, 19X2 and to be paid on January 2, 19X3. What entry is needed?

SOLUTION

December 20:   No entry is needed as it merely sets the time for determining the identity of the stockholders entitled to receive the specific dividend.

January 2 Dividends Payable		12,000	
Cash			12,000

16.13. (a) If the net income of the Black Corporation was determined to be $26,000, what entry would be made? (b) Assume a loss of $5,000.

(a)			
(b)			

SOLUTION

(a)	Expense and Income Summary		26,000	
	Retained Earnings			26,000
(b)	Retained Earnings		5,000	
	Expense and Income Summary			5,000

16.14. What entries are needed to close the accounts below?

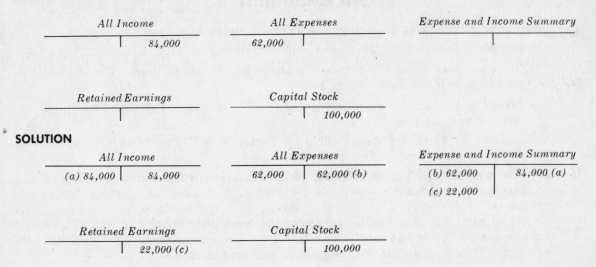

All Income		All Expenses		Expense and Income Summary	
	84,000	62,000			

Retained Earnings		Capital Stock	
			100,000

SOLUTION

All Income		All Expenses		Expense and Income Summary	
(a) 84,000	84,000	62,000	62,000 (b)	(b) 62,000	84,000 (a)
				(c) 22,000	

Retained Earnings		Capital Stock	
	22,000 (c)		100,000

16.15. Based on the information from the above accounts, if dividends of $12,000 were declared, (a) prepare the needed entry, and (b) prepare the stockholders' equity section of the balance sheet.

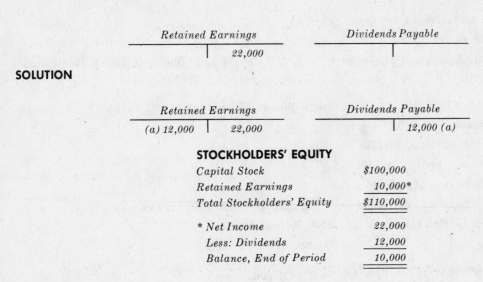

Retained Earnings		Dividends Payable	
	22,000		

SOLUTION

Retained Earnings		Dividends Payable	
(a) 12,000	22,000		12,000 (a)

STOCKHOLDERS' EQUITY

Capital Stock	$100,000
Retained Earnings	10,000*
Total Stockholders' Equity	$110,000
* Net Income	22,000
Less: Dividends	12,000
Balance, End of Period	10,000

Final Examination

1. Journalize the following adjusting data as of December 31:

    (a) Merchandise inventory, January 1, $46,000; December 31, $48,000.

    (b) Office supplies physically counted on December 31 were $1,250. The original balance of supplies on hand was $2,100.

    (c) Prepaid insurance before adjustment, $3,850. It was found that $2,700 had expired during the year.

    (d) Salaries for a five-day week ending on Friday were $3,500. The last payday was on the previous Friday, December 28.

    (e) The company holds a $6,000, 9%, 60-day note receivable dated December 16 of the year just ended.

2. The total payroll for the Fox Company for the week ending April 30 was $17,000. Of this amount, $12,000 was subject to FICA tax. Deductions made: $2,800, federal income tax; $900, hospitalization; the balance was paid in cash.

    (a) Present the journal entry to record the payroll, assuming the FICA tax is 6.13%.

    (b) Present the employer's payroll tax entry, assuming state unemployment tax of 2%, federal unemployment tax of 0.7%. Of the total payroll, $5,000 was subject to state and federal unemployment taxes.

3. Journalize the following separate entries:

    (a) B. Smith discounted his own $4,000 note from City Bank for 120 days at 6%.

    (b) B. Smith discounted at 6% E. Orlian, 120 day, 6%, $4,000 note immediately upon receipt.

4. Prepare a bank reconciliation statement based on the information below:

    (a) Bank balance, $3,400.

    (b) Checkbook balance, $3,120.

    (c) Outstanding checks, $1,140.

    (d) Deposits in transit, $1,800.

    (e) A $1,000 note was collected by the bank; interest, $15; service charge, $5.

    (f) A $16 check was returned for not sufficient funds.

    (g) Check #12 for $82 was incorrectly recorded in checkstubs as $28.

5. Inventory information for Product #248 is given below:

Jan.	1	Balance	15 units	@	$10 per unit
March	17	Purchase	12 units	@	$11 per unit
April	29	Purchase	8 units	@	$12 per unit
Aug.	19	Purchase	12 units	@	$14 per unit
Aug.	29	Purchase	5 units	@	$16 per unit
Sept.	18	Purchase	6 units	@	$20 per unit

    After taking a physical count, we find there are 20 units on hand. Determine the ending inventory cost by (a) First-In, First-Out method; (b) Last-In, First-Out method; (c) Weighted Average method.

6. P & C Printing Company traded in their old press for a new one priced at $18,000, receiving a trade-in allowance of $1,500 and paying the balance in cash. The old press cost $12,500 and had accumulated depreciation of $11,800. (a) What is the entry to record the acquisition of the new machine? (b) What entry would be needed if the trade-in had been only $500?

7. The trial balance of the Schun Corporation as of December 31, is as follows:

Cash	$22,000	
Accounts Receivable	6,500	
Merchandise Inventory	38,100	
Supplies	4,200	
Prepaid Insurance	8,000	
Equipment	15,100	
Accumulated Depreciation		$ 4,400
Accounts Payable		18,200
Capital Stock		20,000
Retained Earnings		17,000
Dividends	2,400	
Sales		98,200
Purchases	42,100	
Purchase Returns		300
Salaries Expense	11,200	
Rent Expense	4,500	
Misc. General Expense	4,000	

Prepare an eight-column worksheet, using the following additional information for year-end adjustments: (a) merchandise inventory on December 31, $42,000; (b) supplies inventory, December 31, $4,000; (c) insurance expired during the year, $2,000; (d) depreciation for the current year, $800; (e) salaries accrued at December 31, $400.

Schun Corporation
Worksheet
Year Ended December 31, 19X2

Account Title	Trial Balance Dr.	Trial Balance Cr.	Adjustments Dr.	Adjustments Cr.	Income Statement Dr.	Income Statement Cr.	Balance Sheet Dr.	Balance Sheet Cr.
Cash	22,000							
Accounts Receivable	6,500							
Merchandise Inven.	38,100							
Supplies	4,200							
Prepaid Insurance	8,000							
Equipment	15,100							
Accumulated Deprec.		4,400						
Accounts Payable		18,200						
Capital Stock		20,000						
Retained Earnings		17,000						
Dividends	2,400							
Sales		98,200						
Purchases	42,100							
Purchase Returns		300						
Salaries Expense	11,200							
Rent Expense	4,500							
Misc. Gen. Expense	4,000							
	158,100	158,100						
Exp. and Inc. Sum.								
Supplies Expense								
Insurance Expense								
Depreciation Exp.								
Salaries Payable								
Net Income								

8. From the information in question 7, prepare all necessary adjusting and closing entries.

9. From the information in question 7, prepare the Income Statement for the Schun Corporation.

10. Prepare the Retained Earnings Statement and Balance Sheet for the Schun Corporation based on question 7.

Answers to Final Examination

1. (a)   Expense and Income Summary   46,000
     Merchandise Inventory   46,000
  Merchandise Inventory   48,000
     Expense and Income Summary   48,000

   (b)   Office Supplies Expense   850
     Office Supplies   850

   (c)   Insurance Expense   2,700
     Prepaid Insurance   2,700

   (d)   Salaries Expense   700
     Salaries Payable   700
     (Monday, December 31: 3,500 ÷ 5)

   (e)   Interest Receivable   22.50
     Interest Income   22.50

2. (a)   Salaries Expense   17,000
     FICA Taxes Payable   735.60
     Federal Income Taxes Payable   2,800
     Hospitalization Payable   900
     Cash   12,564.40

   (b)   Payroll Tax Expense   870.60
     FICA Taxes Payable   735.60
     State Unemployment Insurance Payable   100
     Federal Unemployment Insurance Payable   35

3. (a)   Cash   3,920
   Interest Expense   80
     Notes Payable   4,000*

   (b)   Cash   3,998.40
   Interest Expense   1.60
     Notes Receivable   4,000

$4,000.00	Principal*	
80.00	Interest Income	
4,080.00	Maturity Value	
81.60	Discount	
$3,998.40	Proceeds	

4.

Bank Reconciliation Statement

Bank Balance	$3,400	Check Balance		$3,120
Add: Deposit in Transit	1,800	Add: Notes Receivable	$1,000	
	$5,200	Interest Income	15	1,015
				$4,135
Less: Outstanding Checks	1,140			
		Less: Service Charge	5	
		NSF	16	
		Error	54	75
Bank Balance Corrected	$4,060	Checkbook Balance Corrected		$4,060

5.   (a) First-In, First-Out Method

Sept.	18:	6 units @ $20	=	$120
Aug.	29:	5 units @ $16	=	80
Aug.	19:	9 units @ $14	=	126
Total units	20			$326

    (b) Last-In, First-Out Method

Jan.	1:	15 units @ $10	=	$150
March	17:	5 units @ $11	=	55
Total units	20			$205

    (c) Weighted Average Method

15 units @ $10 = $150	
12 units @ $11 = 132	
8 units @ $12 = 96	$746 ÷ 58 = $12.86 per unit
12 units @ $14 = 168	$12.86 × 20 units = $257.20
5 units @ $16 = 80	
6 units @ $20 = 120	
Total units 58 $746	

6.   (a)

Accumulated Depreciation	11,800	
Machine (new)	17,200	
Machine (old)		12,500
Cash		16,500

    (b)

Accumulated Depreciation	11,800	
Machine (new)	18,000	
Loss on Disposal of Fixed Assets	200	
Machine (old)		12,500
Cash		17,500

7.

Schun Corporation
Worksheet
Year Ended December 31, 19X2

Account Title	Trial Balance Dr.	Cr.	Adjustments Dr.	Cr.	Income Statement Dr.	Cr.	Balance Sheet Dr.	Cr.
Cash	22,000						22,000	
Accounts Receivable	6,500						6,500	
Merchandise Inven.	38,100		(a) 42,000	(a) 38,100			42,000	
Supplies	4,200			(b) 200			4,000	
Prepaid Insurance	8,000			(c) 2,000			6,000	
Equipment	15,100						15,100	
Accumulated Deprec.		4,400		(d) 800				5,200
Accounts Payable		18,200						18,200
Capital Stock		20,000						20,000
Retained Earnings		17,000						17,000
Dividends	2,400						2,400	
Sales		98,200				98,200		
Purchases	42,100				42,100			
Purchase Returns		300				300		
Salaries Expense	11,200		(e) 400		11,600			
Rent Expense	4,500				4,500			
Misc. Gen. Expense	4,000				4,000			
	158,100	158,100						
Exp. and Inc. Sum.			(a) 38,100	(a) 42,000	38,100	42,000		
Supplies Expense			(b) 200		200			
Insurance Expense			(c) 2,000		2,000			
Depreciation Exp.			(d) 800		800			
Salaries Payable				(e) 400				400
			83,500	83,500	103,300	140,500	98,000	60,800
Net Income					37,200			37,200
					140,500	140,500	98,000	98,000

8.
ADJUSTING ENTRIES

(a)	Merchandise Inventory	42,000	
	Expense and Income Summary		42,000
	Expense and Income Summary	38,100	
	Merchandise Inventory		38,100
(b)	Supplies Expense	200	
	Supplies		200
(c)	Insurance Expense	2,000	
	Prepaid Insurance		2,000
(d)	Depreciation Expense	800	
	Accumulated Depreciation		800
(e)	Salaries Expense	400	
	Salaries Payable		400

CLOSING ENTRIES

(a)	Sales Income	98,200	
	Purchase Returns	300	
	Expense and Income Summary		98,500
(b)	Expense and Income Summary	65,200	
	Purchases		42,100
	Salaries Expense		11,600
	Rent Expense		4,500
	Misc. General Expense		4,000
	Supplies Expense		200
	Insurance Expense		2,000
	Depreciation Expense		800
(c)	Expense and Income Summary	37,200	
	Retained Earnings		37,200
(d)	Retained Earnings	2,400	
	Dividends		2,400

9.

Schun Corporation
Income Statement
Year ended December 31, 19X2

Sales			$98,200
Cost of Goods Sold			
Merchandise Inventory, Jan. 1		$38,100	
Purchases	$42,100		
Less: Purchase Returns	300	41,800	
Goods Available for Sale		$79,900	
Less: Merchandise Inventory, Dec. 31		42,000	
Cost of Goods Sold			37,900
Gross Profit			$60,300
Operating Expenses			
Salaries Expense	$11,600		
Rent Expense	4,500		
Insurance Expense	2,000		
Supplies Expense	200		
Depreciation Expense	800		
Miscellaneous General Expense	4,000		
Total Operating Expenses			$23,100
Net Income			$37,200

10.

Schun Corporation		
Retained Earnings Statement		
Year Ended December 31, 19X2		
Retained Earnings, January 1, 19X2		$17,000
Net Income	$37,200	
Less: Dividends	2,400	
Increase in Retained Earnings		34,800
Retained Earnings, December 31, 19X2		$51,800

Schun Corporation		
Balance Sheet		
December 31, 19X2		
ASSETS		
Current Assets		
Cash	$22,000	
Accounts Receivable	6,500	
Merchandise Inventory	42,000	
Supplies	4,000	
Prepaid Insurance	6,000	
Total Current Assets		$80,500
Fixed Assets		
Equipment	$15,100	
Less: Accumulated Depreciation	5,200	9,900
Total Assets		$90,400
LIABILITIES AND CAPITAL		
Liabilities		
Current Liabilities		
Accounts Payable	$18,200	
Salaries Payable	400	
Total Current Liabilities		$18,600
Capital		
Capital Stock	20,000	
Retained Earnings, December 31, 19X2	51,800	
Total Capital		71,800
Total Liabilities and Capital		$90,400

Appendix

Mechanical and Electronic Data Processing

Introduction

From a theoretical point of view the operations of accounting may be analyzed into:

Handling of source documents. Issuing sales invoices, vouching purchase invoices, issuing checks, etc.

Input. Insertion of data into the accounting system.

Processing. Arithmetical calculations, sorting and classification of data.

Output. Results of processing.

Storage. Maintenance of records.

In illustrating the principles of accounting in Chapters 1-8, we supposed the above basic operations to be carried out by hand — as indeed they might be. However, they can be — and to a large extent actually are — performed by means of mechanical or electronic devices.

Mechanical Data Processing

There is hardly a business today that does not use a machine in some part of its data processing. As transactions increase in number, the proportion of machine processing also increases to reduce costs and speed the data processing. For our purpose we will divide machines into three groups.

REGISTERS

Common forms of registers are cash registers and invoice registers. Today's cash registers do far more than help make change. They accumulate cash sales, credit sales, sales taxes, and cash received on account. They can segregate sales into groups, such as hardware, apparel, etc. There are also registers which issue invoices for credit sales or receipt of cash sales but which do not make change. A sizable number of registers are in use today that are connected directly to a computer. These registers may be classified as Electronic Data Processing.

KEY-DRIVEN MACHINES

Under this head come typewriters, adding machines, calculators, and comptometers. These machines are simple to operate and are familiar to most office employees. Thus, sales invoices may be prepared by typewriter, the extensions made and checked by calculator or comptometer, the items totaled by adding machine, and sales statistics also prepared by adding machine. Attachments to key-driven machines allow, along with the primary document, the simultaneous preparation of perforated tapes or cards which can be directly processed on electronic equipment.

ACCOUNTING MACHINES

Though normally provided with keyboards and accumulating counters, these machines are more sophisticated and more costly than typewriters or adding machines. They are capable of processing a number of documents at once. To illustrate the scope of such devices we consider the operation of a typical billing machine.

EXAMPLE

A customer's invoice is to be prepared for goods shipped. The following steps are performed by the machine operator:

1. Sales journal form is placed in the machine and each sales transaction is typed on a line of the sales journal.
2. The following forms are placed in the machine:
    (a) Blank invoice form. Includes customer's copy and carbon and carbon copies for the office.
    (b) Customer's account from the subsidiary ledger.
    (c) Statement to be mailed to customer at the end of the month.
3. The previous balance is picked up from the customer's account.
4. The customer's name, address, terms, etc., are typed on the invoice.
5. For each item sold, the description, number of units, and unit price are typed on the invoice.
6. After the units and unit prices are typed, the operator punches a key and the machine automatically multiplies the units times the price and prints the extension for each item.
7. After all items are listed, the operator presses another key and the machine totals the invoice, prints the total on the invoice, and makes the entry in the sales journal. Also, it enters the new balance on the customer's account and on the customer's statement.

Electronic Data Processing

Electronics, in reference to computers and electronic data processing (EDP), means the flow of electrons, acting as signals in the circuitry of electronic equipment. In mechanical processing the speed of the equipment is limited by the movement of mechanical parts that are subject to friction. The electronic impulses used in computers are not so limited and are many thousands of times faster; some computers can add 250,000 sixteen-digit numbers in one second, or can record the equivalent of 50,000 words in one second. Another important fact is that the electronic computer has a memory or storage bank which makes possible an enormous saving of time in retrieving data. There are various types and sizes of computer systems that use various languages but all of them have the same basic component parts.

COMPONENTS

An electronic data processing system includes the computer and a number of other machines called *peripheral equipment*. The machines are collectively known as *hardware*; *software* includes computer programs, feasibility studies, manuals, etc. The computer may itself be broken down into the following functional units.

(1) *Input unit.* Generally data will be put into the computer by means of punched cards, paper tape, or magnetic tape. The last is by far the fastest method and is the most economical of storage space.

(2) *Storage unit.* The storage unit (sometimes called *memory*) is the unit to which program statements and data are transferred once they leave the input unit. Program statements may move from this unit into the control unit and data may move from this unit into the arithmetic unit and/or the output unit.

(3) *Control unit.* The control unit directs the operations of all the computer components in accordance with the particular *program*. The program is stored within the computer and guides the flow of processing from the input at the beginning until the output at the end of processing.

(4) ***Arithmetic unit.*** The arithmetic unit can do more than merely add, subtract, multiply, and divide. It follows the established program and accepts new data or can recall any needed data from the memory of the computer. It also makes yes-or-no decisions such as: Are two numbers equal? Has sufficient accuracy been achieved?

(5) ***Output unit.*** When the processing is completed the results are made available as desired. The output may be via electric typewriter, line printer, tape, cards, or visual display. The typewriter will produce 10 characters per second, the line printer up to 2,800 lines a minute, with 120 characters per line.

MACHINE LANGUAGE

A computer is used as an extension of a person's mind to allow that person to become more effective. It frees the person from some repetitive tasks that do not require judgement. Since people need to communicate with the computer, they must know how to use the appropriate language. As the parts that control the internal operations of computers have improved over the years, so have the languages.

Electronic computers "understand" only two values, which we may call "current-off" and "current-on", or simply, "off" and "on". The natural language of these machines is then the *binary number system*, which uses only the two digits 0 ("off") and 1 ("on"). Binary numbers are built up by giving these digits place-values. If, for example, the digit 1 is at the extreme right, as in 0001, it has the value 1. If it is moved one position to the left, as in 0010, its value is doubled, becoming 2. If it is moved one more place to the left, making 0100, it doubles again to become 4. If moved still another place, making 1000, it doubles again to become 8. The number which in the decimal system is represented by 5, is represented by 0101 in the binary system.

To bridge the gap between machine language and human language, a number of intermediary languages have been developed. These sufficiently resemble human languages so that the task of instructing the machine is not too difficult. These intermediary languages — called *high-level languages* — are close enough to machine language to permit direct translation into that language by the computer. Three high-level languages which are widely used are FORTRAN (for FORmula TRANslation), COBOL (for COmmon Business Oriented Language), and BASIC (for Beginner's All-purpose Symbolic Instruction Code).

GENERATIONS OF COMPUTERS

The first commercial electronic computer that became available in 1951 marked the beginning of computer generations.

First Generation: 1951–1958. The computers of this generation used vacuum tubes to control their internal operations. These tubes were rather large and generated tremendous heat.

Second Generation: 1959–1964. The computers of this generation used transistors instead of vacuum tubes. The amount of heat generated was greatly reduced and the computers were smaller and more reliable.

Third Generation: 1965–Present. The computers of this generation use miniaturized integrated circuits instead of transistors. These computers are smaller, faster, and lower in price than their predecessors and are programmed almost exclusively in high-level languages. The microprocessor chip has led to the development of microcomputers which currently appear to be the fastest growing product in the data processing industry.

Accounting Applications of EDP

Electronic data processing can be used for practically every accounting operation, but it becomes most profitable where there is a mass of data to be processed, as in payroll preparation, billing customers, and maintaining balances for inventories, accounts receivable, and accounts payable.   There are various other applications that are concerned more with control and analysis than with detailed processing.

PAYROLL

The payroll operation has become more time-consuming in recent years because of a wide variety of withholdings, such as those for income tax, social security, unemployment insurance, hospitalization, pension, and disability. Also, in many manufacturing plants there are premium rates for the night shift, overtime computations, different rates when an employee does different jobs, etc.   When there are hundreds or thousands of employees paid on a weekly basis, the preparation of the payroll can indeed be a major undertaking.

EDP is well-suited to payroll preparation since the repetitive data—the employee's name, address, identification number, pay rate, number of exemptions, types of withholdings—are recorded only once, and thereafter automatically printed when needed. With manual processing this data generally has to be written each week for each employee. With EDP the only new input is the data that will vary, such as hours worked and the job serial number.   The computer calculates all the necessary results, not only what was formerly generated manually by the payroll department, but also such things as the payroll bank reconciliation, many reports to government agencies, and various kinds of management control data.   And all this, of course,   at a fraction of the time required for manual processing.

BILLING

Much of the information needed for preparing bills to customers is repetitive and is readily performed by the computer.   For example, the customer's name, address, and identification number are first stored in the machine.   Then the description of the product and price can be stored.   As deliveries are made, the sales information can be fed into the machine.   Automatically the computer will list the items and summarize all shipments to the customer, calculate prices, print a shipment document, and make out a bill to the customer.

The computer system stores a vast amount of sales information from which summaries can be printed, showing total sales by customer, by period, by product, by salesperson, by territory, or by profitability.   These sales statistics are essential to good management and would require a great amount of time if summarized manually.

MAINTAINING BALANCES

In order to manage a company efficiently it is necessary to control the balances of key functions of the business, particularly inventory, accounts receivable, and accounts payable.   If a sufficient quantity of various inventory components is not maintained, production may be disrupted; if too much is invested in inventory, then working capital will be insufficient and accounts payable cannot be settled.   By the same token, if accounts receivable become too large, working capital is also adversely affected. Many firms maintain all inventory items on the computer: each time goods are received or shipped, punched cards are prepared and a new balance automatically computed.   From time to time reports are printed out, showing purchases, usage, stock levels, and inventory value. Comparable data can be prepared for increases and decreases in the accounts for individual customers and individual vendors.

OTHER APPLICATIONS

There are many types of accounting applications besides those described above.   The general ledger and all other accounting records can be put on the computer.   That is generally the next step after the more repetitive functions have been computerized and are operating satisfactorily. Many companies also have their cost systems and budget systems on the computer.

It should be mentioned that important nonaccounting functions may be computerized in large companies. Purchasing, production, or engineering functions may make continuous or periodic use of the computer, which also allows solution of complex business and management problems that were not previously feasible.

INDEX

Catalog

If you are interested in a list of SCHAUM'S
OUTLINE SERIES send your name
and address, requesting your free catalog, to:

SCHAUM'S OUTLINE SERIES, Dept. C
McGRAW-HILL BOOK COMPANY
1221 Avenue of Americas
New York, N.Y. 10020